Theorizing Faith

Theorizing Faith:

The Insider/Outsider Problem in the Study of Ritual

Edited by

Elisabeth Arweck & Martin D. Stringer

THE UNIVERSITY
OF BIRMINGHAM

UNIVERSITY PRESS

First published in the United Kingdom by The University of Birmingham Press, Edgbaston, Birmingham, BI5 2TT, UK.

ISBN 1-902459-33-4

British Library Cataloguing in Publication data
A CIP catalogue record for this book is available from the
British Library

Printed in Great Britain by MPG Books Limited, Bodmin.
Typeset by Book Production Services, London,

Contents

Acknowledgements

This volume took shape during a conference which was held in June 1999 at the University of Birmingham. The conference was the second meeting organised by the Worship in Birmingham Project, a project which is under the direction of Dr Martin Stringer. The first conference had taken place in summer 1998 on "The Ethnography of Worship" and the title of the conference in 1999 was "Theorizing Faith: The Insider/Outsider Problem and the Study of Ritual", the very title of this volume.

The editors would like to express their thanks to all those who lent their support for the organisation of this conference, in particular Pamela Ogilvie, who acted as the co-ordinator for the conference, Dennis Turner, the (then) Head of the Department of Theology at the University of Birmingham, as well as the Advisory Board and Consultants who are associated with the Worship in Birmingham Project.

The aim of the conference was to bring together both established scholars and research students from a variety of disciplines who have a concern with the study of ritual and the relationship between ritual and faith experience. Therefore the papers were expected to reflect a combination of perspectives—of those studying their own faith community and of those studying the rituals of others. As the conference progressed, it became clear that a number of the papers presented shared common concerns and that they presented a 'natural selection' for conference proceedings. With the exception of the last paper in this collection—Lowell Livezey's "The Ethnographer and the Quest for Meanings"—the papers included in this volume were all read at the conference in 1999.

The editors would like to express their thanks to all those who offered papers to the conference as well as to the contributors to this collection who co-operated patiently in the preparation of their presentations for publication. We would also like to thank Prof. Livezey for agreeing to shed a transatlantic light on the contributions and to round off the collection by providing the insights and experience which the Religion in Urban America Program (RUAP) at the University of Illinois, Chicago—in some ways the American counterpart of the Worship in Birmingham Project—has gained since its inception in 1992.

Elisabeth Arweck & Martin Stringer

1 Introduction: Theorizing Faith

MARTIN D. STRINGER

The Worship in Birmingham Project

When the Worship in Birmingham Project held its first conference in the summer of 1998, the title was "The Ethnography of Worship". This title sums up what the Project is about: it aims to undertake detailed local studies of worship and ritual in different religious communities in Birmingham, using the methodology of participant observation. However, those who responded to the call for papers, and those who subsequently spoke to the conference, were all studying various forms of Christian worship and came from primarily theological backgrounds. All the contributors were excited by the concept of 'ethnography' and were exploring different ways in which the social sciences could be developed and adapted for the study of Christian worship.[1] All the contributors were Christian, and one of the primary areas of discussion for the conference was the question of whether it made any difference that we were Christians studying Christian worship, that we were all, to a greater or lesser extent, 'insiders'.

When we came to hold our second conference, one year later, it was decided that the question of 'insiders' and 'outsiders', in terms of who was studying what, should be the principal theme. The title of the conference was "Theorizing Faith: The Insider/Outsider Problem and the Study of Ritual". The first surprise was that, while the first conference had attracted primarily Christians studying Christian worship from an essentially theological background, this conference attracted a wider range of participants, studying a range of religious traditions, and coming primarily from the context of religious studies or the social sciences. The reason for this, I assumed, was the use of the term 'worship' in the title of the first conference, as opposed to the use of the term 'ritual' in the title of the second conference. What became even clearer, however, as the papers were presented, was the complexity and depth of analysis that surrounded the question of 'insiders' and 'outsiders' in the study of religious communities. It is this question, therefore, which forms the heart of this particular series of papers, all originally presented at our second conference.

The Insider/Outsider Problem

The 'insider/outsider problem' has been a part of the academic study of religion since the middle of the nineteenth century (McCutcheon, 1999). During the first half of the nineteenth century, the study of religion moved from being a branch of Christian theology with its emphasis on the study of Christianity, to being a part of the emerging social sciences, with an emphasis on the study of other religions.

The 'insider/outsider problem' concerned two apparently conflicting positions. On the one hand, there were those who suggested that there was something about 'religion' that meant that those who did not share a 'religious outlook' could not hope to understand the 'real' nature of religion at all. Alternatively, there were those who argued that researchers who were also members of the religion being studied were so involved in what was happening that they could not possibly hope to understand the religion from a truly 'objective' position. Behind this discussion lies a series of problems concerning the nature of religion, the possibility of any kind of 'objective' study of human activity, and the question of what it actually means to be an 'insider' or an 'outsider'. On the whole, it is only the first two of these questions which have been investigated and argued over in the literature (McCutcheon, 1999). The question of what it means to be an 'insider' or an 'outsider' has been either taken entirely for granted or ignored. It is here that this book, and the papers that it contains, enter into the debate, and it is here that I will focus my discussion within this introduction.

Faith

When we ask what it is that makes a person an 'insider' or an 'outsider' in relation to religion, we are, inevitably, also faced with the question of what religion is. This, however, is an almost impossible question to answer. At one level, the question of the 'insider' or 'outsider' comes down to a question of membership. Is an individual researcher a full member of the religious organization that is being studied? However, even this question can be framed in different ways and at different levels. In her paper, Helen Waterhouse asks if it is enough for the researcher to be a practising Buddhist in order to qualify as an 'insider' in the study a particular Buddhist group? Or does that researcher have to be a member of the particular school of Buddhism or even a full member of the group actually being studied? Clearly there are levels of 'insiderness' and 'outsiderness', and where a researcher sits on this continuum will be important to the study in hand. This will be one of the principal areas of discussion in many of the papers that follow. However, even this evades the real question of what it is that makes one an 'insider'. The question of 'membership' could be used in relation to any ethnographic study, and the debate within recent anthropology on the nature of participant observation raises just this question (see the extended discussion of this issue in Peter Collins's paper in this volume). Can we sensibly be a 'participant' observer in a culture that is not our own, within an organization that is not our own, or even in a community that is not our own? This is not a question that is limited to the study of religion and it does not really get to the heart of the questions raised by the insider/outsider debate.

The insider/outsider problem, as it has been traditionally defined, assumes that there is something specific about religion that makes the question of whether the researcher is an insider or an outsider fundamentally important. It is suggested that there is something in religion that clearly and definitively distinguishes the insider from the outsider. In order to investigate what this might be, I would suggest, we need to look at some of those who have held very clear views on this issue. More specifically, we need to look at those who argue that the researcher must be an insider (those who argue strongly for an outsider position are usually less clear and less concerned about the distinctions between insider and outsider anyway[2]). In doing this I want to highlight the work of William Cantwell Smith (Cantwell Smith, 1981). I am focusing on Cantwell Smith, not because I believe he has any specific or unique insight into the question we are investigating, but rather because he is far clearer than many others writing in the field about what it is that distinguishes 'religion', as opposed to any specific religious tradition, from the rest of social activity. What distinguishes religion, or the religious outlook, according to Cantwell Smith, is 'faith'.

Cantwell Smith was trained in the discipline of Comparative Religion, the History of Religions, or what is increasingly called the Theology of Religions. He was concerned to show two things in his writings: firstly, that there is no real distinction between different religious traditions (they are all essentially variations on a theme), and secondly, that there is something fundamentally distinct and unique about religion *per se*. The first argument is based on historical analysis and a careful investigation of the way in which different traditions borrow elements from each other and derive their distinctiveness only through history and development (Cantwell Smith, 1981). However,

Cantwell Smith is not content simply to provide an historical narrative that shows that all religion is fundamentally the same. The 'theological' side of his training still wants to claim some kind of uniqueness for 'religion' taken as a whole. In this Cantwell Smith clearly positions himself as an 'insider' to 'religion' and claims that only such an insider can truly understand 'religious behaviour'. Cantwell Smith uses the concept of 'faith' to distinguish the insider from the outsider, while being notoriously vague in defining exactly what 'faith' is (Heim, 1995: 45). It appears that we have to be 'insiders' in order to understand 'faith' and that no 'outsider' will ever fully grasp what it is. If we are 'insiders', however, 'faith' will be so self-evident as not to need any explanation. In my view, this avoids the issue. It fails to say what 'faith' is. More importantly, it fails even to say what kind of thing faith is.

By drawing on the papers presented in this book, I want to go further than Cantwell Smith was prepared to go. I wish to offer some discussion of what 'faith' might be, what it might mean to be an 'insider' to religion. In order to do this I will not look at 'faith' in some abstract, theological way. Rather I will be asking what it is that those who are insiders share, and what insiders have that outsiders do not. That which is shared, for example, could be a certain kind of experience, or perhaps a particular way of using language. Having looked at what is shared among 'insiders', I want to ask what is not shared between insiders and outsiders. I want to suggest that 'faith', far from being a 'thing' which insiders have and outsiders do not, is rather a construct, a means of excluding those who are deemed not to be 'insiders', most specifically researchers whom the religious communities wish to keep out.

Faith as That Which is Shared

If we take Cantwell Smith seriously, 'faith' is that which is shared between those who are 'insiders' to religion and that which is not shared with those who are 'outsiders'. However, to talk simply of 'that which is shared' raises, once again the fundamental question of ethnography or participant observation. If we take, for example, Peter Collins's study of the Quaker Meeting in Dibdenshaw, we can see that Peter presents himself very clearly as an 'insider'. He claims to share a large number of assumptions with the people he is studying, including, we must assume, their 'faith', although not necessarily their beliefs, which for Quakers can be very diverse. What exactly is it, however, that is being shared? As well as a common religious background, there is a clear sharing of social background, culture, certain class-based assumptions, and even, in this case, a certain intellectual approach to the whole question of religion. It has often been argued that there is a far greater 'cultural' coherence among Quakers than among many other religious groups. This may be due to a common Quaker tradition or to the fact that being a Quaker appeals to a certain kind of person. It is clear, therefore, that far more than 'faith' is shared between Peter and the people studied.

Is it ever possible to distinguish the 'faith' element of what is shared from anything else, either social or cultural, that the researcher might have in common with the group studied? Can we in reality take account of the social and cultural sharing and isolate that which is shared on the level of 'faith'? Reading Peter's paper makes this appear to be very difficult. It is difficult in part because the elements of the community which are related to social or cultural factors and those which are related to faith issues are not distinguished by the members of the community. Friends, like most religious believers, would not see any clear distinction between their 'faith' and the rest of their lives. The way in which they live their lives is, for them, an expression of their 'faith'. Even from a supposedly 'objective' outsider perspective it is very difficult to determine whether, for example, the emphasis on Peace is an aspect of 'faith' or whether, like many others involved in the radical politics of the 1960s, it simply reflects an aspect of a particular social and cultural context that many Friends have grown up with. Peter also makes the point that this kind of discussion presupposes a personal and communal coherence. At one time, and on certain issues, Peter may share common views, culture and even faith with other members of the Meeting. At other times (when he is an academic, for example, or even when he is a 'warden'), he might not.

What is also clear from Peter's paper is that the people themselves, the Friends meeting each week for worship, could not put into words exactly what their 'faith' meant to them. Peter claims to share this inability at least to some extent. But is a shared inability to express something that is felt to be of fundamental importance enough to be described as a shared 'faith'? Some people might object that even this is something that is related to the fact that the group under investigation are Quakers. The focus of Quaker worship is dependent, at least in part, on an expressed inability to voice that which is most important. The worship consists primarily in silence. This, however, both misunderstands the nature of silence in Quaker worship and the widespread nature of the shared inability to express 'faith'. For Friends, the silence of worship is not an expression of any kind of inability to express what faith means to them; rather it is a state of active listening. During ministry, when a member of the congregation stands to speak, the message can be very clear and articulate. The silence of the Quaker meeting is different from the fumbling attempt by people, from many different religious traditions, to say exactly what their 'faith' means to them.

When I studied a Baptist congregation in Manchester, which had a similar social and cultural background to the Quakers in Dibdenshaw, and, incidentally, what became very obvious to both Peter and myself through many interviews and discussions, was the total inability of the members of this congregation to put anything of importance in their 'faith' into words (Stringer, 1999: 95). They knew that I shared, in whatever way, this sense of the inexpressibility of faith, and that in itself allowed us to communicate about worship and what was important to them, primarily through story, allusion, and silence. It was the fact that I was known and trusted, and therefore expected to share in the inexpressibility of faith, that made a discussion of faith possible. It became possible because, in these terms, I was an 'insider', I shared the 'faith' (despite the fact that I am a Catholic and not a Baptist). Yet, can we really leave the discussion at the point where we say, almost with Cantwell Smith, 'yes, faith is shared, but that which is shared is beyond words and therefore can never be discussed let alone analysed'? What is this inexpressible otherness between researcher and researched that, as insiders, we share? Or more specifically, what kind of thing is it?

A Shared Experience

One possibility is that that which is shared is essentially an experience, or more broadly 'experience' (Turner, 1986). This is certainly the conclusion that I came to in relation to my work with the Baptists (Stringer, 1999: 205). That which could not be expressed was experiential, but the kind of experience which could never be put into words. We were able to discuss it, because, fundamentally, both I as researcher and the Baptists as worshippers, knew what this experience was or rather knew what kind of experience we were talking about. A number of the papers in this volume draw on the concept of shared experience as the basis for their analysis. The most obvious is that by Helen Waterhouse in her discussion of the *gongyō* ritual of the Sōka Gakkai International UK. This ritual is closely associated with membership of the Sōka Gakkai and therefore with insiderness. It has to be performed in front of the *gohonzon*, which takes the form of a particular *mandala* that is given to each new member and which must be housed in a special shrine within the house. While it is clear that non-members cannot own a *gohonzon* or enshrine it in their house (even ex-members are expected to return it), any person who so wishes may join in the *gongyō* ritual in front of the *gohonzon*. This ritual is supposed to engender a sense of peace and well-being and is clearly associated with a specific type of experience. Helen tells us that while she is not a member and maintained her official and open outsider position throughout her study of the Sōka Gakkai, she participated in these rituals and, she claims, experienced something of the peace and well-being that is associated with them. She shared the experience associated with the rite, but remained to all intents and purposes an 'outsider'; she certainly did not share the 'faith' of Sōka Gakkai members. It is this, among other things, that leads her to challenge the value of a strict insider/outsider dichotomy.

As I have said, the experience in the case of the Sōka Gakkai is very specific and it is associated directly with the performance of the ritual. In the case of Mathew Guest's paper on 'alternative' worship, however, the experience is much more amorphous, and if anything, deliberately so. Mathew explores the way in which contemporary developments in Christian worship that aim to combine traditional Christian imagery with the style and ethos of rave and club culture both diverge from, and remain consistent with, their evangelical roots. 'Alternative' worship is undertaken within a self-consciously post-modern context where there are no fixed points of meaning. Experience forms the core of the rite. Because of its roots in club culture and its association with the charismatic movement, which Mathew highlights in his paper, 'alternative' worship is clearly a communal experience. However, in this case, while the context for the experience is controlled fairly tightly by the organizers, it is assumed and expected that different people attending the event will experience fundamentally different things, depending on their background and the way in which they plot their own path through the worship. All attempts at offering fixed meanings and sense to the individual experiences are rejected, leaving the worshipper alone to reflect on what has become, by definition, very personal to them. It would probably be difficult to talk about any kind of 'shared experience' in this context. What is more, it is clear that Mathew himself does not really know whether to think of himself, in the role of the researcher, as an 'insider' or an 'outsider' to this worship or its experience. Such terms simply do not make any sense within the context of this kind of worship.

The problem with putting the emphasis on experience, therefore, is that all experience is difficult to define and particular experiences are almost impossible to compare. If I think of my own religious life, experience is clearly very important to me. There are two experiences in particular that I would consider to be central to my own understanding of 'faith'. The first is the experience associated with the elevation of the host at Mass, or, more specifically, the experience of Benediction. Like the Sōka Gakkai experience of *gongyō*, this is an experience associated directly with ritual. In this case, however, the experience is that of being in the presence of God, a presence which is clearly located on the altar. What is important for me is the sense of God being 'out there', being very specifically located in the host. The two papers on Quakers in this volume note the emphasis on the 'God within' among Friends. That is not a concept that has any meaning for me. I cannot relate to any sense of a God that can be 'within' me. For me, God is always 'out there', and in the context of the Mass or Benediction very specifically out there, in the host, on the altar. The Sōka Gakkai experience of the *gohonzon* as being located within its own shrine is clearly very similar to the one that I am trying to express. However, in this Buddhist example, the *gohonzon*, while being very important, is not a location for the presence of the divine and this is bound to create some difference in the experiences being described.

The other experience that is important to me is less specifically related to ritual, but once again concerns the presence of God, and once again it is an external presence. In this case it is my experience of prayer, of stillness, of being with God. My experience is that of being enfolded by God, wrapped around by the wings of God, caring and nurturing, holding me and supporting me. This is the experience of a God who surrounds me. Not of a God who invades my space. Neither of the two experiences are equivalent to Otto's experience of the numinous (Otto, 1928). Neither is tremendous and exhilarating. Each is quiet and certain, consoling and supportive. Neither of these experiences depends on the presence of others. Both are far from the experience of the charismatic or the more ambiguous experiences Mathew describes for 'alternative' worship. I can relate to those who share my kinds of experience. I know what they mean when they talk of such experience. I cannot, however, relate so easily to those who talk of a 'God within', or to those who find the effects of community and enthusiasm central to their understanding of 'faith'. Does this then make me an 'insider' to certain traditions (whether Catholic or Buddhist) and an 'outsider' to others (Quaker and Charismatic)? Does this mean that there are different 'shared faiths'? If this is the case, the logical conclusion must be that all 'experience', and therefore, all 'faith' is ultimately individual and unique, therefore not 'shared' in any way, and this rather defeats the object. What is shared, therefore, cannot easily be expressed as 'experience'.

A Shared Discourse

If that which is shared is not an experience, could we say that what is shared among those who have 'faith' is a 'discourse'? Discourse is a complex word and widely used in contemporary theoretical texts (Stringer, 1999: 61–79). It has many meanings and many different referents, depending on the discipline within which it is used. At this point, I am simply using the term to refer to a way of speaking and/or writing, a way of using language that is related to a specific social group or discipline. Discourse covers all aspects of language, both verbal and visual, and this allows us to talk of 'shared discourses'. A number of the papers in this book talk about the way in which language is used within ritual, surrounding ritual and about ritual, and they highlight the way in which language, or discourse, could distinguish the insider from the outsider. If I go back to my own reflections, what becomes very clear is that I can share some elements of language with those of many different religious traditions which I cannot share with those who have no experience of religion. This is simply because we are all members of religious communities and all use a language which takes for granted some kind of 'other' which has a significant impact on our lives, even if the language itself cannot express the nature of that 'other'. At one level this is related to the kind of experiences I have just been talking about, but it also goes beyond this specific example.

If we look at Bilal Sambur's paper, for example, on the question of ritualism, or legalism, and mysticism within Islam and the place of the philosopher Al-Ghazali in mediating these two terms, I can recognize the basis for this debate, even though I do not share the specifically Islamic context in which the argument is framed. There has been an ongoing argument between those who place more emphasis on the external features of ritual and law and those who place primary emphasis on experience and a change of heart in all the major religions. The principle divisions between Catholic and Protestant Christianity, Mahayana and Theravada Buddhism, Vedic traditions and Bhakti traditions in Hinduism and so on, can all, at a very simplistic level, be framed in the terms that Bilal presents. There are also, undoubtedly, figures such as Al-Ghazali in each of the other religious traditions who have attempted, through similar philosophical arguments, to bridge these two traditions. However, all this distinction and philosophical discussion, as Bilal makes clear, is undertaken from an 'insider' perspective. The very basis for the argument would be meaningless for those who are not steeped in one or other of the great religious traditions. Bilal and I, for example, can debate and argue about the details of this kind of philosophical argument, despite coming from different religious traditions, and, I would guess, different sides of the argument. We share a common language of religion that actually makes the argument itself important.

If we go back to Helen's paper on the Sōka Gakkai, we can see one way in which this same kind of discussion can clearly mark an insider/outsider distinction of its own. The *gongyō* rituals consist primarily of the reading of texts, along with other elements. However, Helen makes it clear that most of those who attend the rituals cannot follow the Japanese dialect in which the texts are written. At one level it is clearly important for participants to be able to follow, to meditate upon and to 'visualize' the content of the texts in order for the ritual to be effective. However, the fact that the people cannot understand what is being said does not appear to matter. This situation is not all that different to the situation that existed within the Catholic Church before the reforms of the Second Vatican Council, or the situation in many other ritual contexts around the world. I have no difficulties with the stance of the Soka Gakkai Buddhists. I can understand their position and can make sense of their ritual, as I attend a Catholic Church in which the liturgy is still celebrated primarily in Latin. Other participants at the conference, however, found the whole idea of attending a rite conducted in a language that they did not understand utterly incomprehensible. These particular participants were themselves committed members of their own faith tradition, primarily Christian and including a number of Quakers. The Muslim participants on the other hand, as well as those of no specific faith, who had studied Buddhist and other rituals, tended to side with the Sōka Gakkai and myself.[3] Who, therefore, within this discussion, is the 'insider' and who is the 'outsider'? What is it that makes me, a British Catholic who prefers Mass in Latin, able to empathize more with the ritual experience of Japanese Buddhists than with British Quakers? Are we really talking the same language?

This discussion raises another set of ideas that are related to discourse and religion. The thinking of the social sciences has saturated much of modern, western Christian thinking. The language that is used by the churches is often similar to that of the social sciences themselves, as Peter makes clear in his discussion of the Quaker speaker who came to talk to the Dibdenshaw Meeting about the concept of 'community'. Reflexivity, self-reflection, the need to 'understand', and make our own in a very individualistic way, the language and experience of religion are common to many traditions within the West, especially those with Christian roots. This can be seen very clearly in the self-consciously 'post-modern' 'alternative' worship discussed by Mathew. Such a position, however, is still alien to many religious traditions in many other parts of the world. There are probably a small number of people in this country that prefer the non-reflexive language and experience of the Japanese/Latin Catholic/Buddhist approach, but we are few and far between. My perspective is probably linked in some way to my sense of an external, 'objective' God, rather than the 'God within' of the more reflexive Quaker tradition. The discussion in itself is, however, not really the point. With reference to Bilal's discussion of Al-Ghazali, I suggest that while it is possible for people of all religions to share a common discourse that would make little or no sense to those who have no religion, the divisions within the religions (and not between them, as we sometimes think) in terms of language and experience are often far more significant and far more relevant for particular individuals than the common discourse of 'the religious'. This clearly raises the question of whether we can talk of faith as a 'shared discourse' in any but the most superficial way.

That Which is Not Shared

If it is so difficult to define 'faith' in terms of that which is shared among all those who claim to be religious or who follow a religion of some kind, is it possible to turn the question around and ask whether it is possible to define 'faith' as something which is not shared between the religious 'insider' and the self-acknowledged 'outsider'? This may seem to be an almost impossible task. However, I would like to offer one possible way of pursuing this in terms of Roy Wagner's discussion of the nature of 'culture' in his *The Invention of Culture* (Wagner, 1981).

At the beginning of the book Wagner describes the fictitious journey of a young anthropologist into the field (Wagner, 1981: 5–6). Her task is to study some village far from home and clearly cut off from much of the outside world. Wagner describes how the anthropologist almost immediately begins to sense something of the difference between her own background and the community she is studying. At first this is experienced as acute embarrassment in terms of the things which everybody else in the community takes for granted and which the anthropologist fails to understand. These embarrassments are seen and felt in little things, such as deportment, greetings, eating habits, etc., and for the first few weeks in the field they make the life of the anthropologist utterly miserable. It is out of this experience, Wagner argues, that the concept of culture is 'invented'.[4]

'Culture', according to Wagner, is defined in relation to points of embarrassment, in terms of difference. It is that which makes the community studied different to that from which the anthropologist originates. Those points where the anthropologist feels no embarrassment are those points where the anthropologist sees no difference, and therefore are points that the anthropologist fails to see. This makes the construction of 'culture' a construction of 'difference', a construction of 'otherness'. This part of Wagner's argument is well known and widely acknowledged. However, Wagner makes a further observation. If the anthropologist is embarrassed, then so is the community visited. If the anthropologist overcomes her embarrassment by constructing or inventing a 'culture' for the community, that community will construct or invent something akin to a 'culture' for the anthropologist. Wagner suggests that the New Guinea Cargo Cults are in some ways a 'native anthropology', an attempt to deal with the difference and otherness of the European (Wagner, 1981: 7).

If Wagner's argument concerning 'culture' is true, could we not construct a similar argument in relation to the concept of 'faith'? If we go back to Cantwell Smith, we will note that he devotes a great deal of his work to the attempt to break down the distinctions between religions and to fit religion into a wider history of cultural and intellectual borrowing across large areas of the world (Cantwell Smith, 1981). Cantwell Smith is reluctant to talk of 'traditions' in terms of specific religions, or even to talk of 'religions' as distinct categories. It is here that he faces a particular problem. He still wants to find something that distinguishes what he sees as 'religion' from the rest of human existence, but he has just presented an argument that tends to deny this. He therefore introduces the concept of 'faith'. It is impossible for Cantwell Smith to say what 'faith' is, as we have seen, but 'faith' is an essential concept. It is that which those who are religious have, and which those who are not religious do not have—and, what is more, the non-religious cannot understand what it is. 'Faith' is that which 'we' (the insiders) have and 'you' (the outsiders) do not have. This is not dissimilar to Wagner's construction of 'culture' as that which 'they' (the other) have and which 'we' (as Anthony Cohen (1994) makes clear in a different discussion) do not have. If anthropologists use 'culture' to distance themselves as 'outsiders' from the community or society they are studying (or at least to distance the reader of their ethnographies from such societies), then 'faith' can be seen as that which the religious use to distance themselves from any kind of outsider interference (especially that of the social scientist). This still leaves us with the question of 'what is faith?' or as I asked earlier, 'what kind of things is faith?'.

Like 'faith', 'belief' is a term which is clearly associated with religion, but which is inadequately theorized within the anthropological literature (Stringer, 1996). Jean Pouillon points out that belief, as a concept, is a distinctively Christian idea (Pouillon, 1982). From the earliest days of the Christian community, the followers of Jesus were called to believe that 'Jesus Christ is Lord'. This became ritualized in baptism, which has always contained a statement of belief, either in Jesus or the Trinity. It also became intellectualized and formed the basis for the principle disputes within the first few centuries of the Christian Church, leading eventually to the development of the creeds with their formulaic 'I/We believe in…'. The Reformation, with its rejection of much of Catholic ritual and its emphasis on 'justification by faith alone' only reinforced the emphasis on belief and the intellectual, personal and deliberate association of the individual with a specific set of doctrines or ideas.

Pouillon goes further than simply stating that 'belief' is a Christian concept from a historical point of view. He argues that there is something distinct about the Christian idea of belief that is not found in other religions (Pouillon, 1982: 5). This, he suggests, is the element of doubt. All forms of belief as used by Christians can be distinguished from the idea of 'knowledge'. We say that we believe something either when we are unsure in ourselves, and therefore don't want to say that we 'know' it to be the case, or when we are aware that others do not share our belief. 'We' believe, but we know that others do not. It is in this latter form that we can see a clear relation between belief and the insider/outsider discussion of faith. This also explains the particular importance of belief to early Christianity. Christianity grew up as a minority religion that had to assert its own identity over and against both Judaism and the range of different religious ideas that were present in the Hellenic and Roman worlds. It was by affirming the statement that 'we believe that Jesus is Lord', when all around not only failed to believe, but tried through more or less violent means to make Christians deny that belief, that Christianity was defined. In these terms, to claim 'belief' is to acknowledge our own position as an 'insider' and therefore to assert a clear boundary between 'us'—the 'believers'—and 'them'—those who do not believe.

'Belief', like 'culture', and, I would argue, like 'faith', implies difference. Belief and faith both assert the difference between 'us' and 'them' and therefore have to do with boundaries. They are related to identity, the understanding of who 'we' are, and are therefore part of the symbolic construction of our own particular communities (Cohen, 1985). 'Faith', it could be argued, is the corporate expression of 'belief'. In contemporary western society, 'belief' is seen to be something very individual, but 'faith' maintains a corporate element, it is that which 'we' share and that which 'you' do not have. It is therefore part of a discourse of exclusion.

Faith as Exclusion

The issue of exclusion and difference brings us back to the discourse on 'culture'. If we follow Wagner in arguing that anthropologists have been involved in a process of constructing the 'other' through the invention of 'culture', any discourse on culture must clearly be a discourse of power in which the one 'inventing' the culture is claiming power over those whose culture is being invented (Wagner, 1981; Fabian, 1983). Constructing a culture for the other is one way of trying to confine them, to control them through description, to place them within a taxonomy of our own making. Having been built on the basis of 'difference', it is also part of the discourse of orientalism (Said, 1995). It is part of a process of exoticization, creating the 'other' as 'different', as 'exotic', as 'savage' (Taussig, 1987). Finally, it is part of a wider process of demystification, taking that which is first constructed as 'other' and then dissecting it, analysing it and describing it, such that it is made accessible and controllable by those who are creating the description. The 'other' is both 'exotic' and 'familiar', 'savage' and 'controllable', an exciting and original way of being human and merely an attraction for tourists.

Creating culture is part of a discourse that is undertaken by dominant groups as part of their domination of the other. 'Faith', I suggest, is almost the opposite. It is part of a discourse undertaken by the dominated, the threatened, in order to retain their distance, their identity and their distinctiveness.

Certain elements of the discourse of exclusion can be seen very clearly in Elisabeth Arweck's paper on the study of New Religious Movements. Here it is the use of words such as 'cult' and 'anti-cult movement' that have allowed one group, the researchers, to distance themselves from, and in many ways to 'exclude' the others. However, we also see the ways in which the groups themselves are trying to maintain this distance, or, alternatively, to build bridges of one kind or another through interaction with social scientists and others whom they allow to study them. It is clear from Elisabeth's paper that the New Religions Movements have chosen, very carefully, how to present themselves within a particular discourse that they feel is attempting to control or even to suppress and destroy them. It is within this kind of discourse that the semi-insider social scientist is being recruited to present the group in the best light.

Jo Pearson picks up a similar theme in her paper on the study of Wicca. She claims that the community itself has suffered at the hands of a researcher who failed to acknowledge the importance of the boundary between insider and outsider. According to Jo, Tanya Luhrmann had presented herself to the group which she studied as a potential insider and had undertaken secret initiation ceremonies. When she came to write up her research, however, Luhrmann presented herself as a complete outsider to them and betrayed the trust that was put in her through the initiation process. She used 'outsider', objective, scientific, language to dismiss the claims, or we might say the 'faith', of the group. Luhrmann asserts her own position as better, more authentic, and superior to that of the Wiccan community. Her discourse is seen by Jo as one of exclusion and oppression. This experience has also led the Wiccan community itself to exclude, although in this case those that are excluded are potential researchers. It is only with researchers such as Jo, who was a fully initiated member of a Wiccan community before she began to undertake her research, that the boundary between insider and outsider has begun to open up once again. However, it is clear that one of the reasons why Jo is trusted as a potential researcher is because, as an insider, she understands the language of 'faith', and respects the discourse on 'faith' within the community, with all the implications that this has for identity and integrity. Elisabeth makes it clear that the position taken by Jo, as an insider who becomes a recognized researcher, is a position that is being established within a number of the New Religious Movements. This enables a form of academic research that preserves the hard-won boundaries fully intact.

In the case of religious groups from the major world religions, unlike many New Religious Movements, there is no obvious sense in which they are being threatened or dominated in any overt way within the West. Members of the major world religions, however, still feel under threat. They are shrinking in numbers, at least in Western Europe. The dominant discourse of most western societies is essentially secular. It is seen to be embarrassing to claim any kind of religious affiliation. In some cases, as with the Jews in the past (and in many cases in the present) and the Muslims within much of the West, the threat is more obvious and more direct. It is important, however, for all the religions to claim something that gives them a sense of identity, a distinctiveness, something that stops them from becoming simply another social movement that is battered by the winds of change and the fickle fads of fashion, as groups which are bound to die when the fashions change. One of the main culprits in this unspoken attack on the religions and the gradual undermining of religion within society has been, for most of the previous century, the social sciences themselves, including sociology and anthropology, and even perhaps religious studies. Some, like Cantwell Smith, have tried to distance themselves from this onslaught, while being major players in undermining the distinctiveness of any religious tradition. They have distanced themselves by playing religion's game and claiming for themselves the undefinable 'faith' that still keeps the religious distinct from the vast majority of most western societies.

Conclusion

If 'faith', as used by Cantwell Smith and others who share his perspective, is part of a discourse of exclusion, and if those to be excluded are, at least in part, those researchers who are self-acknowledged 'outsiders', what does this say for the insider/outsider debate and the future of research on religious communities? One approach is to take the lessons of Jo's paper on Wicca seriously and to recognize that much research on 'other' religions, which is based on the social sciences and religious studies, has been a process of violation and a misuse of trust. This would lead us directly into the position advocated by Cantwell Smith and others and leave us arguing that it is only from an insider perspective that any kind of study of religion can be undertaken. All that we can do, therefore, is to encourage people like Jo to undertake studies of their own religious communities.

While this position may maintain some kind of ethical integrity, it does tend to paint the research community as the villain of the piece and to ignore the very legitimate arguments of those who advocate outsider studies. If the discourse on 'culture' is, in part, a discourse of demystification, an attempt to make the 'other' familiar and accessible, even to break down the boundaries between the self and the other, could we not see the discourse on 'faith' as, at its worst, a discourse of deliberate mystification? Could not the resort to 'faith'—a concept which is almost by definition unknowable, except by direct experience—be a way of avoiding the academic gaze, of saying that here is something which the research community is not allowed to study? This could be seen as a dangerous stance that attempts to prioritize religion over all other areas of social life and will only lead to its increasing marginalization within society.

I would like to suggest that Eleanor Nesbitt's paper in this volume gives us one possible way out of this particular dilemma. Eleanor, like practically all the other contributors, recognizes that the terms 'insider' and 'outsider' are not clearly distinct and that any one researcher will never be a complete 'insider' or a complete 'outsider' in relation to religion. Eleanor, however, looks at a particular group of researchers, namely those who acknowledge a Quaker identity. Many of these researchers are not actually studying Friends, although a couple, like Peter Collins in this volume, clearly are. Eleanor is interested in the way in which a Quaker background or identity affects the way in which the individual researcher undertakes his/her research of a given religious group. She suggests that committed Quakers who happen to be researchers cannot be considered as complete outsiders to any other religious community. In this she is following Cantwell Smith and others in assuming that there is something common among all those who claim to be 'religious', irrespective of the tradition from which they come. This, however, is Eleanor's main point. She suggests that there is something specifically about being 'Quakers' that makes these researchers particularly suitable to the ethnographic research on religion. This element includes factors, such as being good listeners and having an open and tolerant attitude to other religions, both of which are fostered among Friends. Underlying these particular qualities and skills is the more general concept of 'empathy'; Quakers, it appears, are particularly good at 'empathizing' with the 'other'.

'Empathy' provides a way of trying to undermine or counteract the impenetrability of the boundary between the insider and the outsider as far as religion is concerned. If we acknowledge that some insiders feel threatened by research and construct some concept of 'faith' or 'mystery' that says 'there is something here that you are never going to understand unless you become one of us', it is clear that the first thing that the researcher has to do— whether an insider, an outsider, or somewhere in-between—is to acknowledge that need for 'mystery', to empathize with it and to respect it. The implication of this is that the discourse becomes less one of boundaries, who is in and who is out, as one of identity. Who are the 'we' who claim this 'faith'? How is that 'we' constructed, maintained or controlled?

How, therefore, can the researcher respect, or empathize with, the 'we' of religion, and how can they write in such a way that allows those who acknowledge the 'we' to join in the conversation? Cantwell Smith argues that we should write nothing about a religion that members of that religion cannot say 'yes' to (Cantwell Smith, 1981: 97). There are two criticisms of this particular position. Firstly, as Bilal's paper makes clear, is that different members of the same 'religion' may wish to say 'yes' to very different things, and so who is to decide which voice is listened to? Secondly, such a position immediately closes off any form of dialogue. An aggressive, dismissive, arrogant, outsider voice can also cut off all forms of dialogue, and that has led us to much of the problem that we currently face. That is why I suggest that we need to be sensitive enough to provide a text that allows the 'other'— whether that other is an insider or an outsider, or both—to engage in the conversation. This is not to dismiss the importance of difference, which must always be acknowledged, nor is it part of a process of exclusion or domination. What I am advocating is a process of study that acknowledges the other, is sensitive to the use of words, such as 'culture', 'faith', 'belief', and even 'religion', and that opens up conversations between the religious and the researcher that are ultimately fruitful to both. That, I hope, is what all the papers that follow within this volume, and the wider work of the Worship in Birmingham Project, aim to do.

The Papers in the Volume

The seven essays within this book have been divided into two blocks of three with Peter Collins's paper acting as a link between the two. The first three deal primarily with ritual, either theories of ritual or studies of specific rituals. It is from the perspective of the study of ritual that these papers engage with the insider/outsider question. The second set of essays each begin with the theoretical questions raised by the insider/outsider question and then go on to relate that to those who are studying ritual. Peter in some sense tries to do both and hence forms a natural link between the two.

We have begun with Bilal Sambur's discussion of the work of Al-Ghazali on ritualism and mysticism. This paper picks up a number of the questions raised towards the end of this introduction, about the fundamental core of religion, but does this within the specific context of a particular religious tradition. The paper shows that it is possible to be an 'insider' or an 'outsider' to different parts of one's own religion, and that it is possible—through the work of scholars such as Al-Ghazali—to overcome some of these internal boundaries. We then move on to two studies based on the analysis of particular religions. Mathew Guest looks at the 'alternative' worship scene, a form of radical Christian worship that deliberately aims to break down the boundaries between insiders and outsiders, while Helen Waterhouse looks at the *gongyō* ritual of the Sōka Gakkai and asks questions about her own positions as a partial insider, at least to the experience, of such a ritual. Helen's discussion also begins to raise some of the more personal questions that are explored further in the second set of essays.

Peter Collins reflects on his own experience as an 'insider' researcher within the Quaker Meeting where he was both warden and researcher. This allows Peter to engage with some of the anthropological literature on insider and outsider research and to question the apparently coherent nature of the researcher. Peter also includes a detailed analysis of a particular act of worship and hence looks back to some of the earlier discussion on ritual as well as forward to the more theoretical discussions of ethnographic research in the final three papers.

Jo Pearson opens the second set of papers by raising a very specific problem in relation to her research within the Wiccan community. Jo shows how previous research, by one who claimed to become an insider and yet remained an outsider led to considerable distrust and uncertainty among the community; as such it was only from her pre-research position as an insider that Jo could undertake the study of the community at all. Elisabeth Arweck takes up a number of the themes raised by Jo, but widens the discussion to look at a wider range of New Religious Movements. She shows how the construction of these movements as 'cults' has led to considerable mistrust between the communities and the academic community, which is only now beginning to break down, not least because of researchers, such as Jo who come out of these communities to engage with academia. Finally, Eleanor Nesbitt's paper looks much more closely at the researchers, particularly at those researchers who claim a Quaker identity. She asks how far this particular form of 'insiderness' helps, hinders or in other ways affects the nature of the research. She also asks how far the research, usually on communities other than Quakers, affects the religious journeys of the researchers themselves.

The book is rounded off by a short paper from Lowell Livezey who is Director of the Religions in Urban America Program in Chicago (RUAP). Like the Worship in Birmingham Project, although set on a larger scale, RUAP is designed to undertake detailed ethnographic studies on religious communities throughout Chicago. RUAP is far more developed than the Worship in Birmingham Project and the first findings of the Project have already been published (Livezey, 1996). Lowell's contributon provides observations on the workings of RUAP, its methods and conclusions, and it is from that perspective, of having been involved in a far larger comparative analysis, that he is able to reflect on the papers and themes of this volume.

Notes

1   See Stringer for a discussion of ethnography in relation to the study of Christian worship (Stringer 1999, 42–61).
2   The insider/outsider problem is discussed with much more vigour in a discipline, such as 'religious studies', where most practitioners are insiders to one religious tradition or another, than it is among anthropologists, for example, or even sociologists, where it is assumed that the researcher is always an outsider. See, for example, the range of extracts chosen by McCutcheon (McCutcheon, 1999).
3   This discussion is similar to that conducted among liturgists and social scientists at the time, with the social scientists defending the use of Latin or traditional English on the grounds that the associations of the rite were more important than the meaning of the words (see Martin, 1980 and Stringer, 1991).
4   Wagner uses the word 'invented' to refer to a process by which that which is already there is revealed to the researcher, rather than to suggest creation out of nothing. This does not, however, weaken the argument that I am developing (see Wagner, 1981: xvi).

References

Cantwell Smith, W. *Towards a World Theology: Faith and Comparative History of Religion.* New York: Orbis Books, 1981.

Cohen, A. P. *The Symbolic Construction of Community.* London: Routledge, 1989 (originally published in 1985 by Ellis Horwood, Chichester).

Cohen, A. P. *Self Consciousness: An Alternative Anthropology of Identity.* London: Routledge, 1994.

Fabian, J. *Time and the Other: How Anthropology Makes its Object.* New York: Columbia U. P., 1983.

Heim, S. M. *Salvations, Truth and Difference in Religion.* New York: Orbis Books, 1995.

Livezey, L., ed. *Religious Organizations and Structural Change in Metropolitan Chicago: The Research Report of the Religion in Urban America Program.* Chicago: The University of Illinois at Chicago, 1996.

Martin, D. *The Breaking of the Image: A Sociology of Christian Theory and Practice.* Oxford: Blackwell, 1980.

McCutcheon, R. T., ed. *The Insider/Outsider Problem in the Study of Religion: A Reader.* London: Cassell, 1999.

Otto, R. *The Idea of the Holy: An Inquiry into the Non-Rational Factor in the Idea of the*

Divine and its Relation to the Rational. Oxford: Humphrey Milford, 1928.

Pouillon, J. "Remarks on the Verb 'To Believe'." In Izard, M. & Smith, P., eds. *Between Belief and Transgression: Structuralist Essays in Religion, History and Myth.* Chicago: The University of Chicago Press, 1982: 1–8.

Said, E. W. *Orientalism: Western Conceptions of the Orient.* London: Penguin Books, 1995.

Stringer, M. D. "Situating Meaning in the Liturgical Text." *Bulletin of the John Rylands University Library of Manchester* 73 (3), 1991: 181–195.

Stringer, M. D. "Towards a Situational Theory of Belief." *Journal of the Anthropological Society of Oxford* 27 (3), 1996: 217–234.

Stringer, M. D. *On the Perception of Worship: The Ethnography of Worship in Four Christian Congregations in Manchester.* Birmingham: The University of Birmingham Press, 1999.

Taussig, M. *Shamanism, Colonialism, and the Wild Man: A Study in Terror and Healing.* Chicago: The University of Chicago Press, 1987.

Turner, V. W. "Dewey, Dilthey, and Drama: An Essay in the Anthropology of Experience." In Turner, V. W. & Bruner, E. M., eds. *The Anthropology of Experience.* Chicago: University of Illinois Press, 1986: 33–44.

Wagner, R. *The Invention of Culture.* Chicago: The University of Chicago Press, 1981.

2 From the Dichotomy of Spiritualism/Ritualism to the Dichotomy of Insider/Outsider

BILAL SAMBUR

Introduction

Religion is a complex phenomenon which has many dimensions. This complexity makes it difficult to understand religion as a whole. Although this difficulty remains, scholars never give up studying and analysing religion. For example, Ninian Smart, a phenomenologist of religion, presents seven dimensions of religion in order to get a better picture of the religious anatomy.[1] Muhammad Iqbal (1877–1938) on the other hand, tries to define religion in holistic terms saying that "religion is neither mere thought, nor mere feeling, nor mere action; it is an expression of the whole man" (Iqbal, 1998: 2). Whether religion is defined or analysed in terms of its totality or in terms of its partiality, it is all too easy for those studying religion, as well as for those practising it, to reduce its complexity to a series of simple dichotomies, expressed, for example, in questions such as 'are the spiritual and the ritual[2] compatible with each other?' or 'is the spiritual superior to the ritual?'.

The history of religion shows that it is a 'noble dream' for religious people to experience the dimensions of their religion without ignoring others. There always seems to be a tension between the ritual and spiritual dimensions of religion, for example. The advocates of religious rituals do not sacrifice their religious practices for the sake of spirituality, and the advocates of religious spirituality do not sacrifice their spiritual ways for the sake of rituals. This is a controversial issue between Muslim Sufis and Muslim jurists. The Sufis claim that they are 'the followers of the heart'. The jurists say that the practice of religious rituals is an inevitable command of Islamic law. This points to a further dichotomy between 'heart' and 'law'.

Similarly, there has been a dichotomy between the insider and the outsider view of the study of religion. Those who claim that religion can only be understood from the insider view do not understand, and stand opposed to, those who claim that an outsider view is more objective.

This paper seeks to present the approach of Imam Al-Ghazali concerning the question of spirituality and ritual and to raise some questions about the 'insider/outsider' dichotomy based on Al-Ghazali's views.

Al-Ghazali was born in 1058 (450 A.H.) at Tus, a town near the modern Mashhad in Iran. He studied theology, philosophy, logic, dialectic, and jurisprudence under the supervision of 'Abdu'l-Malik al-Juwaini, one of the most distinguished scholars of his time. In 1091 (484) he was appointed as the rector of the Nizamiyyah College in Baghdad. At the zenith of his career, in 1096 (488), he gave up all his wealth and position, left Baghdad and spent ten years in solitude. During this time, he wrote his *magnum opus*, *Ihya' 'Ulum al-Din* ("The Revival of the Religious Sciences"). In 1107 (499), he started to teach again and wrote an autobiographical work, *al-Munkidh min al-dalal* ("Deliverance from Error"). He died in 1111 (503) at the age of 53.[3]

Why were Al-Ghazali's views chosen for this examination? The reason is that Al-Ghazali's position in classical Islamic thought is indispensable. As Goldziher states, "since the twelfth century, Al-Ghazali has been the final authority" for mainstream Islam (Goldziher, 1981: 245). Al-Ghazali attempted to combine the spiritual life with the legal code of Islam. The marriage between Sufism and Law is his great achievement. Therefore, he is called the great reconciler of Orthodox Islam (Schimmel, 1978: 95–96). If Al-Ghazali is the great reconciler of the heart and the law, we need to ask how he explains religious rites spiritually, without violating Islamic law. In order to answer this question and to understand Al-Ghazali's approach regarding religious rituals and spirituality, I will examine the Muslim practice of ritual prayer (*salat*). Ritual prayer in Islam has spiritual as well as legal dimensions. Ritual prayer is also one of the principal ways of expressing Muslim religious identity. Therefore I will not only present Al-Ghazali's view concerning the spiritual and legal aspects of ritual prayer, but I will also try to explore the meaning of this ritual in Muslim life in the light of Al-Ghazali's ideas.

In the second half of the paper, I will attempt to apply the same 'reconciling' techniques to the question of the insider/outsider approach to the study of religion.

Al-Ghazali and Ritual Prayer

Al-Ghazali's spiritual interpretation of Islamic rites is based on the two cardinal sources of Islam, the Qur'an and the prophetic model of Muhammad (*sunna*). Lazarus-Yufeh claims that although Islamic rituals had no spiritual meaning in Islam, Al-Ghazali gave them spiritual meanings and fixes them properly in Islamic doctrine. In other words, he argues that Al-Ghazali achieved the Islamization of non-Islamic rituals (Lazarus-Yufeh, 1981: 34–36). Lazarus-Yufeh ignores Qur'anic and Prophetic principles in Al-Ghazali's explanations and presents him as an 'inventor'. However, Al-Ghazali does not invent anything new, he is only a systematic interpreter of Islamic practices, since their form and content are determined by Qur'anic doctrine and Prophetic model.

As mentioned earlier, for Al-Ghazali the real confrontation was between the legalists and the spiritualists. Metaphorically speaking, religious rites provide the playground for this confrontation. He believes that there is a need to reconcile legal and spiritual matters with each other, According to him, there is a mutual relationship between legal and spiritual matters that could be compared with the relationship between body and spirit. For him, legal principles establish the body of Islamic rites, the spiritual principles establish their soul. When the spirit leaves the body, it becomes a corpse and the soul leaves like air. Schimmel succinctly summarizes Al-Ghazali's view as follows:

> All that al-Ghazali teaches … is only to help man to live a life in accordance with the sacred law, not by clinging exclusively to its letter, but by an understanding of its deeper meaning, by sanctification of the whole life, so that he is ready for the meeting with his Lord at any moment … This teaching—a marriage between mysticism and law—has made al-Ghazali the most influential theologian of medieval Islam. (Schimmel, 1978: 95)

In the light of Schimmel's view, we could say that the Law (*shari'ah*) is the answer to the question of *how* Muslims can practise religious rites, like pilgrimage and ritual prayers. Sufism is the answer to *why* they practise religious rites. The law is necessary for the practice of form, while Sufism is necessary for the understanding of the content.

In his most important work, *Worship in Islam* (*Ihya 'Ulum al-Din*, Al-Ghazali, 1925), Al-Ghazali first explains the prescribed conditions of ritual prayer, then argues their inner mysteries. As "ritual goes back beyond the dawn of history" (Whitehead, 1930: 10), ritual prayer also goes back to the earliest period of Islam. Ritual prayer may be defined as the daily duty of Muslims, which is performed five times a day and requires ablution, bodily movements—mainly standing, bowing and prostrating, reading verses from the Qur'an, and some other prayer formulae. Muslims claim that the Prophet first taught his companions how to practise ritual prayer and that his prescription has been transmitted to other generations through the first companions. The Prophet said to "pray as you see me do (pray)". The main form and content of ritual prayer in Islam have had extraordinary stability from the beginning to today, regardless of time, place, and social states. It is practised in almost every part of the world in the same form. Fazlur Rahman has coined the term 'living tradition' for ritual prayer and other practices of Islam which were transmitted from the Prophet through generations (Rahman, 1979: 54). According to Al-Ghazali, it is one of the essential religious duties of parents to teach their children how to practise ritual prayer, because ritual prayer plays a decisive role in the way children gain and maintain their religious identity (Al-Ghazali, 1996, Vol. 2: 152).

Ritual prayer is rich in symbolism and filled with meaning. Therefore, it is perceived as a universal presentation of Islamic doctrine at the deepest level.[4] The Prophet describes ritual prayer as the 'centre pole of religion' and in the list of the 'five pillars', ritual prayer is placed second after the testimony of Islamic monotheism (*shahada*). Muslims believe that the monotheistic testimony of Islam is the basis for a natural and sincere relationship with God. Ritual prayer, as the second pillar, presents a natural act of this relationship and provides a frame of reference for a Muslim. It could even be said that in ritual prayer, the Islamic faith is experienced in a total manner. It could be called 'belief in the flesh'. The close relationship between monotheistic testimony of Islam and its prescribed prayer shows how the Islamic creed forms into ritual. Al-Ghazali thinks that practising ritual prayer, or not practising it, shows whether an individual is a Muslim or not. The practice of ritual prayer shows that one is apparently a member of the universal Muslim community (*umma muslima*). In Al-Ghazali's understanding, giving up ritual prayer is almost equal to being a non-Muslim. In his thought, the act of ritual prayer is an activity of a Muslim's functional membership in society. Ritual prayer is a kind of religious ID.

The meaning of ritual prayer is not to have holiness in itself, but to be in a kind of unconditional surrender to God. Whoever prays lives with God. Whoever abandons prayer abandons God. Therefore, ritual prayer is the act which makes Muslims see themselves in the presence of God.

I recall an incident when one of my Muslim colleagues told me that "prayer is not like relations between us, it is like unconditionally meeting with God. It presents God's holiness, which we explore five times a day." Al-Ghazali reports the following saying of the Prophet: "whoever meets God as a miser of prayer, God will not pay attention to any of his works" (Al-Ghazali, 1996: 44), because to miss ritual prayer means to lose the opportunity to have a relationship with God.

Islam does not only pay attention to the legal rules of ritual prayer, but also to its spiritual dimension. However, Al-Ghazali knows that the outward observation of the legal rules of ritual prayer is one thing and full realization of its meaning is another. He therefore starts by explaining the legal rules of ritual prayer. We draw the following principles from his explanations:

1. Prayer formulae must be uttered word perfect.
2. The place of ritual prayer must be cleaned and properly used.
3. The Divine verses of the Qur'an must be correctly recited and in proper sequence.
4. The entire process of ritual prayer—ablution, standing, bowing and prostration—must be performed completely, accurately, orderly and timely. Errors in any of these acts may invalidate prayer.[5]

As these principles show, each individual should be a 'great artist' of ritual prayer, while performing prayer. Al-Ghazali not only requires outward stipulations for the human body, but he also presents the necessary conditions for the human heart. As the Qur'an says, "their flesh and blood reach not God, but the devotion from you reacheth Him" (*The Qur'an*, 22: 37). For Al-Ghazali, without the heart, ritual prayer could become a mechanical habit or a religious fossil. For that reason, ritual prayer cannot stand only in its own ritual realm, but it must stand at the centre of the heart. There is no centre for ritual prayer except the heart. Without the heart, there would be emptiness at the centre. In Islam, God is always present. Ritual prayer brings the individual into the presence of God, not God into the present. Because of this aspect of ritual prayer, it is called the 'ascension of a Muslim' (*al-mi'raj*). Al-Ghazali asserts that the presence of the body is not enough, the presence of the heart (*hudhur-i qalb*) is essential, since the heart is the place where the principal reality of the human is kept. The location of ritual prayer in the heart means that it is located in the primary ground of the human being. In the ground of the heart, individuals should know and show their servanthood to God. Al-Ghazali argues that the main qualities of the true servant's heart are these:

1. The 'presence of heart', which means that the heart must be liberated from everything except God.
2. 'Apprehension', which means to understand the meaning of Qur'anic verses and prayer formulae.
3. To magnify God as a servant.
4. To feel a sense of awe and fear in the presence of God's majesty.
5. To be hopeful for God's reward.
6. To be aware of one's shortcomings and sins.[6]

Al-Ghazali asks people to transcend the ritual and establish a spiritual kingdom in their heart. Ritual prayer plays the role of a vehicle towards spirituality. For him, ritual prayer should be an outward and visible sign of ethical and spiritual sovereignty. Al-Ghazali expects the individual not only to be a 'man of God', but also an ethical 'man among the people' at the end of ritual prayer. According to Al-Ghazali, ritual prayer should prevent people from doing evil and it should lead them to good. Ritual prayer is an instrument of morality, which can deepen it and keep it alive. Al-Ghazali wants people to actualize the deepest ground of their being on an ethical and spiritual level. He expects nothing less from ritual prayer than spiritual and ethical renewal.

Ritual prayer is not only an individual act, it is also a social one. According to the Prophetic paradigm of Islam, social prayer in the mosque is considered twenty-seven times more meritorious than individual prayer. Prayer five times a day presents the need for a regular and mutual affirmation of unity for the Muslim community. According to Islam, Muslims should have the desire for Muslim brotherhood and sisterhood. Ritual prayer, as a social rite, is the expression of this desire. All Muslims participate in social prayer as equal and independent individuals who submit themselves to the transcendental authority of God. Homogeneity and equality are the main aspects of social prayer in the mosque, because there is no hierarchical order in this communal prayer. Ritual prayer in the mosque is neither a ritual of 'status reversal' nor of 'status elevation' (Turner, 1969: 94). All Muslims have an egalitarian and independent status in the mosque. For Al-Ghazali, the egalitarian structure of social prayer shows that everybody occupies a significant place in Muslim society. This respectful attitude towards Muslim individuals allows them to consider themselves as honourable members of society.

Al-Ghazali thus tries to break the one-dimensional approaches of Sufis and legalists to the relationship between the ritual and the spiritual. As ritual prayer shows, religious rituals have a multi-dimensional character, because rites involve many things at the same time. Ritual prayer is concerned with ethical, spiritual, eschatological, and social aspects. This is the heterogeneity of ritual prayer. Al-Ghazali presents spirituality and morality as the basic ground for religious rituals. He maximizes spirituality and morality, but minimizes formality. Al-Ghazali's formulation is 'simple rites, but high spirituality and morality'.

Al-Ghazali and the Insider/Outsider View of Religion

Al-Ghazali approaches the dichotomy between what can be considered the ritual and spiritual aspects of human behaviour as an insider. He argues that the ritual and spiritual dimensions of humanity complement each other during the meaning-making process of ritual prayer. As a religious instructor, he asserts that even if the spiritual dimension were to disappear, one should continue to perform one's ritual practice until meaning is found in the experience. However, such a conclusion seems to be self-evident and theological in nature, because Al-Ghazali's suggestion is more concerned with the ultimate ends of the ritual and spiritual aspects of prayer. He does not, however, clarify or provide details of what really occurs in the performance of prayer as a ritual act or as a spiritual state. Such clarification would be much more helpful for students of religious studies, if they are to come to grips with the often complex and contested theoretical, definitional, and methodological aspects of religion.

How useful, therefore, is an insider's approach to fundamental and important religious issues, such as prayer? Can an insider really tell us what is happening in the religious life of an individual or community? Who can we claim to be an 'insider'? For example, the dichotomy that existed between spiritualism and ritualism can still be seen within the Muslim community today. Both jurists (*Fuqaha*) and Sufis are concerned Muslims and they both claim that their religious experience is drawn from the very heart of Islam. In other words, Sufis would consider themselves as insiders, but they would view Muslim jurists as outsiders, and vice versa. Furthermore there are many Muslims today who approach the study of Islam by looking through the eyes of Western social scientific theory, which is considered an outsider's perspective within the broader Muslim community. How then should we identify and define the modern Muslim researcher? Would s/he fall in the insider or the outsider camp? It is obvious that the position of what might constitute an insider or outsider varies depending upon the perspective that is held.

Researchers, such as Otto and Cantwell Smith, claim that it is the insider who should hold the primary position for the proper understanding of a religion. Cantwell Smith, for example, asserts the unique authority inherent in the insider's position in religious studies:

> No statement about Islamic faith is true that Muslims cannot accept. No personalist statement about Hindu religious life is legitimate in which Hindus cannot recognize themselves. No interpretation of Buddhist doctrine is valid unless Buddhists can respond 'Yes! That is what we hold.' (Cantwell Smith, 1981: 97; see also Cantwell Smith, 1959: 43)

Cantwell Smith's claim raises the following question: 'is being an insider to be the measure of all things concerning religion or anything else?' If the perspective espoused by an insider is to be considered the primary authority in matters of religious study, then does his/her religious experience speak for the entire religious community and represent their view of reality as well? Can the Sufi speak for the jurist, or the jurist for the Sufi? Who is the insider whose 'Yes! That is what we hold' is to be sought? Does the insider, therefore, say everything there is to say, either about the nature of God or the human condition? What if something is left unsaid? Given these questions, Cantwell Smith's approach and the authoritative voice he gives to the insider is not really convincing, especially in the light of one's total understanding of any religion, whether approached from an insider or outsider's perspective, for both are by definition limited.

At least two very different elements are at work here and there should be no confusion regarding their distinctiveness. To *value* an insider's view is one thing, but to *authorize* it is quite another.

In contrast to Cantwell Smith's approach, although the outsider should value the insider's view, s/he should not be dependant on the affirmation or qualifying 'yes' of the insider in order to validate his/her own views. If s/he seeks the insider's 'yes' in matters of religion, then s/he accepts that religion is the sole property of the insider, or a particular sub-set of insiders, and that no-one has access to this property without their permission. Thus, if religion is considered the property of only a limited number of insiders, can any religion make claims of universality and make their religion both meaningful and relevant to the lives of others? For example, Islam presents itself as a religion not just for Muslims, but for the rest of humanity. This means that whether one finds oneself as either a Muslim or non-Muslim, insider or outsider, everybody should be able to study and interpret the teachings of Islam, and thus has the right to say 'yes' or 'no' to Islam. There is no need for an outsider to ask Muslims, Christians, Jews, Hindus or Buddhists for self-authorisation, because all of humanity should have equal access to the knowledge that these religious traditions possess. However, the outsider's point of view should not and cannot be formed independent of the insider's perspective.

Scholars engaged in the study of religion have often lent an undue amount of authority to the insider's point of view, while asserting that the difference between the insider and outsider is one of quality rather than degree. Some argue that religion itself is a special category of experience that must be evaluated as an autonomous province of human life. The question arises, therefore, whether religion should be looked upon as merely another human construction like the economy, society, or the state. Or is it something more? According to Eliade, religion is a *sui generis* category that cannot be reduced to any other human process like culture, psychology or sociology. It cannot even be compared with other human categories. It is unique by nature, therefore it must be understood on "its own plane of reference" (Eliade, 1999: 98). Almost a century before Eliade was writing, Feuerbach had rejected such an idea and claimed that all religion is anthropological, in other words it is entirely consigned to a human process. He states:

> Man—this is the mystery of religion—projects (vergegenständlicht sich) his being into objectivity, and then again makes himself an object to this projected image of himself thus converted into a subject; he thinks of himself as an object of himself, but, as the object of an object, of another being than himself. (Feuerbach, 1957: 29)

While Eliade's aim is to avoid reductionism in order to save the transcendental concepts bound up in religion, such as God, Feuerbach attempts to reduce God to a human image, which draws our attention to the central role that human beings play in religion.

In the world of the faithful adherent, these two opposing and distinct approaches to the study of religion are displayed in the following way. Eliadian thought can be detected when insiders proclaim that their religious experience is transcendental by nature and comes from God, as opposed to outsiders who maintain that whatever the insider boasts of is only in the final analysis their own construction, including God, and has no reality except in the mind of the believers. This dichotomy raises a number of questions: is it possible to ever come to terms with, and truly understand, the human experience, or is it possible for mortal human beings to understand the divine? Is it necessary for insiders to attribute everything that they experience to God, and likewise, is it paramount that outsiders always strive to find a human origin for whatever the insider says comes from God? In other words, is it the proper attitude on the part of the outsider to start his/her research under the pre-formed assumption that all things coming from organized religion should be simply assigned to the category of human construction? Further, is it proper for the insider to presume that everything s/he experiences in his/her daily life emanates from a divine source? Can all religions really claim to be *sui generis*, as Eliade claims? Are all religions merely products of human design and imagination, as Feuerbach claims? Can both theories be valid and be seen at work in different religions, in various cases and stages within the broader religious experience?

The researcher should not feel compelled to attribute either a human or a divine element to every religious phenomenon s/he encounters, but should be open to the possibility of finding both along the way and within a variety of religious contexts. Whether the outsider really maintains that religion is a mere human construct or not, is not or should not be the central issue, but rather how valuable they consider the contribution of the insider's religious life to be for the wider community. As an insider, Al-Ghazali draws our attention to the spiritual, ethical and social value found in the performance of ritual prayer. How then can we come to understand such an insider's evaluation of a commonly viewed ritual act or function? To begin this process we first need to separate the question of origin from the question of value.

The act of ritual prayer is performed in almost exactly the same manner in most parts of the Islamic world. Al-Ghazali does not say that only the physical acts of ritual prayer are held in common, but that there is a commonality of meaning behind these acts, which is understood by all Muslims. This presents the outsider with a fundamental question: does every act of ritual prayer, such as prostration, bowing, standing, etc., have exactly the same meaning in every part of the Muslim world? According to Al-Ghazali, the deeper meaning attached to ritual prayer is hidden within various Islamic texts, such as the Qur'an, and in certain Prophetic utterances (*hadith*, pl. *ahadith*), as well as in the performance of the act of prayer itself. However, Al-Ghazali seems to ignore the wealth of meaning that resides with individual Muslims, and this might be important (see Stringer, 1999: 2–3).

If the outsider really wants to understand what is going on in the world of the insider, how does s/he begin this process? Is there a moment in time when the outsider can truly say 'That is it! Now I understand'?

It is necessary to question the process whereby the outsider comes to an understanding of the insider's view, in order to see if it truly represents authentic 'facts' with regard to the insider or is nothing more than the fiction or fantasy of the outsider. Is it valid to question the motives, religious and cultural background of the outsider engaged in a study of religion? It would seem just as valid as him/her questioning the motives and religious background of the insider. If the religio-cultural background of the outsider is that of a Westernized Christian, is it possible for him/her to look at any other religion, except through the glasses of a Western-Christian culture? Doing so would make one's understanding of another's religion largely one of one's own construction, rather than the other's reality. For example, the terms 'worship' and 'prayer' are Christian, not Muslim terms. If a researcher examines the Islamic terms '*Ibadah*' and '*Salah*' through the Christian perception of what worship and prayer mean, then his/her understanding would be constructed on a Christian rather than Muslim foundation.

Some people maintain that to know and understand one religion is sufficient to aid one in coming to a fruitful knowledge of other religions. Harnack, for example, represents such a one-sided approach when he asserts that "Christianity is not one religion among many; it is religion. He who does not know this religion, knows none, and he who knows it and its history knows all" (cited in Heiler, 1938: 121). It has been pointed out that many religious studies in the West have resulted in nothing less than a superficial, stereotype, sometimes fictitious and normative understanding of other religious systems in the world.[7] Perhaps it is true that because some religions are more complex and diverse by nature than others, they do not readily lend themselves to the application of the same religious approach or methodology when undergoing any in-depth study. This does, however, not mean that a Muslim cannot gain anything more than a normative understanding of Christianity, or that a Christian or an atheist cannot come to a 'competent' understanding of Islam. If this were the case, the major religions of the world would be worthless and of no value at all to the common man or woman. For all these religions are made up of literally millions of faithful adherents and on the whole their faith is a simple one.

In summary, as the study of religion is a serious endeavour, it should not be approached from the fieistic subjectivism of the insider, any more than it should be approached from the anthropological objectivism of the outsider. One of the hardest tasks for a human being is to be totally objective when engaged in the study of anything. Human beings are relentless in their struggle to understand and know as much as possible about themselves and the world they live in, and this is especially true where the study of religion is concerned. Therefore, it is important to note that both the view of the insider and the view of the outsider offer different approaches to often the same questions, and neither should be seen as superior or of more value than the other. As Al-Ghazali provided the means for the reconciliation between the spiritual and ritual on the basis of the necessity of both for a full understanding of ritual prayer, we ought to look for some means of reconciliation between the insider and the outsider view on religion as part of a deeper understanding of religion in all its forms.

Notes

1 The seven dimensions are: 1. the ritual or practical dimension, 2. the doctrinal or philosophical dimension, 3. the mythic or narrative dimension, 4. the experiential or emotional dimension, 5. the ethical or legal dimension, 6. the organizational or social dimension, and 7. the material or artistic dimension. (Smart, 1997: 10–11).

2 In this paper I am using the term 'ritual' to define the outward practices of the religion, those governed by law in Islam, those which have to be performed according to certain norms. The term 'spiritual' is to be understood as relating to the inner elements of the religion, those to do with the heart in traditional Sufism.

3 For further information about Al-Ghazali's life, personality, and thought, see Sambur, 2000; Watt, 1971; Smith, 1994.

4 This position regarding ritual prayer in Islam is a good example for Monica Wilson's argument. She says that "Rituals reveal values at their deepest level … men express in ritual what moves them most, and since the form of expression is conventionalized and obligatory, it is the values of the group that are revealed. I see in the study of rituals the key to an understanding of the essential constitution of human societies." (Wilson, 1957: 241)

5 For Al-Ghazali's explanation of external practices of ritual prayer, see Al-Ghazali, 1996: 63–84.

6 Concerning the conditions of heart in the thought of Al-Ghazali, see Al-Ghazali, 1996: 93–98.

7 According to Wach, Western religious studies have produced fictive and normative understandings of World Religions. He criticizes such Western stereotypes and gives some of these images as examples: "Islam, for example, means to many the personal teachings and practices of Mohammed, or a somewhat austere, otherworldly, fanatic faith accompanied by rigid sanctions. Buddhism is understood either as a lofty, highly rational ethical ideal supposed to have been taught by a twin brother of Socrates or as the thinly veiled polytheism of the masses of North and East Asiatic people. Hinduism, for which it seems so difficult to find any constitutive features, appears as an enormous mass of heterogeneous concepts and idolatrous practices, though some may feel inclined to identify it altogether with either an ancient or a modern version of the monistic metaphysics of the Vedanta school. Confucianism, viewed most frequently as the application of a faithfully kept body of the sayings of the great sage, is conceived as a replica of modern Western 'humanism', purged of all that smacks of 'metaphysics' and 'superstition'." (Wach, 1947–48: 263)

References

Al-Ghazali, Imam. *Ihya 'Ulum al-Din.* New Delhi: Islamic Book Service, 1996. Translated by E. E. Calverley as I. Al-Ghazali. *Worship in Islam: Al-Ghazali's Book of the Ihya on Worship.* Madras: The Christian Literature Society for India, 1925.

Cantwell Smith, W. *Towards a World Theology: Faith and the Comparative History of Religion.* Maryknoll, NY: Orbis Books, 1981.

Cantwell Smith, W. "History of Religions—Whither and Why?" In Eliade, M. & Kitagawa, J. M., eds. *The History of Religions: Essays in Methodology.* Chicago: University of Chicago Press, 1959.

Eliade, M. "A New Humanism." In McCutcheon, R. T., ed. *The Insider/Outsider Problem in the Study of Religion.* London, New York: Cassell, 1999: 95–103.

Feuerbach, L. *The Essence of Christianity.* New York: Harper & Row, 1957.

Goldziher, I. *Introduction to Islamic Theology and Law.* Princeton, NJ: Princeton U. P., 1981.

Heiler, F. *Prayer: A Study in the History and Psychology of Religion.* London: Oxford U. P., 1938.

Iqbal, M. *The Reconstruction of Religious Thought in Islam*. Lahore: Sh. Muhammad Ashraf, 1998.

Lazarus-Yufeh, H. *Some Religious Aspects of Islam*. Leiden: Brill, 1981.

Rahman, E. *Islam*. Chicago: Chicago U. P., 1979.

Sambur, B. *Prayer in the Psychology of Religion, with Special Reference to Al-Ghazali, Ibn 'Ata Allah, and Iqbal*. Unpublished PhD thesis, Department of Theology, University of Birmingham, 2000.

Schimmel, A. *Mystical Dimensions of Islam*. Chapel Hill: University of North Carolina Press, 1978.

Smart, N. *Dimensions of the Sacred: An Anatomy of the World's Beliefs*. London: Fontana Press, 1997.

Smith, M. *Al-Ghazali: The Mystic*. London: Luzac, 1994.

Stringer, M. D. *On the Perception of Worship: The Ethnography of Worship in Four Christian Congregations in Manchester*. Birmingham: University of Birmingham Press, 1999.

Turner, V. W. *The Ritual Process: Structure and Anti-Structure*. London: Routledge & Kegan Paul, 1969.

Wach, J. "Spiritual Teaching in Islam: A Study." *Journal of Religion* 27–28, 1947–48.

Watt, M. *Muslim Intellectual: A Study of al-Ghazali*. Edinburgh: Edinburgh U. P., 1971.

Whitehead, A. N. *Religion in the Making*. London: Cambridge U. P., 1930.

Wilson, M. *Rituals of Kinship among the Nyakyusa*. Oxford: Oxford U. P., 1957.

3 'Alternative' Worship: Challenging the Boundaries of the Christian Faith[1]

MATHEW GUEST

Introduction

Enmeshed in interpretative frameworks that emphasize post-modern fragmentation, individualism and de-traditionalization, it is sometimes easy to lose sight of the social and conceptual boundaries which define religious identity and shape religious change (Bauman, 1998: 57–58; Heelas *et al.*, 1996). Religious innovation does not imply a randomly experimental approach to 'spiritual capital', but implies change that is tempered by convictions about which cultural phenomena are worthy of spiritual significance. Contemporary cultural change seems to have broadened the possibilities in this respect, but it has not thrown them wide open for all people. New religious initiatives need to be grounded in their specific social manifestations, subject to the social class, cultural identity and religious background of participants, to the experiences to which they are most open, and to which they are most disposed.

Bearing this in mind, this paper deals with the 'alternative' worship movement in the UK as a site of religious change. Located within the organisational structure of the 'mainstream' churches, and yet adopting a radically experimental approach to worship, the movement embodies a tension between tradition and a culturally driven ideology of progression. Moreover, although expressing no desire for schism or organisational independence, 'alternative' service groups provide the context for a radical rethinking of the conceptual boundaries of the Christian faith. In line with the notion that religious innovations are parasitical upon the traditions out of which they grow, it is the intention of this paper to interpret the ritual and ideological innovations of 'alternative' worship as the result of an appropriation and transformation of Protestant evangelicalism. Furthermore, although the two movements seem asymmetrically opposed in some respects, it can be argued that 'alternative' worship is dependent upon evangelicalism for its historical heritage as well as for the theological and cultural assumptions that underpin the vision of Christianity that it seeks to express. Just as notions of the 'sacred' only exist in the form of relationally or situationally defined categories (Smith, 1982: 55), so—it seems—do representations of faith. First, however, it will be necessary to trace a brief history of 'alternative' worship in order to set this development within its context.

A Brief History of 'Alternative' Worship

'Alternative' worship originated primarily with the pioneering 'Nine O'Clock Service' (NOS),[2] which began in the charismatic church of St Thomas's, Crooks, in Sheffield, in the mid-1980s. NOS advocated a radical evangelical theology and claimed to be revisiting the essence of Christianity, as lived by the early church through committed discipleship and close-knit community living. Most notably, NOS attempted to challenge the moral and religious complacency that it perceived in Western culture at large as well as in the established church. However, it was the worship at NOS which secured its reputation as inspirational, and which drew so many people to its events.

NOS services were distinguished by a radical use of multi-media technology. Ambient and dance music was used, in vogue with the developing popular music scene of the time, and a conscious effort was made, on the part of the leadership teams, to keep up-to-date with the latest trends in sound technology and image reproduction. For many, this combination of factors formed an event that was closer to a night-club than any conceptions of 'church'; many who had previously felt alienated from traditional church worship found a welcome haven in NOS, where the boundaries between Christianity, the church and pop culture had been effectively and deliberately blurred. Those hundreds of young people who travelled across the country to take part in this pioneering service responded in different ways. Some moved to Sheffield and committed themselves to the NOS community more whole-heartedly, while others were inspired to inaugurate similar projects within their own local areas. It is these scattered local groups that have developed into the 'alternative' worship movement.

Around the time when NOS was enjoying its heyday, several other developments were emerging within Christian circles in the UK, which had an impact on this nascent movement. Dave Tomlinson, a former House Church leader, began to perceive the doubts and misgivings of many Restorationist Christians with respect to the fundamentalism and authoritarian leadership that were central to the House Church style (Walker, 1988: 112, 116). He responded by establishing 'Harry', a Christian arts festival that encouraged a more experimental approach to worship, using the media of story and debate to provide a 'safe' ecclesiastical space in which young people could express and explore these doubts. In 1995, Tomlinson published *The Post-Evangelical*, in which he argues that a great number of evangelicals have become disillusioned with the conservative, exclusivist approach to truth, authority and the church, which characterizes evangelicalism. He suggests a more experimental, exploratory approach to faith and worship, in accordance with a post-modern understanding of truth as multi-dimensional, and of tradition as subject to perpetual subversion and revision, if it is to retain any relevancy within contemporary culture (Tomlinson, 1995: 131–132). Tomlinson also established *Holy Joe's*, a Christian discussion group run along the same lines as 'Harry'; it is based in a pub in South London, and holds an 'alternative' service on a regular basis.

Although NOS had begun by advocating a strongly charismatic approach to worship, inspired by John Wimber's 'signs and wonders' theology (Percy, 1996), its later services were more inspired by Matthew Fox's 'Creation Spirituality', which emphasizes ecological concerns, a holistic spirituality and a radically immanentist understanding of the sacred (Fox, 1991). Although surviving 'alternative' services shy away from Fox's work, they demonstrate a willingness to experiment with new sources of spiritual significance, including Celtic traditions, and they demonstrate a political awareness of 'green' issues. Services are mostly multi-media based, incorporating video imagery, sound mixing, and the use of incense, in order to facilitate a worship event in which all the senses are involved. Usually held once or twice a month, 'alternative' services are for the most part organized and led by a small planning group who design worship afresh at each occasion, according to the theological theme of the day. Consequently, there is a tendency towards creativity and liturgical revision rather than towards any notion of ritual consistency. Moreover, leadership roles within the act of worship are often shared and any directive teaching is given minimal space, if any at all—a feature that reflects the distrust of person-based, 'parental' authority that Tomlinson observes in many 'post-evangelicals' (Tomlinson, 1995: 54–55).[3]

It is difficult to ascertain the exact number of 'alternative' services across the UK at the present time. Some practitioners have mentioned a number of over a hundred, but the complexities of self-definition mean that those services which claim the label 'alternative' for themselves may be radically different from one other in worship style and ritual emphases. A useful framework for classifying such worship groups might indicate two divergent trends. Firstly, there are services which adopt multi-media technology primarily in order to attract young people into a church environment in which they feel more comfortable. Such services are regularly held in churches throughout the country, and at large-scale events, such as those organized by *Soul Survivor*, a movement which has fostered youth ministry through festivals and church outreach initiatives since 1993. However, in terms of proclaimed teaching, leadership style and expressed attitudes towards Biblical authority, these initiatives seldom express any serious divergence from the 'mainstream' evangelical community. Secondly, there are groups which incorporate experimental worship into a broader shared project of rethinking the notions of church, cultural identity and Christian faith. These groups fit closer into Tomlinson's 'post-evangelical' category and many developed out of a first-hand experience of NOS. Such groups are the main concern of this paper, as they establish the contexts in which evangelical identities are explored and negotiated in a ritual context.

Worship groups are scattered throughout the country, although they are for the most part located in urban areas. Attendance tends to be on a fairly small scale, with regular services attracting around 20–50 people. Those who attend come from various social and religious backgrounds, although most long-standing participants appear to have some background in evangelicalism and often in charismatic Christianity. It is also fair to say that most are university educated and from the middle classes, a tendency that reflects the factors of technical expertise and a critical, intellectual perspective of religion, both of which are common within 'alternative' worship circles.

Following the collapse of NOS in 1995, a study day was held on 'alternative' worship at Lambeth Palace (see Fig. 1). One of the reasons why the study day was arranged was to give the church hierarchy the opportunity to see that the problems inherent in the Sheffield group arose from its authority structures rather than from its worship. The church establishment has since viewed 'alternative' worship with toleration and acceptance, although very few clergy are centrally involved in worship groups, and services receive minimal attention from the church press. On a local level, most 'alternative' worship groups today exist under the auspices of a host church, which may provide facilities and financial support as well as some pastoral supervision. The majority are attached to Anglican parishes, although some have their homes in non-conformist churches.[4] Although the 'alternative' worship movement is predominantly a UK phenomenon, parallel developments have emerged in the Antipodes and more recently in the USA (Roberts, 1999: 13). Moreover, while the UK movement maintains inter-group contact through visits and collaborative projects, based at events such as *Greenbelt* and *Time of Our Lives,* the international movement is united in virtual interaction through the alt.worship e-mail discussion list, which acts as the forum for the exchange of worship ideas as well as for the debate of theological issues.

Methodology

As is clear from the above overview, 'alternative' worship is as much a social movement as it is a development in progressive ritual. Moreover, I wish to argue that it is most thoroughly analysed from a dual perspective that incorporates both dimensions. It is based around and orchestrated by localised small groups, which interact on the basis of shared attitudes both in and around the event of worship, as well as in other social contexts. Within this emerging Christian sub-culture, the actual event of worship is but one context among several, in which a reworking of Christian identity is actively negotiated. I would tentatively delineate primary contexts as the 'event' (incorporating all organized episodes of worship), the small group discussion, and the national and international network (incorporating face-to-face and 'virtual' interaction). A considered examination of any 'alternative' group will perceive lines of influence that frequently pass between these three contexts of social activity.

In accordance with this broad picture, the portrait of 'alternative' worship that follows is based on two main sources of data. Firstly, I have explored the nature of the broader 'alternative' worship movement by way of an extensive study of service literature,[5] internet sites, e-mail discussion, and observation of 'alternative' worship events. I have also interviewed several individuals who have had considerable experience of 'alternative' worship in various church contexts across the country. Secondly, in order to explore more deeply the culture of 'alternative' worship within a single group setting, I have engaged in participant observation among an 'alternative' worship group based in a large town in the north of England. There are several reasons why I chose this particular group as my case study; the most important reason is related to its ecclesiastical situation as a worship group attached to a large and thriving evangelical Anglican church. Guided by my intention of exploring the cultural dialectics that occur between 'alternative' worship and evangelical Christianity, this situation seemed well suited to a comparative analysis that may contrast the two groups by their worship and shared attitudes, and to the exploration of the nature of any interaction that may occur between them. My fieldwork at this stage has extended to over three months duration and has incorporated participant observation of all services held by both the evangelical church and the 'alternative' worship group. I have also attended various group meetings and have engaged in numerous conversations with participants in both 'camps' in varying contexts.

I chose to conduct my fieldwork overtly for two main reasons. Firstly, I feel that it is important, on ethical grounds, for the researcher to be as honest as is practically possible about his/her intentions. Secondly, in order to ensure

1. As part of the 'Alternative' Worship Study Day in Lambeth Crypt in 1995, a service entitled 'Are you receiving me?' was held, organised by groups from Bristol, Leeds, London, Oxford and York. The service involved a prayer ritual during which participants lit candles for those who are suffering or are separated from God. These candles were then offered at an altar constructed from broken TV sets and decorated in topical newspaper cuttings. The ritual as shown here is recreated by the *Visions* group, who performed it at one of their own services in York the week after the Lambeth event. (courtesy of Richard Horton/*Visions*)

2. A 'Labyrinth' service held by the *Live on Planet Earth* group as part of the 'Reimagining Worship' conference for UK 'alternative' worship groups in May, 1998. Suggested meditations are placed at intervals around the labyrinth. The ironic OHP caption on the far right is reflective of the way western consumerism is undermined in some 'alternative' services; critique is often expressed through ambiguity and symbol, rather than through any verbal diatribe. (courtesy of Steve Collins)

3. A *Visions* service visual arrangement, typically juxtaposing radically divergent images: a motorway complex, a waterfall, angels, the Turin Shroud and a pair of hands cupped around the warmth of a naked flame. All of this is flanked by constantly changing TV images, and illuminated by a characteristically simple, open but provocative verse from the Bible. (courtesy of Richard Horton/*Visions*)

4. During the Visions service in York, the whole east wall of the church building is transformed by projected visuals and video images. Here, nature-centred images of trees and water droplets are juxtaposed with an orthodox icon of Christ. In reflection of the group's use of Celtic tradition, the orthodox 'Jesus prayer' is also displayed, its simplicity and innocence enhanced by the medium of child-like handwriting. (courtesy of Richard Horton/*Visions*)

some sort of thematic focus, I wanted to conduct formal interviews as part of the fieldwork. Consequently, I have been open with all the people with whom I have spoken about what I am doing and about my personal beliefs. This approach has helped gain the trust of many people, and has had the added advantage of opening up avenues of discussion that have been stimulating and insightful. It has also enabled me to observe the different ways in which the two communities receive outsiders and relate to their external environment (see Hobbs & May, 1993: xii). I considered myself in particular to be an outsider who did not share the apparent beliefs of those people within either group—at least this was my initial preconception. However, my subsequent research has revealed a more complex picture.

I do not consider myself a Christian and have been plain about this fact with respondents within the community. I have portrayed myself rather as an interested agnostic who is nonetheless sympathetic to some aspects of Christianity, but who has difficulties accepting other, more conservative values. My attitude could perhaps be described as that of a liberal humanist. It is important to note that I have not announced my non-Christian status to either community uninvited, but have responded to questions about my personal beliefs if and when asked. This has allowed me to gauge responses to my presence as an unknown newcomer, and also to gauge initial responses to outsiders generally (as least in as much as this was practically possible). Reactions to my presence within the two communities have been markedly different.

After reading about the guarded suspicion with which some researchers of conservative Christianity have been received in the past (e.g. Peshkin, 1984), I was justifiably anxious about how I might be viewed within the evangelical community. However, I was happily proven wrong and experienced both warmth and helpful, open co-operation from both church staff and parishioners. Most people with whom I have spoken have been curious about my research and have expressed an interest in speaking further. Furthermore, once acquainted with my status as a researcher, the vast majority of people then asked if I was a Christian. My often convoluted answers have prompted more interest, some encouragement towards conversion and certainly no condemnation, but the question has been a recurring one and has appeared in straightforward language: are you a Christian?

My reception within the 'alternative' group has been very different. Despite my continuous presence both in services and in small group discussions, I have only been asked once about my personal beliefs. The group is small and it was not long before I was known by all the core members, with whom I have spoken at length, both in 'religious' and social contexts. I have assisted in the setting up of services and contributed to group discussion. I have been asked about my research, and the group is positive about my presence (to the point of asking me to lead one of their small group discussion sessions[6]) and yet, virtually no questions have been raised about my personal religious identity.

Although these impressions are merely based on my experience within a single local community, they introduce some recurring issues with which the remainder of this paper will be concerned. In particular, they illustrate the evangelical conception of conversion as a straightforward transformation of identity—'Christian' being the operative category, the invocation of which is assumed to safely indicate a certain status, the nature of which is unquestioned. By contrast, the 'alternative' tendency is towards the unquestioning acceptance of individuals, regardless of background or faith. Direct questions about personal faith are perceived as judgmental and intrusive. Moreover, there is a reluctance to discuss identity openly in such clear-cut terms.

These initial reactions shed light on the boundaries manifest in each group, which separate insiders from outsiders, and on the criteria upon which this division stands. Although the evangelicals welcomed me, their rhetoric suggested that they conceived my identity as categorically different from their own. I may have shared common ground with many members of the congregation—not least a university education and a knowledge of theology—but the categorical dichotomy of Christian/non-Christian was a perpetual reminder of my being different, an outsider. By contrast, no such clear-cut distinctions were evident within the discourse shared among the 'alternative' group. Indeed, the possibility of such categories seemed to be the very subject of discussion at times. Ostensibly, the group ethos is to welcome people from any background, although there are, of course, boundaries of group inclusion. However, these are implicit and related to the 'sub-cultural' mood of worship events. Although I found some sense of affinity with dimmed lighting, video projections and contemporary ambient dance music, it was clear that many individuals from more conservative backgrounds would not have felt so comfortable. Indeed, in explaining why they did not attend the 'alternative' service, most evangelicals referred to its 'weird' style rather than any theological argument. Consequently, some 'alternative' worship can be interpreted as culturally alienating for a great number of people.

The insider/outsider distinction is a useful theoretical lens through which the transformation of evangelicalism within 'alternative' worship groups can be viewed. The predominant shift appears to be from exclusivism to inclusivism, marked by an openness to outsider influences and to outsider involvement. The development of 'alternative' worship out of evangelicalism is, however, more complex than this. In order to explore this process, I shall focus on three thematic dimensions that appear to mediate, in various manifestations, the problematization of evangelical Christianity among 'alternative' worshippers: authority, reflexivity, and community.

Progressive Dimensions: Authority

The success of Protestant evangelicalism during the 1980s was marked by several key features which characterized its theology and wider mission, and which distinguished it from the liberal Protestantism of the time. Descriptions of evangelicalism vary, although all focus on the importance of scripture as the inspired word of God, the centrality of the cross as the basis of salvation, a stress upon actively living the Gospel message, and the essential experience of conversion as the door to the Christian life (Bebbington, 1989: 1–17). During the 1980s, these maxims were predominantly interpreted and enacted along conservative lines within many evangelical circles in the UK. The Bible was taught as the primary, if not the sole, source of divine authority, before all other possible sources of divine inspiration, which were therefore to be measured against it. Moreover, salvation was conceived in exclusivistic terms—formulations that deviated from the evangelical conception (most notably those that de-emphasized the living Christ or the crucifixion) were often judged as illegitimate. Moreover, those deemed to be 'unsaved' were often considered to be destined for hell, usually understood as an actual place of punishment rather than a state of being. The boundaries that marked insiders from outsiders were explicit and unequivocal—even if members were not expected to make some public statement of commitment, it was clear through shared discourse and received teaching what 'insiders' were expected to believe.

In addition to these features, the conflation of evangelical and charismatic developments in the early 1980s transformed British evangelicalism (Bebbington, 1994: 371). The emerging generation of young evangelical leaders, many of whom had been influenced by the House Church Movement, expressed a new combination of theological conservatism, social and political awareness and charismatic spirituality.[7] The importance which charismatic gifts assumed in the world of British evangelicals, intensified by the influence of John Wimber and later the Toronto Blessing (Percy, 1998: 141–162), awarded a new status to personal experience as a source of divine inspiration and spiritual guidance. It also fostered a renewed faith in the reality of supernatural power as it may be manifested in the social world as well as in church.[8]

The emergent charismatic evangelicalism, as manifested in expressed theology and worship practice, stressed two main sources of authority for the church: scripture and experience. The Bible, appropriated as the inspired account of God's work on earth through Jesus Christ, was taught as foundational to Christian faith, as an authority independent of personal or institutional mediation. In actual fact, of course, certain Biblical themes were stressed over others, according to the theology that was taught by evangelical preachers, a theology that often incorporated a moral conservatism and an exclusivist stance on other faiths. Moreover, a conservative interpretation of scripture such as this required consistent media through which it might be expressed and defended against liberal polemic. Evangelicalism catered for this by way of its active community of preachers, effectively reaching a wide audience through the increasingly popular tradition of evangelical conferences and festivals, such as 'Spring Harvest' (Tomlinson, 1995: 19–21). Significantly, it was through the medium of personal leadership, transmitted in preaching as well as spiritual guidance and Bible study, that the understanding of the authority of scripture was inculcated and sustained. The success of 1980s evangelicalism was not merely founded on the Bible, but on the directive style of the leaders (often young and enthusiastic) who preached its message as they had appropriated it. Consequently, the stress on Biblical authority veils another source of social power within evangelicalism: that expressed in the personal conviction of successful preachers.

'Experience' was invoked as authoritative in two related, yet distinct senses. In a perennial sense, 'experience' referred to the life world of the developing individual, in which and through which, it was taught, one may sense God and His work as a present-day reality. Such an understanding grounds the common evangelical tendency to attribute the occurrence of banal, everyday events to supernatural causes. The second understanding relates to charismatic gifts, the conception of which is based upon the former understanding of experience. However, charismatic gifts are manifest in the form of particular norms of performance, often within a congregational context. The occurrence of charismatic gifts is therefore subject to social pressures that persist in communal contexts, and expressions of power may effectively be contested or embraced in relation to group dynamics. What is important for our purposes is that divine authority is perceived as accessible and communicable through inter-personal media (Percy, 1998: 73). Moreover, it is experienced as something to be shared and understood, and consequently incorporates the notion of an authority for others as well as for oneself.[9]

Contrary to popular misconceptions, the 'Nine O'Clock Service' (NOS) appears to have maintained a ritual and theological structure that endorsed the above sources of authority in a traditionally evangelical vein, at least prior to its absorption of creation spirituality and post-modern thought in the early 1990s. Some of the other long-standing 'alternative' groups appear to have developed out of a similar state, originally combining traditional evangelical authority structures with multi-media worship. However, during the past ten years, 'alternative' worship has been the context for the development and rethinking of such notions of authority, as expressed in ritual as well as in group discourse. In particular, there has been a widespread shift away from expressions of authority as directive, imperative sources of teaching. Personally delivered instruction is often viewed with suspicion and at best as one 'reading' among many others. Biblical teaching is treated critically—not with cynicism, but from a perspective that welcomes new interpretations, fresh nuances in the text, and an authentic dialogue between Biblical stories and the post-modern culture that defines our identity. Furthermore, leadership roles within groups are mostly unofficial, shared and de-emphasized. Whereas 'mainstream' evangelicalism has built itself upon a tradition of authority embodied in influential preachers, many 'alternative' worshippers remain thoroughly suspicious of institutional or charismatic authority.

Such developments suggest a move away from a hegemonic understanding of authority towards a more democratic, open understanding, which suggests authority as negotiated and relative, rather than received and absolute. The 'truth' of Christianity is not seen as simply available in the sermons of an 'inspired' preacher or as residing in prescribed readings of the Bible, significantly mediated through the middle-class, Western preconceptions of conservative evangelicalism. Indeed, the 'truth' of Christianity is seen as something that cannot be easily encapsulated in rhetorical formulae. Rather, Christian identity is represented as a processual phenomenon, subject to development and exploration, with the final arbiter of authenticity being the individual. As a consequence of this, faith is frequently conceived in terms of a journey, a pilgrimage with no prescribed route or defined end.

The most vivid ritual expression of this understanding of personal faith may be found in the widespread use of the 'labyrinth' by 'alternative' groups. This tradition originally derives from the maze-like floor pattern in Chartres Cathedral, which was traversed in medieval times by candidates the day before their baptism or confirmation. The labyrinth (as modelled on Chartres) has been a feature of Grace Cathedral, San Francisco, since 1991, and NOS may have followed this example in its own initiative soon afterwards. In 'alternative' services, the labyrinth is used as an aid for prayer and meditation—slowly and silently participants move around the labyrinthine floor pattern at their own pace, moving to the centre as they approach God, stopping in the middle to sit and be with God, and eventually moving back 'into the world', supposedly renewed by the experience. Some 'alternative' labyrinths are entirely blank, with only a Bible at the centre for guidance, while others include 'stations' that suggest prayer rituals and meditations (see Fig. 2). However, all suggest ritual and spiritual direction as person-centred, guided primarily by the experience and perception of the individual participant.

The shift in 'alternative' worship away from directional expressions of authority also relates to a refusal to embrace rhetorical representations of the Christian message as straightforward, univocal and binding. Out of a tradition of Christianity that has concentrated on the Word as the primary medium of divine communication (Coleman, 1996), 'alternative' worship embraces the image as a means to inspiration, reflection and spiritual insight. In accordance with this ethos, the symbolism used in worship events is often deliberately ambiguous and provocative (see Fig. 3). Occasionally, irreverent and controversial images are juxtaposed with images traditionally associated with purity or holiness, in an expressed effort to subvert our understanding and provoke a rethinking of the Christian tradition. *Grace*, an 'alternative' service based in Ealing, have used a particularly controversial image during their communion service: a picture of Jesus surrounded by gay men dressed in leather. As one of the organisers commented: "It's quite a shocking image ... and again irreverent, but plays well, begging the question who would Christ have shared his table with?" (Baker, 1999: 46)

The expression of Christian identity as essentially an exploratory process is accompanied by a tendency for 'alternative' service groups to adopt a broad perspective in which various traditions of significance may be legitimately incorporated into worship and into one's faith. Indeed, the ritual resources of 'alternative' worship are sometimes so eclectic that some uninformed outsiders have been tempted to compare it to the New Age movement. *The World Service*, previously based in London, once ran an event addressing the topic of 'Holy Ground', which included the use of Islamic art next to Christian stained glass as wall decoration. *Visions*, an 'alternative' group in York, often draw from the Celtic tradition in the form of prayers as well as projected images (see Fig. 4). And *The Nine O'Clock Community* (NOC), organised by former members of NOS in Sheffield, have incorporated a wide variety of spiritual traditions into their worship, including a performance of Samhain, an ancient pagan festival associated with the remembrance of ancestors and the coming of new life.

Despite the common tendency to draw from a wide variety of traditions as well as from the themes and media of pop culture, those within 'alternative' worship rebut any accusation that they have become 'New Age'. 'Alternative' worship is seen as the context in which our vision of Christianity is broadened and liberated from conservative traditions that constrain our appreciation of a living God. Furthermore, the intense use of material symbolism, suggested by some as indicative of a return to sacramentalism (Roberts, 1999: 18), together with the renewed emphasis on the image (see Fig. 3), suggest that 'alternative' worship is not an exercise in revising the mainstream church as a whole, but that it is concerned with reclaiming sources of significance eclipsed by the overly rhetorical theology of Protestant evangelicalism.

A further consequence of the resistance to directive forms of authority and to definitive portrayals of Christianity relates to the perception of evangelism in 'alternative' groups. Many 'alternative' worshippers would deny that their activities are primarily intended to attract more young people into the church (Ward, 1999: 14). Indeed, while this may be a by-product of the 'alternative' approach, for most, the expressed aim is to provide a worship environment in which disillusioned Christians might make sense of their faith. This ethos is based on the argument that the church is out of touch with post-modernity and needs to adopt a less rigid and more open approach to spirituality in accordance with the wider cultural climate. However, the fact that 'alternative' worship resists any 'pat' expressions of Christianity and shrinks from 'pushy', discursive forms of evangelism, has meant that it has no active mission strategy. Services are not widely promoted, nor do organisers typically gauge their success by numerical attendance. Consequently, 'alternative' groups remain small, with probably little prospect for significant demographic growth in the near future.

In conclusion, the authority structures of evangelicalism have undergone a significant transformation through 'alternative' worship. Most notably, absolutist notions of truth and essentialist expressions of faith, often mediated through directive evangelical preachers, have been undermined by a symbolic stress on ambiguity, a ritualized shift towards individual-centred spirituality, and a resistance to any simple, 'packaged' expression of the Christian message. The emergent movement is characterized by ritual experimentation and a broadly inclusive attitude towards sources of spiritual significance.

Progressive Dimensions: Reflexivity

I have argued that 'alternative' worship, as a development in the Christian community in the UK, is revisionist. That is, it represents an attempt to revise and rethink, in ritual and discursive forms, the traditions that its participants have inherited. In particular, it is shaped by an effort to challenge some key features of evangelical Christianity. However, the ethos that drives the revisionist trend is frequently carried further to such an extent that a 'theology of questioning' becomes a desired end in itself rather than a means to some final resolution or agreed truth (Tomlinson, 1995: 132). In many ways, the discursive exchanges and ritual innovations encompassed by 'alternative' worship reflect the post-modern urge to subvert received assumptions, question established authorities, and experiment with new possibilities of meaning (Beckford, 1992). Many of those most centrally involved in the movement are versed in post-modern literature and thought (Roberts, 1999: 17–19; Howard, 1996: 26–27). Indeed, many organizers would explain 'alternative' worship as an attempt to bridge the gap between the church and post-modern culture. This is certainly an important factor in accounting for its particular emphases, although explicit references to 'post-modernity' and to authors associated with this field also suggest a particular social location for 'alternative' worship among the educated middle classes (Beckford, 1992: 20).

Reflexivity can also be claimed as an intended feature of the many new rituals performed in 'alternative' services. The one-way delivery of the sermon is frequently rejected in favour of participatory exercises that suggest and provoke rather than inform. Prayers and meditations are frequently based on sensory experience and improvisation, and participants are often encouraged to engage actively with material symbols as an aid to reflection on a suggested issue (see Fig. 1). One ritual in which I participated was developed from the theme of Peter as the rock of the church. Rather than listen to a sermon on leadership, we considered the idea of the church as many rocks, symbolized by a series of small stones placed on the centre table. We all picked one and examined it, reflecting on the suffering of others as well as ourselves, before placing the rocks in a small fountain at the front of the hall. This was to symbolize how God transforms us from rough, damaged individuals into a beautiful community. Such an inventive rite sheds new light on Catherine Bell's claim that the loss of authentic sources of community in the contemporary world has led to a rise in ritual 'entrepreneurship' (Bell, 1997: 224).

In addition to the active encouragement of reflection, the general form of services undermines clear-cut or definitive presentations of Christianity, thus demanding some reflexive engagement from the participant. The multi-media technology of services facilitates the simultaneous bombardment of a continuously changing series of sounds, words and images—effectively subverting the possibility of a univocal, substantive message. Moreover, little effort is made to offer interpretations of the symbolism used; images may reflect a service theme, but the juxtaposition of sharply varying images frustrates the possibility of any unified meaning. Moreover, worship environment and ritual form are typically arranged anew for each service, so that the notion of a consistent substantive message that one might appropriate over the course of weeks is arguably undermined (Rappaport, 1993).

There is a strong ethic of experimentation in 'alternative' worship, born out of a desire to communicate more and more effectively to participants, and born out of a resistance to the simple rehearsal of tradition. 'Alternative' services embody a paranoia about 'effective' ritual—about constructing a successful event, whereby success is not measured in terms of the numerical popularity of services, but by the conviction on the part of those who participate that it 'worked' for them. However, as this quality is difficult to gauge and impossible to describe adequately, service-planning groups are working with no specifically defined goal in mind. Combined with some insecurity brought on by low numbers and the potential for disagreement among key members who are, after all, united in a project that has no established guiding principle, the picture is one of perpetual innovation and ritual change—reflexivity without closure.

Discussion on the alt.worship e-mail list further demonstrates a shared willingness to radically question the fundamentals of the Christian faith through discursive media. Similar to Tomlinson's projects at *Holy Joe's* and 'Harry', this list provides a safe place in which 'progressive' Christians may voice doubts about key issues and suggest innovative solutions (Roberts, 1999: 11–12). Indeed, although some contributions are controversial, it is rare for messages to appear that challenge or strongly object to another point of view—the overall tone is one of acceptance and exploration, a feature that reflects the unspoken 'post-evangelical' ethic of allowing space for innovation and resisting judgement or condemnation at any cost. Recent contributions have challenged certain Biblical teachings on ethical issues, argued against the notion of a gendered God, and proposed an inclusive attitude towards other religions. Perspectives seem to range from the liberal evangelical to the post-Christian, and post-modernity is often referred to as an index of culture or as a cultural movement from which we may learn to question certain received categories.

Progressive Dimensions: Community

The fact that 'alternative' worship takes place in groups scattered across the country, and the possibility, discussed above, that the spiritual identity of those who attend may be seen as individualistic, privatized or post-traditional, may lead one to the conclusion that this is a rather fragmented movement, perhaps destined for dissolution. This may be the case. However, there are conditions in place that have so far ensured the continuance of 'alternative' worship as a development with some degree of unity and shared purpose. Many participants share some common history, having moved among the social networks surrounding *Greenbelt* festival, NOS and 'alternative' worship conferences;[10] continued inter-service collaboration takes place from time to time.[11] The Internet is used extensively, as a means to community cohesion and service promotion, and this reflects the fact that many participants possess considerable technical expertise. All in all, the emergent picture is of an 'imagined community' of 'alternative' Christians connected by a perception of shared attitudes and worship tastes (Anderson, 1993; Stringer, 1999: 67).

However, the theme of 'community' within the movement runs deeper than this. Locally based 'alternative' groups are close-knit, and a significant amount of time and commitment is invested in fostering continued group cohesion and mutually supportive relationships. This takes place within the context of small group meetings, commonly linked to worship groups, as well as social events. Moreover, participants invoke a sense of community and group identity in explaining their continued involvement. This can be partly explained as an inevitable consequence of the marginalized status of many groups, who need to establish and sustain close inter-personal links in order to persist as a social collective (Becker, 1963: 81). In this sense, an emphasis on community does not so much mediate a negative reaction to evangelicalism as compensate for the social consequences of partial detachment from it.

However, I would argue that an emphasis on community among 'alternative' worshippers might be traced to an ecclesiological style that has its basis in their evangelical heritage. In speaking of evangelical developments during the 1970s and 1980s, David Bebbington stresses the shift towards communitarian involvement as a lauded virtue of the British movement. This can be explained to some extent by the pervasive influence of the charismatic notion of 'unity in the Spirit' and by the strong evangelical stress on actively living out the Gospel message. Many churches established traditions of group activity outside Sunday worship as a further context for ministry, mission and group fellowship. House groups, Bible study classes, away days, church holidays, youth clubs and church-organized social occasions all served to strengthen group cohesion (Bebbington, 1989: 243–244).

By the late 1980s, evangelical church life had come to be equated not just with regular church attendance, but with wider involvement in other group activities that had a Christian purpose or an ecclesiastical source of organization. Such was the experience of many who subsequently became involved in 'alternative' worship. With the close-knit small group as an established context of faith-based interaction, 'alternative' worshippers had the confidence to initiate groups of their own, without the fear of being perceived as schismatic or sectarian. Free from excessive ecclesiastical interference and free from any shared conservative theology or organizing principle, 'alternative' worship could develop on the level of 'culture' (Martin, 1990: 274), in accordance with group creativity and the evolving attitudes of key participants.

However, it is tempting to over-emphasize the extent to which 'alternative' worship groups serve as a focus for community belonging. Key participants, involved in the organization of services, may form close-knit groups, but a sizeable proportion of attendees only participate on an occasional basis. Moreover, initial research suggests that many of those who participate, including organizers, regularly attend other places of worship. These factors suggest that 'alternative' services are not being treated as the sole ritual and pastoral basis of Christian identities, but more as a cultural resource—a source of meaning without strong demands of commitment and without explicit criteria of belonging.[12] However, the fact that many 'alternative' service groups have survived the duration of the 1990s suggests that there is strong active commitment at their core.

Conclusion

I have argued for a transformation of evangelical Christianity within the 'alternative' worship movement, particularly as mediated through the themes of authority (undermined and questioned as a consequence of negative experiences), reflexivity (endorsed as a post-modern medium of desired change), and community (restored out of a common marginality). Each of these themes has been the basis of revision through discursive interaction as well as in and through ritual, effecting a shift from exclusivism, authoritarianism and essentialism to an inclusive, experimental approach to faith that resists any form of conceptual enclosure. It is, however, important to resist the suggestion that 'alternative' worship exists as a simple oppositional reaction to evangelicalism, borne out of 'post-modern' attitudes to religion and truth. Indeed, in many ways, its character owes as much to evangelicalism as it does to a negative perception of its theologies and styles of authority.

In an interesting essay on ritual, Pierre Bourdieu makes the important point that for a ritual to function successfully—for it to communicate the message and effect the transformations that it intends—those participating must recognize the authority on which it is based (Bourdieu, 1997: 113). Although it might appear that 'alternative' worship invokes no claims to ritual authority as such, it still relies on particular established norms for its activities to be recognized as meaningful and legitimate episodes of Christian worship. To some extent, legitimacy has been secured by precedent, the experiments at NOS effectively pioneering 'alternative' worship and opening up the possibility for re-traditionalization within mobilized groups around the country. At a deeper level, it is a tradition of 'experience'—partially rooted in evangelical Christianity—which has effectively nurtured 'alternative' worship into an accepted 'tradition' and which serves as the basis for the legitimacy granted to it by those who participate.

The understanding of subjective 'experience'—emphasized as a source of spiritual authority by charismatics and as the context of divine guidance for other conservative Christians (Percy, 1998: 155)—has persisted in 'alternative' circles, but has also undergone significant transformation. Firstly, 'experience' is not seen as a source of authority that is binding for others. This can be explained by the widespread suspicion in 'alternative' groups of charismatic power as a potential means of manipulation. Secondly, as the medium in which truth and God might be located, 'experience' is not interpreted through unquestioned categories of tradition, but is the means by which such 'categories' might be first ascertained and explored. Whereas evangelical interpretations of experience are generally invoked as supporting the fundamentals of belief—God's presence at particular times may be questioned, but his substantive nature is not—'alternative' worshippers tend to draw from experience as an inductive resource, effectively developing and exploring theological possibilities in the light of subjective experience. Church tradition is treated as but one framework among many which may be employed in order to make sense of, and find meaning in, the cultural experience of individuals. As one organizer of 'alternative' worship informed me: "[Our service] is primarily about a spiritual search, for worship that has integrity, a spirituality that sits cohesively into our world, and a form of Church community *that works in our culture* (my emphasis)."

Such radical 'inculturation' has effectively expanded the conceptual boundaries within which Christianity can be conceived. Ideological inclusivity demands a rethinking of the insider/outsider distinction, and understandings of 'faith' as an expression of identity seem to require considered revision and exploration in the light of recent cultural change. What is perhaps clear from the above discussion is that manifestations of 'faith', as negotiated and expressed in discourse, are not simply reflective of the tradition on which they are based, but emerge out of a dialogue between pervasive relations of power within specific religious and cultural contexts.

Notes

1   I would like to acknowledge the assistance of the Economic and Social Research Council for funding the research upon which this paper is based. I also wish to offer my thanks to the editors as well as to Simon Coleman and Paul Roberts for insightful comments on these issues, as presented in an earlier draft.

2   Unfortunately, the only extensive published work on NOS is the journalistic account provided by Roland Howard in *The Rise and Fall of the Nine O'Clock Service* (1996). Howard's book is marred by his unconcealed agenda that seeks to 'expose' the power trappings of the contemporary charismatic church. Consequently, his portrayal of NOS is generally negative and its reliability questionable. Although I had to consult Howard's book as the only available published source on NOS, I have also spoken to several individuals who were either members of NOS or who attended its worship events at some point. I have subsequently pieced together a rough picture of the worship at NOS that I believe to be reliable. I have deliberately withheld from commenting on the alleged power and sexual abuse that took place within the NOS community, as I do not feel that this is relevant to the present paper.

3   The distrust of person-centred authority, expressed as a suspicion of manipulation and abuse, was exacerbated and intensified for many 'alternative' worshippers following the exposure of abuses of power that were rife at NOS.

4   I know of no 'alternative' services that are held in connection with any Roman Catholic church, a fact that reflects the origins of 'alternative' worship and its continuing dialogue with Protestant Evangelicalism, the tradition that shapes its activities and forms the background culture of many participants.

5   Although extensive service literature has been made available to me by organizers, primarily in the form of group magazines, service orders, notes kept from discussion sessions, and promotional material, there is very little written on 'alternative' worship that may be referred to as secondary literature. In fact, the only academic account of 'alternative' worship is contained in Paul Roberts's short booklet, *Alternative Worship in the Church of England* (1999). Roberts's work is a useful and sensitive portrayal by someone active within the movement. His interpretative framework is very much in accordance with the argument that 'alternative' worship is a ritualized response to post-modernity.

6   In accordance with the open, inclusive ethos of the group, I was asked to contribute a presentation primarily on the basis of my knowledge as an academic researcher.

7   Dave Tomlinson traces this development to the appointment of Clive Calver as leader of the Evangelical Alliance in 1983. Calver was an unashamed charismatic, had connections with the House Church Movement and was instrumental in involving young leaders of a similar persuasion (Tomlinson, 1995: 17–19).

8   This had negative as well as positive dimensions, the emerging charismatic mind-set incorporating notions of satanic evil as well as divine blessing. This may be exemplified in the popular 'Marches for Jesus' during the 1980s as well as in the notion of 'spiritual warfare'.

9 This is only a rough sketch of what was a far more complex movement. However, the elements stressed are pertinent to this paper, as they are common to the perception of evangelicalism entertained within 'alternative' worship circles.

10 *Greenbelt* is a Christian arts festival which has been held annually since 1974. Originally held at Charlsfield in East Anglia, the festival has shifted between several venues over the years, before finally moving to Chelmsford Race Course in 1999. The main ethos of the festival has been the expression and celebration of the Christian Gospel through the media of contemporary pop culture and the arts; it is this emphasis that drew many who subsequently became involved in 'alternative' worship. 'Alternative' worship has had a central place at the festival since NOS performed its famous 'Passion in Global Chaos' set in 1992. Each year, 'alternative' worship groups continue to lead services, debates and other creative events at the festival.

11 In particular, groups in London— notably *Grace, Epicentre, Holy Joe's, The Host Community*, and *Vaux*—have worked together across denominational lines within the context of various events.

12 Further research will need to explore this issue, particularly in relation to the possibility that 'alternative' worship may be 'used' by many people as supplementary to sources of Christian worship and belonging. If this is the case, an actual 'theology' of alternative worship may only extend to those most intimately involved in its organization.

References

Anderson, B. *Imagined Communities: Reflections on the Origin and Spread of Nationalism.* London: Verso, 1993.

Baker, J. "Rhythm of the Masses." In Ward, P., ed. *Mass Culture: Eucharist and Mission in a Post-Modern World.* Oxford: The Bible Reading Fellowship, 1999: 33–53.

Bauman, Z. "Postmodern Religion?" In Heelas, P. (with the assistance of D. Martin & P. Morris), ed. *Religion, Modernity and Postmodernity.* Oxford: Blackwell, 1998: 55–78.

Bebbington, D. W. *Evangelicalism in Modern Britain: A History from the 1730s to the 1980s.* London: Unwin Hyman, 1989.

Bebbington, D. W. "Evangelicalism in its Settings: The British and American Movements since 1940." In Noll, M. A., Bebbington, D. W. & Rawlyk, G. A., eds. *Evangelicalism: Comparative Studies of Popular Protestantism in North America, The British Isles, and Beyond, 1700–1990.* Oxford, New York: Oxford U. P., 1994: 365–388.

Becker, H. S. *Outsiders: Studies in the Sociology of Deviance.* New York: The Free Press, 1963.

Beckford, J. "Religion, Modernity and Post-Modernity." In Wilson, B. R., ed. *Religion: Contemporary Issues.* London: Bellew, 1992: 11–23.

Bell, C. *Ritual: Perspectives and Dimensions.* New York, Oxford: Oxford U. P., 1997.

Bourdieu, P. "Authorised Language: The Social Conditions for the Effectiveness of Ritual Discourse." In Bourdieu, P. *Language and Symbolic Power* (edited and introduced by John B. Thompson). Oxford: Polity Press, 1997: 107–116.

Coleman, S. "Words as Things: Language, Aesthetics and the Objectification of Protestant Evangelicalism." *Journal of Material Culture* 1 (1), 1996: 107–128.

Fox, M. *Creation Spirituality: Liberating Gifts for the Peoples of the Earth.* New York: HarperCollins, 1991.

Heelas, P., Lash, S. & Morris, P., eds. *Detraditionalization: Critical Reflections on Authority and Identity.* Oxford: Blackwell, 1996.

Hobbs, D. & May, T., eds. *Interpreting the Field: Accounts of Ethnography.* Oxford: Clarendon Press, 1993.

Howard, R. *The Rise and Fall of the Nine O'Clock Service.* London: Mowbray, 1996.

Martin, D. *Tongues of Fire: The Explosion of Protestantism in Latin America.* Oxford: Blackwell, 1990.

Percy, M. *Words, Wonders and Power: Understanding Contemporary Christian Fundamentalism and Revivalism.* London: SPCK, 1996.

Percy, M. *Power and the Church: Ecclesiology in an Age of Transition.* London: Cassell, 1998.

Peshkin, A. "Odd Man Out: The Participant Observer in an Absolutist Setting." *Sociology of Education* 57 (October), 1984: 254–264.

Rappaport, R. "Veracity, Verity, and Verum in Liturgy." *Studia Liturgica* 23, 1993: 35–50.

Roberts, P. *Alternative Worship in the Church of England.* Cambridge: Grove Books, 1999.

Smith, J. Z. *Imagining Religion: From Babylon to Jonestown.* Chicago, London: University of Chicago Press, 1982.

Stringer, M. D. *On the Perception of Worship: The Ethnography of Worship in Four Christian Congregations in Manchester.* Birmingham: University of Birmingham Press, 1999.

Tomlinson, D. *The Post-Evangelical.* London: SPCK, 1995.

Walker, A. *Restoring the Kingdom: The Radical Christianity of the House Church Movement.* London: Hodder & Stoughton, 1988 (2nd ed., 1st ed. published in 1985).

Ward, P., ed. *Mass Culture: Eucharist and Mission in a Post-Modern World.* Oxford: The Bible Reading Fellowship, 1999.

4 Insider/Outsider Perspectives on Ritual in Sōka Gakkai International–UK

HELEN WATERHOUSE

Introduction

This paper is concerned with questions of method relating to the study of ritual in performance. Its intention is to challenge the idea that the division between insiders and outsiders may be represented by a neat line, with all insiders on one side and all outsiders on the other side. I shall argue that the insider/outsider dichotomy, while useful, does not possess this elegant simplicity. In order to show this I offer three observations: firstly, that there are many outsider perspectives which vary in their motivational basis and consequently in their level of empathy with insider accounts; secondly, that there are many insider perspectives and that these may present significant contrasts; and thirdly, that there are areas which fall between the two categories. Insider/outsider is therefore more of a continuum than a dichotomy. This analysis is applicable across a range of religious forms, but here it is based specifically on the observation of one religious movement, the Sōka Gakkai. I shall illustrate the analysis by using the ritual of Sōka Gakkai International, as practised in the UK, as a case study.

Method and Methodology

The account of Sōka Gakkai practice which follows is based on continuing fieldwork, a major part of which was carried out in 1994. Over a period of six months I attended all Sōka Gakkai fortnightly meetings for one local group and carried out nine recorded interviews with members, mostly—but not exclusively—from within that same group. This formed part of a case study of Buddhist practice across all six Buddhist groups operating in one British town (Waterhouse, 1997). The fieldwork provided an opportunity to experience, at first hand, a range of Sōka Gakkai practices, including ritual practice, at fortnightly study and discussion meetings. I also attended a residential course at the movement's headquarters at Taplow Court (near Maidenhead) with a group of practitioners from another part of the country. Since that time I have maintained links with the organization mainly, but not exclusively, through its academic wing, The Institute of Oriental Philosophy.

The research was assisted by the fact that my life circumstances resemble those of members of the group. If I were to start to practise Buddhism within Sōka Gakkai, I would be quite unremarkable in many respects. Around 60% of the membership are women. Approximately 4–5% of the movement as a whole are within a couple of years of my own age. 65% have had a religious background, and around a quarter have been to university, just as I have (Wilson & Dobbelaere, 1994). Because that is the case, what I shall discuss here are the fine distinctions that operate within a cultural group, rather than the more overt differences which operate between groups.

Research within proselytizing groups, such as Sōka Gakkai, brings both opportunities and problems. It is relatively easy to gain access to such groups, since part of their ethos is to make available the practices they carry out and the ideas they promote. Others have pointed to difficulties inherent in researching such groups, which arise from the group members' desire to effect the conversion of the researcher, in just the same way in which they would wish to see any outsider converted (Gordon, 1987; Pollner & Emerson, 1983).[1] While this was potentially a factor within my research, I cannot claim that this tendency made fieldwork among the Sōka Gakkai particularly problematic. There was no overt pressure to join, although I was aware that my 'conversion' to the practice of Sōka Gakkai would have brought pleasure to those I was researching.

There is perhaps an explanation for the question of why researching this organisation did not lead to the kinds of difficulties sometimes inherent in researching proselytizing organisations, in which distinctions are made between insiders and outsiders. The explanation is that there are those within the Sōka Gakkai UK hierarchy who are interested in promoting an active rapport between the practice of Sōka Gakkai Buddhism and the academic study of Buddhism. This interest is focused in the movement's academic wing, The Institute of Oriental Philosophy, which organizes conferences and lectures by academics who are outsiders to the movement.[2] The president of the international movement, Daisaku Ikeda, is often photographed with prominent academics and world figures. It seems that this gives the movement a certain cachet in its own eyes. The inclination to associate with academic study is also evident in non-official sources. For example, in a personal web-site, a Sōka Gakkai member claims—somewhat naively—that the existence of sociological accounts of the movement provides proof that it is not a 'cult'.[3]

While I remain an outsider to the organization, my relationship with it has been both professional and personal. Together with the interest in academic accounts within the movement, this has facilitated the input of two long-term 'academically literate' practitioners in this account. Their observations on my presentation of their ritual practices have been incorporated at a number of places, but more interestingly, they have both affirmed my analysis to be acceptable from the perspective of an insider.[4] In her contribution to this volume, Elisabeth Arweck discusses the position of 'insider academics', in particular insiders who take up academic study, as well as the difficulties which may arise when insiders are allowed to comment on outsider/academic accounts of their organizations. Soka Gakkai clearly illustrates some of the points she makes. Arweck further points out that a researcher's detachment may be weakened by sustained contact with a religious group. It is not easy to determine when and whether such weakening occurs, and I am aware that this has been a potential pitfall in my involvement with Sōka Gakkai. Although not in sympathy with the organization's aims, I am nonetheless conscious of my own reaction against some of the more sensationalized accounts of the movement, which appear from time to time in press accounts. I hope to have been sufficiently reflexive in the research process to avoid the worst pitfalls, but am conscious of tensions for which, as Arweck points out, there are no real solutions. The ambiguity of the role of outsider/researcher will be addressed later in the paper, but before offering any analysis, I should first describe the movement under discussion and specifically the central ritual practice of *gongyō*.

Sōka Gakkai

The Sōka Gakkai (Society for the Creation of Value) is a lay Buddhist movement which was started in Japan in the 1930s by the radical Japanese educationalist Tsunesaburō Makiguchi (1871–1944). Makiguchi found that the liberal educational theories he had developed[5] could be enhanced through association with the religious practice of the Nichiren Shōshū (Orthodox Nichiren Sect).[6] Nichiren Shōshū is a priestly lineage which claims to uphold the true teachings of Nichiren (1222–1282). Nichiren was a thirteenth-century Buddhist monk whose teachings are outlined below. No one form of Buddhism has more followers in contemporary Japan than the sects which claim allegiance to his teachings.[7] Whereas Nichiren's concerns were in part nationalistic, modern-day movements which embrace his teachings, including the Sōka Gakkai, have extended their concerns well beyond Japan.[8] The Sōka Gakkai is the most successful of the many post-war lay religious movements in Japan (Bocking, 1994: 118) where it claims up to 16 million members. The international movement, too, has a substantial following which is spread throughout the rest of the world. It is represented in 148 countries[9] in five continents and is thus the most successful Nichiren movement outside Japan. There is a reported membership of 30,000 in Europe[10] and of 330,000 in the US[11]. Sōka Gakkai is therefore a substantial religious movement.

My concern in this paper is specifically with the Sōka Gakkai in the UK. The British organization was established in 1961 with just two members, both of whom were Japanese women who had followed their English husbands to Britain. In 1975, when the British movement gained legal status as a registered charity, there were 200 members. Richard Causton, who joined the movement in 1974 and was its leader until his death in 1995, saw it grow rapidly to become one of the largest Buddhist groups in Britain. Wilson and Dobbelaere suggest that it is "almost certainly the school of Buddhism with the largest body of support in Britain" (Wilson & Dobbelaere, 1994: 13).[12] In 1995, the estimated British membership of Sōka Gakkai was 6,500, of whom 3,500–4,000 were described as "active"[13]—in other words in regular attendance at meetings and thus engaging in community expressions of Sōka Gakkai ritual. The remaining members may maintain a loose affiliation with the organization and practise on an irregular basis. I shall return to this important distinction below.

Sōka Gakkai Ritual

Nichiren studied within the Japanese Tendai school of Buddhism. Tendai is an eclectic form of Buddhism, which—like its Chinese forebear, T'ien-tai— placed Buddhist texts in a hierarchy. Nichiren was well educated in Buddhist scriptures and philosophy and came to believe that not only a particular Mahāyāna Buddhist text, the Lotus Sūtra (*Saddharmapuṇḍarīka Sūtra*) represents the highest, most advanced and final teaching of the Buddhas,[14] but also that other forms of Buddhism taught in Japan at that time were corrupt.[15] None of the Mahāyāna Sūtras, including the *Lōtus Sutra*, is recognized as canonical or authentic by the Theravādin Buddhists of south-east Asia, but many East-Asian Buddhists, not only followers of Nichiren, believe that to recite, copy or promulgate this Sūtra is sufficient for salvation.[16]

According to Nichiren, the Sūtra is not merely *sufficient* for salvation as taught by some sects, it is *necessary* for salvation. Nichiren believed that he was living in the degenerate age, the last day of the law (*mappō*), a period predicted by the historical Buddha of India. He taught that it is possible to overcome the degeneration of this age, but only through the transformatory power of the *Lotus Sūtra* which can turn the degenerate age into an age in which salvation is easily achieved. He believed that recitation of the *Lotus Sūtra* would enable Japan to enter a stable and peaceful state (Dollarhide, 1982: 9–19) and claimed that other salvific techniques taught by Buddhas cannot be efficacious in this age and only have the status of provisional teachings. He taught that the *Lotus Sūtra* is so powerful that simply to repeat its name is sufficient for salvation. The Sūtra's name in ancient Japanese is *myōhō-renge-kyō*, which with the addition of an honorific—becomes the mantra of Nichiren's Buddhism, *nam-myōhō-renge-kyō*. This mantra is chanted in individual and group ritual practice.

The central ritual performance of Sōka Gakkai, called *gongyō*, is focused on the *Lotus Sūtra* and is the formalized repetition of two chapters from the Sutra. The text of *gongyō* is chanted in a form of ancient Japanese, which is never translated into the vernacular and which very few people, including contemporary Japanese people, can understand.[17] *Gongyō* also includes a number of prayers and incorporates the repetition or chanting of the mantra *nam-myōhō-renge-kyō*, called *daimoku*. The mantra may also be chanted outside of, or instead of, *gongyō*.

The symbolic focus for all ritual practice is the *gohonzon*. In Japanese, a *honzon* is an object of worship: the prefix 'go' is an honorific. In physical terms, the *gohonzon* is usually a paper copy, produced by the most up-to-date photographic printing methods, of the mantra *nam-myōhō-renge-kyō*. The mantra is embodied on the page in the form of a mandala in which it is surrounded by the ten worlds of Tendai philosophy[18] represented by the names of Buddhas and Bodhisattvas and inscribed in ancient Japanese and Sanskrit. For practitioners, the *gohonzon* is far more than a paper scroll; it is a precious symbol of potential enlightenment and it is for this reason that it is the object of worship. It has been described as "a map of a human being manifesting Buddhahood" (*UK Express* 310, April 1997: 15). According to Nichiren Shōshū orthodoxy, all *gohonzon* derive from the original *gohonzon* inscribed by Nichiren on 12th October, 1279 (Matsuda, 1983: 141–142). While Nichiren's mantra *nam-myōhō-renge-kyō* is not secret and available for anyone to use, the *gohonzon* is strictly controlled by the organization; copies are made available only when individuals have proven a degree of dedication to the practice and received a home visit to check that a suitable site is available, on which to place the *butsudan*, the wooden cabinet which houses the scroll.[19]

Figure 1 (Courtesy of Sōka Gakkai International-UK Publications Dept.)

Figure 1 shows an altar with the *butsudan*, housing the scroll, at the top. Altars vary in size and complexity. Japanese practitioners especially may have large ornate altars, while British practitioners are more likely to have smaller, simpler versions. The example in Figure 1 falls somewhere between the two being comparatively large, but simple. It is not permitted to take photographs of the *gohonzon* itself, which is why the *butsudan* is closed in this picture. Symbols placed on the altar are each interpreted by the organization (*UK Express* 343, January 2000: 40–44). Evergreen branches symbolize permanence and vitality, which are the aspects of life that members try to develop. Cut flowers are not used, since they wither and die. Candlelight signifies the Buddha's wisdom and incense represents his compassion. Incense sticks are kept in the long box between the candles. On ceremonial occasions, people may offer three pinches of powdered incense representing the three kinds of *karmic* action: thought, word and deed. Water, contained in the bowl, represents traditional Buddhist offerings and fruit offerings, which—like all the symbols—are optional, but serve the same purpose. On the floor in front of the altar is the bell. This is rung to signal transitions in the ritual, but it also represents an offering of pleasant sound.

Rolled in tubes, *gohonzon* are distributed to new members at joyful ceremonial occasions. In 1991, the Sōka Gakkai split from the priesthood of the Nichiren Shōshū sect. Since that time, this ceremony has been led by senior lay leaders, instead of by Japanese priests. Before the distribution takes place, members are instructed on how they should care for the *gohonzon*. For example, they are told not to wave the tube around in triumphal fashion, but to treat their *gohonzon* with care and respect, until it can be enshrined in the home *butsudan*. After a member has received the *gohonzon*, it is enshrined in the *butsudan* by a senior practitioner at a further ceremony (*okuri*) which requires careful ritual performance, including the recitation of *gongyō*. Members may invite friends to share in this momentous occasion. Such is the reverence with which the scroll is regarded that those who handle it directly during the enshrinement and on other formal occasions hold a leaf in their mouths, in order to prevent droplets of saliva falling on it. Members are told that the *butsudan* is ideally placed in a quiet room and that, if it must be in a room used for purposes other than *gongyō*, it should not be positioned where the practitioner may be distracted by pictures or ornaments.

After the *gohonzon* has been enshrined, the *butsudan* is opened exclusively for the purpose of ritual practice and always with due ceremony. Members are encouraged not to leave the *gohonzon* unattended because of the risk of fire, theft or other damage. When members are away from home, the *gohonzon* is carefully removed from the *butsudan*, wrapped for protection in several layers of paper or foil and taken to another member's house or to a Sōka Gakkai centre, so that it can be cared for correctly. If an individual stops practising *gongyō*, the *gohonzon* is ideally returned to the organization and may be held in store at the Taplow Court headquarters. This certainly happens in some instances; when practitioners cease to practise, they may retain a respect for the *gohonzon* and may wish to have their personal copy correctly stored. However, it seems unlikely that all ex-practitioners are assiduous in this regard.

Doing *gongyō*

When performing *gongyō*, the member starts to chant *nam-myōhō-renge-kyō* while lighting candles and incense. The chant continues as the doors of the *butsudan* are opened and the member kneels or sits facing the *gohonzon* holding prayer beads (*juzu*) which are periodically rubbed together. Most members follow the liturgy in a small *gongyō* book which they keep, together with the beads, wrapped in a decorative cloth (*fukuson*). The formal recitation begins, accompanied by the sounding of a bell at designated places. Inexperienced chanters often struggle with the unfamiliar words and the order of *gongyō* practice as laid out in the book; however, practice brings speed and experienced practitioners will perform the recitation quite quickly. The performance takes about half an hour, although it can be extended indefinitely by the inclusion of a long period of *daimoku* in the middle. Some practitioners may write a translation of the Japanese words in their books, but this is not usual—most members are entirely unaware of the meaning of the words spoken.

Members are advised to perform *gongyō* in front of the *gohonzon* every morning and evening, the form for each being slightly different. Recent 'guidance' from the president of the international movement, Ikeda, has removed a former emphasis on strict adherence to twice daily *gongyō* and many members affirm that the organization's advice on the form of *gongyō* is not as strict as it used to be. Wilson and Dobbelaere's sociological survey of the movement showed that just over half the membership practise over ten times per week, with a further 28% practising between 8 and 10 times weekly (Wilson & Dobbelaere, 1994: 174).

Gongyō is practised either individually or at group meetings. Communal recitations may be led by any member, or indeed non-member,[20] provided s/he is familiar with the liturgy and the correct order for the recitation, and all members are encouraged to play their part in leading *gongyō*. In spite of the formalized nature of the practice, the atmosphere at communal recitations is relaxed. In my experience, if members make an error or lose their way in the liturgy, they simply find the correct place in the *gongyō* book and continue, sometimes with smiles of reassurance from their companions. Members are encouraged to do 'good' *gongyō*, which usually means getting the Japanese pronunciation accurate. Even so, experienced practitioners often admit that they 'tend to rattle through it'. However, more important than this is that the motivation which underlies the ritual is correct; the practitioner is expected to chant with faith and determination.

The ultimate aim of the chanting practice is to experience enlightenment or Buddhahood in every moment of life. While this is the aim, in the short term, members may be less ambitious, reporting that all aspects of their lives are enriched and empowered. I leave it to a practitioner to describe this:

In a sense I don't need to be able to explain it. I simply get up in the morning and with almost one hundred percent constancy, I set aside an hour in the morning, between six thirty and seven thirty and I do *gongyō* and chant for half an hour. And that sets me up, not just for the day, but as an ongoing thing, as part of my life. And I just feel that when I do that, and because I do that, I do what I do … with more respect and much more effectively. I am empowered if you like... I can't prove it to anyone else but I don't think I need to. To my own satisfaction I know it works for me. At the very bottom line that is all I need to say about it. (interview with member, April 1994)

I should also add, since this is probably one of the most widely reported aspects of Sōka Gakkai practice, that part of the empowering process which practitioners describe may involve the attainment of material as well as non-material goals. Press accounts of the movement often concentrate on this aspect, including the fact that some members have chanted for cars or for money. Also, experience of the practice is not always positive. Members report that *gongyō* practice is sometimes uncomfortable, especially when they set out to challenge, through practice, aspects of their personality or life circumstances, which they would rather ignore.

Outsider Perspectives

Having provided a short account of Sōka Gakkai ritual I shall return to my three-fold analysis concerning the insider/outsider dichotomy. The first part of this analysis is that not all outsiders who study religious rituals are the same. This is for two reasons: firstly, researchers have individual differences and contrasting skills. For example, Lofland suggests that small, female researchers are likely to appear to the subjects of their research as in need of assistance and instruction. They thus have a different experience of fieldwork from that of the older, male, professorial 'expert' who does not appear to be in need of being taught (Lofland, 1971). While Lofland's gender categorization is unfortunate, I agree with his underlying sentiment and have always found that some of the most useful fieldwork conversations and relationship building takes place when my perceived academic status is at its lowest, for example, over a washing-up bowl.

David Gordon's paper on fieldwork with proselytizing groups lays out contrasting approaches to researching those who try to persuade outsider researchers to become insiders. His own strategy was to argue openly with members about their beliefs in order to maintain sufficient distance from them and in order to avoid personal stress (Gordon, 1987). He sets up this strategy in direct contrast to that of Robbins *et al.* (1973) who were anxious to avoid the discussion of their own beliefs. The fact that these researchers were comfortable with contrasting approaches to members of the same religious organization (The Jesus People) indicates that outsider researchers employ contrasting techniques in order to achieve a similar purpose. Methodological literature within sociology now seems to prefer Gordon's method to that of Robbins *et al.*; it is, however, likely that these two approaches will continue to suit researchers of contrasting temperaments and with contrasting degrees of commitment to religious or ideological positions of their own. There is no one 'right' way to carry out participant observation, because individual researchers differ—outsiders differ and the result of this is that outsider accounts, which emphasize qualitative aspects of a religious movement, including human relationships, will differ or—at least—emphasize contrasting elements.

Apart from individual differences in temperament or life circumstances, not all outsiders have identical motivations for their study. There are, I think, broadly three motivations for studying the rituals of a religious organization such as the Sōka Gakkai. Firstly, insiders or potential insiders may study Sōka Gakkai rituals in order to learn how to perform them or how to perform them better. This is clearly an insider position which is motivated by the desire to perform the rituals in ways that will bring the benefits that the movement promises. Secondly, outsiders may study these rituals in order to discredit them. Members of other religious groups, or of the 'anti-cult movement', or anti-religionists, or people who believe their family and friends have been damaged by these rituals may take this line, as may ex-members of the movement and some journalists. We need not look beyond British Buddhism for evidence of this. In the present climate, a significant number of Buddhist groups are jostling for adherents. Like the celebrated Buddhist scholar Edward Conze,[21] practitioners of forms of Buddhism other than that taught and practised by Sōka Gakkai may claim that Sōka Gakkai Buddhism is not authentic Buddhism at all[22] and, very often, they will base this judgement on the nature and aims of Sōka Gakkai ritual. Sōka Gakkai is not a special case, British Buddhism at the turn of the millennium is sectarian in nature and, partly in order to validate the practices of their own particular group, practitioners may challenge the authenticity of another group.[23]

This is incidentally one of the reasons why it is problematic to claim, as many practitioners do, that in order to study Buddhism at all, one must be a practitioner (Hayes, 1999: 172). If Buddhism were a monolithic structure in which all rituals were identical, this claim would still be problematic; however, Buddhism is not monolithic. It is gloriously diverse and its rituals form part of that diversity. If we were to accept that outsiders cannot study Buddhism, the very diversity of Buddhism would logically require the further disaggregation of who can study which parts of the whole.[24] Theravada Buddhists are outsiders to Tibetan Buddhism. Nyingmapa Tibetan Buddhists are outsiders to Gelugpa Tibetan Buddhists and so on—we could end up with a situation where researchers could study only the rituals performed within their own lineage. There are those who argue that Buddhist ideas can be studied in a non-sectarian environment[25] together with meditation practice; however, this is really only an option for forms of Buddhism which do not lay emphasis on sectarian differences or, for example, specialized mantric practices. There are all kinds of difficulties inherent in the position of a person who claims that only Buddhists can study Buddhism, because we are all outsiders to some degree, although possibly some of us are further outside than others.

Jo Pearson argues in her contribution to this volume that it is useful to have both insider and outsider perspectives in the study of any religious tradition and I agree with her, but the point still remains that not all outsider perspectives are the same. Between the two extremes of insider and crusading outsider lies a middle ground, the perspective of the interested observer who neither wishes to embrace nor to condemn, but to learn. Sections within Religious Studies have traditionally occupied this middle ground. I would certainly position myself as someone interested in what Sōka Gakkai ritual is and what it means, according to official accounts, but also as interested in the way in which members of the movement experience that ritual as well as interested in the elements of Sōka Gakkai ritual which are not necessarily emphasized in the movement's accounts of itself. In providing this account it has not been my intention to reduce Sōka Gakkai practice to sociological or psychological explanations, or to ridicule or condemn it. I believe this account to be complementary to official insider accounts. There are two reasons why this is the case. The first and the most straightforward of the two is that the account of Sōka Gakkai ritual presented here is based on observation, but also on insider accounts of what it feels like to experience this practice. The second is that the informants in the study have been selected by me and neither they nor I have been subjected to any editorial control from the organization. Many of the informants have no formal representative role within the movement. This can be viewed negatively as promoting confusion about Sōka Gakkai practice or it can be viewed positively as adding depth to officially sanctioned accounts. The accounts of ritual included here have been limited in the interests of brevity. However, I could have included broader personal interpretations of carrying out Sōka Gakkai ritual, for example, contrasting interpretations of what we might call the magical elements within the ritual. An outsider account of this movement is free to include narratives which divert from the official account of ritual, it can therefore complement insider accounts to provide a rounder, more complete picture (Griffiths, 1991: 24). The outsider participant-observer position is not without its complexities, as Elisabeth Arweck shows in her contribution to this volume.

In arguing that outsider accounts are valuable I should make it clear that I am not claiming that as an outsider I can make observations on Sōka Gakkai ritual which no insider could make. Participant observation as an insider throws up different kinds of challenges from those experienced by an outsider, as Jo Pearson's contribution shows.

What Does It Mean to Be an Insider in Sōka Gakkai?

The second challenge to the insider/outsider dichotomy is that not all insiders are the same. It is necessary at this point to consider what it means to be an insider in this movement. In order to do this I shall make use of an outsider observation about the movement in general and an insider definition of what it means to practise Sōka Gakkai Buddhism. I shall first consider the outsider observation. In their sociological study of Sōka Gakkai in the UK, Wilson and Dobbelaere suggest that insiders of Sōka Gakkai "more readily refer to someone as having started to practise, or as having 'stopped practising', than as having become, or ceased to be, a member" (Wilson & Dobbelaere, 1994: 173). This is the case. However, if asked specifically about what it means to be a member, practitioners are likely to associate membership with owning a copy of the *gohonzon*. One member told me that

A member is somebody who formally applies to become a member to Sōka Gakkai International UK and then they receive a membership certificate and then at some time, usually about twice a year, we have made available *gohonzon*. (interview with member, November 1993)

This throws into doubt what it means to be an insider in this organization. Insidership is determined either by ownership of the object of worship or by the activity associated with that. When asked in 1995 how many members the movement had, the Vice-General Director, Kazuo Fujii, made a similar distinction by giving statistics for those who have a copy of the *gohonzon*, the symbolic representation of Nichiren's mantra *nam-myōhō-renge-kyō*, but also an estimate of the number of those who are active in the organization. The former is clearly the easier statistic for the organization to provide, since it keeps records of the number of *gohonzon* issued and of the persons to whom they are issued. It cannot know how many members have ceased to practise, but retain their copy of the *gohonzon*. This shows that there are at least two categories of insider: those who have the means to practise and those who are involved in the movement's activities.

If we look in more detail at what it means to be active within the movement, the situation is complicated further. Practice within Sōka Gakkai does not only mean chanting *nam-myōhō-renge-kyō* or performing *gongyō* or attending group meetings. In 1988, Richard Causton, then director of Sōka Gakkai–UK, described practice within the movement as follows:

> ... *practice* for oneself and others means to perform *gongyō* twice a day and to chant *Nam-myōhō-renge-kyō* 'to your heart's content', while making efforts to teach others about this Buddhism and to work for their fundamental happiness, whether they practise Buddhism or not. (Causton, 1988 : 243, emphasis in the original)

We can note that in addition to *gongyō* and chanting, Causton includes proselytizing and altruism in his description of practice. Members, he says, should make 'efforts to teach others about this Buddhism and to work for their fundamental happiness'. This description comes within the standard English language work about Sōka Gakkai Buddhism in a chapter headed "The Essentials of Practice" (Causton, 1988). In this chapter, Causton discusses the role of faith and study indicating that all three aspects of Sōka Gakkai Buddhism, practice, faith and study are essential for insiders, if they are to practise in the ideal way. If practice determines who is an insider, then all three elements of practice, as described by the movement's former director, should ideally be present. While it is possible to observe levels of *gongyō* or *daimoku* practice and levels of study, I think it is difficult for either insiders or outsiders to quantify faith. A rather graphic illustration of this point is that one of the informants for the research, on which this account is based, spoke with great assurance in an interview about his role in the movement and his understanding of the ritual practice. However, since the interview took place, he has left the movement; therefore, although he was an insider at the time of the interview, he is now definitely an outsider. Not all insiders are the same and individual insiders do not remain the same over periods of time. One of my insider readers has pointed out that within the movement's activities, it is possible for those we might consider as insiders to feel like outsiders under certain circumstances, thus adding a sense of social belonging or some other aspect to what insider status might mean.

As we have seen, Wilson and Dobbelaere have shown that members vary significantly in the frequency with which they perform *gongyō*. Just over 80% of the members, who returned their questionnaire survey, practise at least seven times per week (Wilson & Dobbelaere, 1994: 174). Of those who returned the survey completed, a total of 626, or 8%, said they practised less than four times per week (ibid: 39). 362 recipients of questionnaires failed to return them completed (ibid: 39). The survey was sent out to members who have retained their copy of the *gohonzon*; therefore, many recipients of the questionnaire could have been non-active holders of the *gohonzon* who have failed to return the object of worship to the organization. This being the case, it is likely that a large percentage of those who failed to return a completed survey, a total of 374 people, are among the estimated 1,500 members who are no longer active. It is clear then that not all insiders are the same in respect of ritual practice.

The category of insider is not straightforward for this movement and being an insider does not lead automatically to a deeper or more encompassing understanding of Sōka Gakkai ritual in just the same way that being an outsider does not lead to greater objectivity. Insiders differ and perform, understand and account for ritual practices to contrasting degrees and in contrasting ways.[26]

Insider/Outsider Ambiguity

Finally, I shall argue that there is a position between insider and outsider which is occupied by potential converts and by those who leave the movement and which can be occupied by outsider researchers. In order to explain this argument, it is necessary to say more about the chant *nam-myōhō-renge-kyō* and the way in which it is used. Within the context of Buddhist tradition, *nam-myōhō-renge-kyō* represents a tantric transformatory mantra for which the sound itself, regardless of its meaning, is sacred and intrinsically powerful. Indeed, Nichiren claimed that scholars who argue the view that there is no value in reciting *nam-myōhō-renge-kyō* with faith, but without understanding the meaning "will be unable to avoid the deepest hells" (Rasplica Rodd, 1980: 83). Shimazono suggests that Sōka Gakkai has been successful in transferring to other cultures precisely because it presents a "straightforward magical practice" (Shimazono, 1991: 105).

There is therefore no need for new practitioners to have any understanding of the practice before they begin to chant. As Bocking observes, "it is well known that potential converts are encouraged to chant '*namu-myōhō-renge-kyō*' even without the *gohonzon*, to see for themselves the effect *daimoku* practice has, 'proof' being one of the signs of the true teaching" (Bocking, 1994: 122). Nichiren's mantra is not secret or subject to financial transaction, as it is, for example, in Transcendental Meditation, and the only way to begin practising

Sōka Gakkai Buddhism is to begin to chant, either in private or in group meetings. In this movement, the first step to becoming an insider is to begin to chant. There is therefore a transition period in which potential converts are neither complete outsiders nor complete insiders. They have begun to chant, but have not received the *gohonzon*. In the same way, participant observation involves chanting at Sōka Gakkai meetings. That is the participant part of the method. Given that Nichiren taught that the mantra has power regardless of intention, a participant observer, like a potential convert, is neither a complete outsider nor a complete insider, but occupies—at least for a temporary period—an ambiguous area in-between.

When carrying out fieldwork on Sōka Gakkai I slipped easily into the local group, was expected at meetings and became involved very quickly in activities and even in decisions about activities. The insider/outsider dichotomy did not rigidly apply, because, when at meetings, I joined in with, and indeed enjoyed, *gongyō* practice. Often in participant observation situations within religious groups, leaders are aware of a researcher's presence at meetings and of her/his intentions, while ordinary members are not (Gordon, 1987: 273). During this research, all those in attendance at meetings were aware of my status, just as they are always aware of the status of a potential convert. This is enabled by the fact that part of the monthly discussion meetings is for those present to share their experiences with the group. This involves a short introduction at each meeting at which time members usually say how long they have been practising. Therefore, at every meeting, I had to explain publicly my status and further, according to the logic of the movement, every time I joined in *gongyō* practice I was inviting personal experience of it, just as members and potential members were.

In other respects, my experience of attending Sōka Gakkai meetings was clearly not the same as that of a potential new member. For example, most potential converts know little of Buddhism or of Nichiren's particular teachings, whereas I had been teaching Buddhism to undergraduates. However, in terms of the observation and, to an extent, the experience of performance of the ritual, there were significant similarities. Experience of the practice was as open to me as it was to other new chanters. Potential converts who begin to chant and participating researchers occupy an ambiguous status between that of outsider and insider.

Conclusion

I have argued that the terms 'insider' and 'outsider' do not represent a simple dichotomy. Insiders vary just as outsiders do. However, insider status also varies in degree. This does not mean that the terms 'insider' and 'outsider' are not useful ones. At one level we know what they refer to. Yet, in order to avoid misleading generalizations, it is useful to remember that they are umbrella terms which embrace variety. In respect of the Sōka Gakkai at least, there exists an ambiguous area between the two categories, which may be occupied by potential converts or by a researcher. While insider status in this group, which incorporates all three aspects of practice (faith, ritual performance and study), offers a sustained experience of promised effects, a taste of that experience is not denied to those who operate on its periphery.

The question this leaves open is how far this analysis can be extended to other religious groups. My experience of other British Buddhist groups suggests that insider status can be more carefully guarded. While this analysis of the Sōka Gakkai has received the sanction of insider readers, a similar exercise on another group may not have been so well received, especially one in which practitioners claim to have had experiences deriving from ritual practice, which are not open to outsiders or even to those who have lately begun the practice. Many meditators, for example, claim ineffable transformatory experiences based on ritual practice, which are frequently used to divide those who know from those who do not know, namely insiders from outsiders. However, the fact that ambiguous areas exist within the Sōka Gakkai opens up the possibility that they also exist in other religious organisations.

Notes

1   For example, Rochford describes the distress he felt when he was among the Hare Krishna members he was researching (Rochford, 1985: 23–24)
2   For example, the lecture series "The Wisdom of the East" and two symposia which took place in 1995 and 1999 respectively on "New Religious Movements: Challenge and Response" and "Re-Presenting Buddhism". Papers from the former are published in Wilson & Cresswell, 1999.
3   The web-site is http://members.aol.com/watchbuddh/books.htm (viewed 10th June, 1999).
4   I am grateful to Wendy Jermyn and Jamie Cresswell for their input to this paper.
5   See Educational Department of Sōka Gakkai (n.d.: 55–70) for an explanation of Makiguchi's Theory of Value.
6   For an historical account of the movement, see Metraux, 1988.
7   30% of Japanese Buddhists living in Japan are connected with forms of Buddhism based on Nichiren's teachings. This compares, for example, with only 8% connected with Zen schools (O'Brien & Palmer, 1993: 27).

8 The peace pagodas in London (Battersea Park) and Milton Keynes were erected by another Nichiren inspired group, Nipponzan Myohoji.

9 Sōka Gakkai web-site: http://www.sgi.org (viewed 28th January, 2000).

10 See *UK Express* 278, August 1994.

11 SGI USA web-site: http://sgi-usa.org/aboutsgi-usa.html (viewed 18th January, 2000).

12 This observation has been criticized by Harvey as being unsubstantiated (Harvey, 1995: 357). There are other British Buddhist groups which are probably as large as the Sōka Gakkai, in particular the Friends of the Western Buddhist Order and the New Kadampa Tradition; however, statistics on Buddhist groups are difficult both to gather and to interpret, partly because insider/outsider categories are fluid.

13 Interview with Kazuo Fujii, Vice General Director of Sōka Gakkai, 30th March, 1995.

14 Like other Mahāyāna sutras, the *Lotus Sūtra* makes this claim for itself, e.g. in Chapter 10 of Kumarajiva's version of this text (Hurvitz, 1976).

15 See Dollarhide (1982: 86–105) for a translation of the text by Nichiren, entitled "The Three Calamities called the Nembutsu, Zen and Shingon Sects".

16 See Williams (1989: 142) for an engaging traditional illustration of the power of the Lotus Sūtra.

17 One of my insider readers asked me to point out that the organization does have translations of the *Lotus Sūtra* and English language commentaries on it. Increasingly, the international organization is promoting an understanding of the content of the *Sūtra* and it would be wrong to think that practitioners chant the *Sūtra* mindlessly. The *Lotus Sūtra* is a complex and abstruse text. Although I would not want to suggest that members chant mindlessly, my research to date suggests that in spite of the availability of translations of the *Lotus Sūtra*, most members do not make its study a priority and are not familiar with its content.

18 These are the life conditions in which any living being may manifest and are, in ascending order: hell, hunger, animality, anger, humanity or tranquillity, heaven or rapture, learning, realization, bodhisattva and buddhahood.

19 Some members, particularly those who travel about the country on Sōka Gakkai business, may also be given an *omamori gohonzon*; as far as members are concerned, these are small versions of the *gohonzon* which may be worn around the neck and are therefore very convenient when travelling or for group *gongyō* practice at a Sōka Gakkai social or cultural event held in a public place. A more conventional understanding of an *omamori* is that it is a protective amulet or charm (Bocking, 1995: 138).

20 I was recently invited to lead *daimoku* chanting at a meeting in the home of Sōka Gakkai members, in spite of the fact that they are aware that I do not practise outside of meetings attended for research purposes.

21 Conze claims that with Nichiren, Buddhism "evolved its very antithesis out of itself" (Conze, 1980: 114).

22 In the Spring 1995 edition of *The Forest Hermitage Newsletter*, Ajahn

Khemadhammo, an ordained Theravada monk, described the Sōka Gakkai as "awful rubbish" and "an alarming aberration". The Ajahn is of course entitled to his opinion as a Buddhist practitioner, however, scholarly work on British Buddhism would be incomplete without taking account of Sōka Gakkai–UK, since it is one of the largest Buddhist groups in the country. A recent volume on American Buddhism appropriately includes a chapter on Sōka Gakkai in the US (Hammond & Machacek, 1999: 100–114). In a broad-ranging review of Buddhism in America in the same volume, Seager argues that "It may well be that Sōka Gakkai is now at the forefront of the Americanization of Buddhism and, given the reported size of its membership, may yet make a claim as to being the defining movement in American Buddhism" (Seager, 1999: 250). While I cannot agree with Seager's conclusion, the fact that this idea has been voiced at all indicates the significance of Sōka Gakkai within Western Buddhism.

23 See Waterhouse (1997; 1999) for accounts of the contrasting ways in which British Buddhists may legitimize their practice.

24 However, see Corless (1990) for an interesting view on teaching Buddhist ideas to undergraduates while avoiding aspects specific to lineage.

25 Robert Goss (1999) has written an account of Buddhism as taught at the Naropa Institute in the US, in which he cites the views of Judith Simmer-Brown. Simmer-Brown lectures on Naropa's Engaged Buddhism programme. She does not insist that her students are Buddhists, but she does insist that they meditate. Presumably this means that she wants her students to engage with the teachings and consider them on a personal level. I believe this indicates the problems associated with the idea that meditation is not grounded within a particular religious tradition.

26 A representative from a very different branch of Buddhism made a related observation at a meeting convened by the Friends of the Western Buddhist Order (FWBO) in February 2000. She remarked that, in her branch of British Tibetan Buddhism, men and women new to monastic orders may be the most eager to answer outsiders' questions in spite of the fact that they know less than their more experienced colleagues.

References

Bocking, B. "Of Priests, Protests and Protestant Buddhists: The Case of Sōka Gakkai International." In Clarke, P. & Somers, J., eds. *Japanese New Religions in the West*. Folkestone: Japan Library, 1994: 118–149.

Bocking, B. *A Popular Dictionary of Shinto*. Richmond, Surrey: Curzon, 1995.

Causton, R. *Nichiren Shōshū Buddhism*. London: Rider, 1988.

Conze, E. *A Short History of Buddhism*. London: George Allen & Unwin, 1980.

Corless, R. "How is the Study of Buddhism Possible?" *Method and Theory in the Study of Religion* 2 (1), 1990: 24–41.

Dollarhide, K. *Nichiren's Senji-sho*. New York: Edwin Mellen, 1982.

Educational Department of Sōka Gakkai. "Sōka Gakkai and the Nichiren Shō Sect." *Contemporary Religions in Japan* 1 (1), n. d.: 55–70.

Gordon, D. "Getting Close by Staying Distant: Fieldwork with Proselytizing Groups." *Qualitative Sociology* 10 (3), 1987: 267–287.

Goss, R. E. "'Buddhist Studies at Naropa': Sectarian or Academic?" In Williams, D. R. & Queen, C., eds. *American Buddhism*. Richmond, Surrey: Curzon, 1999: 215–237.

Griffiths, P. J. *An Apology for Apologetics*. New York: Orbis, 1991.

Hammond, P. & Machacek, D. "Supply and Demand: The Appeal of Buddhism in America." In Williams, D. R. & Queen, C., eds. *American Buddhism*. Richmond, Surrey: Curzon, 1999: 100–114.

Harvey, P. "Review of B. R. Wilson & K. Dobbelaere: *A Time to Chant*." *Sociology* 29 (2), 1995: 256–257.

Hayes, R. "The Internet as Window onto American Buddhism." In Williams, D. R. & Queen, C., eds. *American Buddhism*. Richmond, Surrey: Curzon, 1999: 168–179.

Hurvitz, L., transl. *Scripture of the Lotus Blossom of the Fine Dharma*. New York: Columbia U. P., 1976.

Lofland, J. *Analysing Social Settings*. Belmont, California: Wadsworth, 1971.

Matsuda, T., ed. *A Dictionary of Buddhist Terms and Concepts*. Tokyo: Nichiren Shoshu International Centre, 1983.

Metraux, D. *The History and Theology of Sōka Gakkai: A Japanese New Religion*. New York: Edwin Mellen, 1988.

O'Brian, J. & Palmer, M. *The State of Religion Atlas*. New York: Touchstone, 1993.

Pollner, M. & Emerson, R. "The Dynamics of Inclusion and Distance in Fieldwork Relations." In Emerson, R. M., ed. *Contemporary Field Research*. Boston: Little Brown & Co., 1983: 235–252.

Rasplica Rodd, L. *Nichiren: Selected Writings*. Hawaii: University of Hawaii, 1980.

Robbins, T., Anthony, D. & Curtis, T. "The Limits of Symbolic Realism: Problems of Empathetic Field Observation in a Sectarian Context." *Journal for the Scientific Study of Religion* 12 (3), 1973: 259–271.

Rochford, E. B. *Hare Krishna in America*. New Brunswick: Rutgers U. P., 1985.

Seager, R. "Buddhist Worlds in the U.S.A.: A Survey of the Territory." In Williams, D. R. & Queen, C., eds. *American Buddhism*. Richmond, Surrey: Curzon, 1999: 238–261.

Shimazono, S. "The Expansion of Japan's New Religions into Foreign Cultures." *Japanese Journal of Religious Studies* 18 (2–3), 1991: 105–132.

Waterhouse, H. *Buddhism in Bath: Adaptation and Authority*. Leeds: Department of Theology and Religious Studies, University of Leeds, 1997.

Waterhouse, H. "Who Says So? Legitimacy and Authenticity in British Buddhism." *Scottish Journal of Religious Studies* 20 (1), 1999: 19–36.

Williams, D. R. & Queen, C., eds. *American Buddhism*. Richmond, Surrey: Curzon, 1999.

Williams, P. *Mahāyāna Buddhism*. London: Routledge, 1989.

Wilson, B. R. & Cresswell, J. *New Religious Movements: Challenge and Response*. London: Routledge, 1999.

Wilson, B. R. & Dobbelaere, K. *A Time to Chant*. Oxford: Oxford University Press, 1994.

5   Connecting Anthropology and Quakerism: Transcending the Insider/Outsider Dichotomy

PETER COLLINS

Introduction

I carried out my first ethnographic fieldwork in a Quaker meeting in the North of England (Collins, 1994). I was already a member of the Society of Friends (a Quaker) and resident warden of the same meeting. Although I would not claim that my position was unique, such 'insider research' remains a relatively unusual practice in anthropology. In writing up this research I chose to divide each of the first ten chapters into three parts: in the first section, I simply presented a conversation, usually between Quakers, relating to a particular aspect of meeting; in the second section, I reflected on this conversation as 'Simon' (a member of the meeting and warden or 'insider'); in section three, I continued this spiral of interpretation as 'Peter' (anthropologist or 'outsider'). It was a novel, partially autobiographical and rather mechanical, heuristic device which I revisit in what follows. However, my primary aim in this paper is to discuss the insider/outsider dichotomy in terms of methodology and epistemology, before going on to suggest that the distinction is redundant from the ontological perspective which I favour.

Observing and Participating: The Anthropologist as Partial Member

The insider/outsider conundrum finds its natural home in the practice of anthropology. It remains a key issue in so far as the discipline was founded on the distinctiveness of the anthropologist as someone who aspires to be neither 'insider' nor 'outsider', but who occupies that space indicated by the backslash (between insider/outsider). During the early decades of this century anthropology strove to legitimize itself as an academic discipline by being 'scientific' and science was, perhaps above all else, 'objective'. Objectivity depended on securing a posture *vis-à-vis* one's field of study best characterized as distanced. Subjectivity was to be avoided at all costs— although Malinowski's diaries, published in 1967 (Malinowski, 1967), reveal the difficulties of sustaining this pretence. Whether the anthropologist was likened to an engineer observing the workings of a machine or a physiologist scrutinizing a living organism, an unemotional detachment between observer and observed remained central to the analogy.

Early accounts implied a relatively straightforward relationship. Descriptions of the anthropologist entering the field are often graphic and beautifully told: the beginnings of an adventure in strange lands, populated by exotic (and sometimes quixotic) peoples. That told by Raymond Firth (1963; first published in 1936) arriving at the Pacific Island of Tikopia in 1929 is a *locus classicus:*

> In the cool of the early morning, just before sunrise, the bow of the Southern Cross headed towards the eastern horizon, on which a tiny dark blue outline was faintly visible. Slowly it grew into a rugged mountain mass, standing up sheer from the ocean. Then as we approached within a few miles it revealed around its base a narrow ring of low, flat land, thick with vegetation. The sullen grey day with its lowering clouds strengthened my grim impression of a solitary peak, wild and stormy, upthrust in a waste of waters. (Firth, 1963: 1)

Each account serves as a strong metaphor for the anthropologist as 'outsider' going 'into' the field. Unfortunately, the 'waste of waters' had already been muddied for many anthropologists—by missionaries, administrators, slave traders, and traders of all kinds. The categories 'us' and 'them' had been blurred long enough for the purity of the 'insider/outsider' dichotomy to be a fiction. The fiction was maintained in early ethnographic accounts by simply omitting to mention colonial encounters—whether past or present. Firth is in fact an exception: he includes unusually forthright sections on the 'foreign elements of culture introduced', although his account remains typically objectivist.

During the 1960s, anthropologists began to see the relationship between the terms 'insider' and 'outsider' as less of a dichotomy and as more of a continuum. Until then, the implicitly held premise was that anthropologists commence their fieldwork from a position, which we may call 'outside'. Few would claim to reach a degree of belonging they could confidently call 'inside'. 'Going native' is rare and its meaning is obscure, but it does imply that movement along a spectrum is possible, maybe even likely. 'Insider research' of one sort or another remains relatively unusual, but as experimental ethnography increases, instances will undoubtedly multiply (see e.g. Ellis & Flaherty, 1992; Ellis & Bochner, 1996). Between these two positions lies what is often considered the 'natural' environment of the anthropologist, the in-between, the margin, the interstices, the penumbra—call it what you will, but don't dare call it 'the outside' or 'the inside'! Anthropologists have, in defining their field, generally taken for granted the all too solid existence of an 'outside' and 'inside' in order to position themselves, advantageously, in that zone of shadows between the two. If all goes well, they will find accommodation on the edge, not in the centre of town, will have local friends, but not family, will have access to those in power, but will never be trusted by them, will have planned from the outset their time and means of departure, and will remain 'professional strangers' (Agar, 1980). Lévi-Strauss (1976) famously called himself 'an amputated man'—detached from French society and certainly no Amazonian Indian—doubly outside (and therefore doubly objective?).

Geertz's account of his first days in Bali is equally evocative, but slightly more intricate:

> Early in April of 1958, my wife and I arrived, malarial and diffident, in a Balinese village we intended, as anthropologists, to study. A small place, about five hundred people, and relatively remote, it was its own world. We were intruders, professional ones, and the villagers dealt with us as Balinese seem always to deal with people not part of their life who yet press themselves upon them: as though we were not there. For them, and to a degree for ourselves, we were nonpersons, specters, invisible men. (Geertz, 1973: 412)

Geertz and his contemporaries began to adopt an increasingly reflexive perspective and make explicit their own impact on the field. It was increasingly recognized that the terms which comprise dichotomies, such as 'objective/subjective', 'mind/body', 'emic/etic', 'insider/outsider', are social constructions which do not represent immutable truths and which are not neutral either, theoretically or politically. Bell (1992) alerts us to the fact that the insider/outsider dichotomy is mapped onto a further dichotomy which colours the way we see others. In relation to ritual,

insider : outsider :: action : thought

Such metaphors are important, not only because they reflect the way we understand the world, but—as Lakoff and Johnson (1980) so brilliantly show—because they are constitutive of that world. The idea is not new, as Soskice (1985) indicates in her account of religious metaphors. She claims that this 'strong metaphor theory' can be traced through Vico to Nietzsche, Barfield and Derrida. Lakoff and Johnson argue that our conceptual system is fundamentally metaphorical. Metaphor is pervasive in everyday life, not just in language, but in thought and action. Metaphors structure the way we perceive and understand the world and the ways in which we relate to others—even though we are hardly conscious of it. Furthermore, the metaphorical concept is systematic: the generic metaphor 'argument is war', for example, colours all our perceptions of disputation. In a more relevant example, they show us that the visual field is systematically metaphorized as a container—or a series of containers. And so it has come to seem 'natural' to divide the world up into those who are insiders and those who are outsiders. (Lakoff & Johnson, 1980)

This natural division is exemplified in what is probably the most blatant oxymoron of all those which grace the discipline of anthropology: participant observation—a term coined by Malinowski (1922). It describes what is generally regarded as the discipline's defining research method. However, does the anthropologist participate and then observe, or participate as well as observe, or observe as a participant, or participate as an observer? In any case, observation would seem to equate with 'outsiderhood', participation with 'insiderhood'. For much of its history, anthropology has encouraged its practitioners to dance a somewhat ironic polka with 'the field'. This remains so, partly due to the increased toleration shown by the discipline in relation to what may constitute an appropriate 'field'.

The idea of doing anthropology at home (in one's own country) was assumed, for some time, to be impossible. The distance required for objectivity would necessarily be reduced to zero, the anthropological space occluded. Despite this assumption, British anthropologists have carried out ethnographic fieldwork in Britain, and since the early 1980s, this has become an increasingly common practice—for a variety of reasons; examples include Cohen, 1987; Okely, 1983; Rapport, 1993; Strathern, 1981; Stringer, 1999. Partly because of the shortage of funding and partly due to the discovery that 'home' is a delightfully heterogeneous place, it is increasingly felt that social rather than physical distance might suffice as a means of objectifying 'the other'. It goes without saying that 'home' is a relative expression. Depending on circumstance, home for me might be the Solar System, Planet Earth, Europe, Britain, the United Kingdom, England, the North East, County Durham, Pittington, High Pittington, Hallgarth Road, the Quaker meeting, Durham University, Wales, Cardiff, the football club—and this is to limit the concept to mean only physical place (cf. Evans-Pritchard, 1940). The anthropologist even 'at home' has plenty of scope for 'playing the *vis-à-vis*' (Boon, 1982). We all experience multiple belongings, each of which may be used to gain a purchase on understanding others.

The insider/outsider dichotomy (or spectrum) can be expressed in terms of similarity and difference. Our relations with others are always marked by a certain playfulness involving the marking of first one and then the other—regardless of when, where and with whom these interactions take place. In assuming that distance between self and other is primarily social, anthropologists can generally establish a measure of difference between themselves and their subjects (and vice versa of course—this is a two-way process). On the other hand, a certain degree of similarity must be assumed, if we anticipate even a minimum level of communication. My own experience was unusual in so far as I was carrying out fieldwork 'at home' in a particularly precise sense. This was 'privileged access' (Agassi, 1969) to a high degree. Embodying both self *and* other, we might expect the social and spatial distance between the self of the anthropologist and the other inhabiting the field to be completely eclipsed. This was not the case. Each of us is bound always to be both self and other. No matter how many similarities exist between self and other, there will always be differences. Greta, a fellow Quaker, and I are both Quakers, she is, however, English and not Welsh, a woman and not a man, in her eighties and not her thirties, widowed and not married, retired and not employed, a local and not an incomer, and so forth. These differences themselves contribute to what we mean when we agree to call ourselves Quakers—a partially shared identity, a similarity, but only up to a point. Indeed, it is a similarity, only because we choose to describe (and inscribe) it as such.

Although ethnography is textual (Geertz, 1988; Van Maanen, 1988), it is also a lived experience and typically full of ethical dilemmas, complex emotions, power struggles, epistemological puzzles and ontological confusion. These are primarily existential issues which face us all during social interactions, they are—as I will show—exemplified in my own fieldwork experience.

Meeting as Experience and Discourse

While I agree with Stringer's argument that academics tend to underestimate the experiential aspect of worship (Stringer, 1999), there is no denying that the Quaker meeting for worship is at the same time a thoroughly discursive event. Furthermore, rituals are not abstract phenomena, they take place in particular places at particular times. Like all ritual events that are regularly repeated, they can be described by means of generalization, glossed as 'the same', but each can be portrayed as singular and unique. An event or interaction can take place, which may significantly influence a participant's belief or practice, for instance—even though it may pass unnoticed by everyone else present. Worship consists not only in the shared experiences of the group, but also in the unshared experiences of individual participants. Bearing these things in mind I will describe a particular meeting for worship.

One Sunday morning in 1992, I pass (as warden and anthropologist) into the Quaker meeting house from the warden's flat through the door which might be understood as the physical representation of the backslash (between insider/outsider), except it does not make sense to suggest that I am moving from the 'outside' to the 'inside'. I may or may not be 'in the field', but the field is, in a significant sense, always 'in me'. I check my pocket for notebook and pencil. Having spent a few hours cleaning up the place the previous day, the rooms are neat and tidy and laid out in the customary way. They are carefully prepared and presented as they always are—Friends attending worship this morning will find no nasty surprises, but an environment which is orderly and familiar. I assume that my expectations and their expectations coincide. The small library and collections of papers and pamphlets are carefully arranged. Before removing some out-of-date notices from one of the pinboards, I make a list of them and remind myself to file them later. I catch sight of, read, and straighten a poster containing a quote from the works of the American Quaker John Woolman. Opposite the front entrance, the chairs and tables are ready in the Children's Room (this is what *we* call it) for that time after meeting when Friends gather for a cup of tea and a biscuit. As I was taught by the previous (and pragmatic) warden, the furniture is arranged like this *also*, because it means less work when other groups come in and use the building. I look out across the garden at the parish church, a magnificent Victorian gothic edifice which towers over our modern and unornamented meeting house. I continue my rounds, as warden, anthropologist and member of the meeting—some tasks relate to one of these roles, others are less easily classifiable.

The meeting room is warm—a little too warm? Operating the central heating is an art. I open a window. I consider hiding the pole just in case Roger takes it upon himself to open all the windows, to the dismay of elderly Friends. I have arranged the chairs in the meeting room in two concentric circles, two or three arranged further back, rounding off the corners and placing them where some Friends prefer to sit. In the middle of the room, providing a focal point, the rectangular table is bare, apart from a Bible and some copies of *Christian Faith and Practice* (a collection of Quaker writings).

Later someone will bring in a small vase of flowers: *always* a small vase of flowers. I wonder why this is so and sense a yearning to see something quite different provided as the focus of our attention. The meeting room is quiet; the central heating pipes make no sound; the bare white walls are soundproofed. The meeting house is ready. I stop to listen to a blackbird and am mindful that we are asked to come to meeting 'with heart and mind prepared' ('Advices and Queries', in *Quaker Faith and Practice*, 1995: paragraphs 1.01–1.02). Preparing the meeting house is my preparation for meeting. How much of this action constitutes ritual and to what extent is it shared? Is it sensible to ask whether these questions derive from the anthropologist or the Quaker? I am 'at home', an insider, and yet I reflect continually on the building, its artifacts, the events that take place here and those who participate in such events—is this what distinguishes the outsider? Is it possible to determine, during such times, whether my standpoint (and/or actions) are emic or etic (Headland, Pike & Harris, 1990)? It is more likely that such terms tend to oversimplify.

The doorbell disturbs the peace and quiet and I am slightly irritated until I remember that it is probably Iris, who sometimes arrives early by bus. I open the door and welcome her with a smile and a handshake; we fall into conversation about mundane things—the weather, the car-park, the beech hedge. She enquires after my 'studies'—I respond with a shrug and a smile. It is 10.15 am. During the next 45 minutes or so, a steady trickle of Friends arrive at the meeting house. I greet each one in turn—a smile, a handshake, a brief verbal exchange. Who is doing the greeting? The warden? An elder? An anthropologist? To paraphrase Griffiths, the collectivity 'Quaker' is striated multifariously: Quakers may be men, women, black, white, heterosexual, homosexual, employed, unemployed, able bodied, disabled, young, old, and so forth. Differential membership of these social categories ensure that any claim to 'insiderhood' rests on the suppression of these 'contradictory positionings' (Griffiths, 1998: 363).

I introduce a newcomer to one or two 'old hands' who say a little about themselves and ask tentatively about the newcomer's familiarity with Quakerism. It turns out that this is her first time at a Quaker meeting which one Friend briefly describes while handing her a small explanatory leaflet. As the time reaches 11 o'clock, she is guided along the concourse and into the meeting room. I notice, with unusual clarity, how sensitive and how kind Quakers are: I feel a sense of empathy and identity, which is beyond words. Without announcing or in any way experiencing a change of role, I talk to this Friend about a recent Elders and Overseers meeting, to another about my daughter who will be attending children's meeting (which runs parallel to the adult meeting), complain about the form of the local football team to another, am asked about the stopcock in the men's lavatory, hear a rather *risqué* joke, and make mental notes about interactions I will later write down as fieldnotes. There is clamour. I mill about and watch others doing the same, coming into and breaking off from conversations. There is laughter. One or two smaller circles are discussing matters which may be personal or private. The clerk (who is responsible for reading out notices following meeting) is collared by a number of Friends who either have notices which they want read out or want an opportunity to address the meeting directly. Children meandering in and out of the adults' room eventually find their way into the Children's Room in which a couple of Friends are preparing painting materials. Children are critically interstitial. I experience this meeting and the talk-in-interaction in which I am involved as a unity and certainly sense no schizophrenic shifting from 'insider' to 'outsider' persona.

The notice-board tells visitors that Meeting for Worship begins at 11 am. One or two Friends leave leaflets concerning events and issues, which they think to be of interest, on tables in the concourse, or they pin notices to the wall, about a choral concert, an anti-nuclear rally, the problem of homelessness. Most Friends crowd in just before the appointed time—elders and overseers (and sometimes others) begin to herd people along the concourse into the meeting room a few minutes before 11, and at this point voices are lowered. One or two, arriving a few seconds late, continue their conversation into the meeting room— eyebrows are raised in their direction. Friends know, but sometimes forget, that meeting 'actually' begins at that time when the first person arrives in the meeting room and settles down for worship, no matter when. Friends seldom talk to one another once in the meeting room; children are expected, at a certain age, to remain quiet—until they are taken out to children's meeting after about ten minutes. As I enter the meeting room, the self-as-adept waxes and the self-as-warden wanes. Up until this point I have welcomed latecomers and ensured that they refrain from entering meeting should spoken ministry have commenced— a role I could occupy as warden only because I am also a member of the meeting. As anthropologist I am, of course, happy to remain on the lintel a little longer. I pass the children as they make their way out and take my seat—not the same in which I sat the previous week. Even in ritual as tightly organised as this one, there is room for manoeuvre.

Much of the hour passes in silence, broken insignificantly by the rustle of clothing and the muffled hum of cars passing along the road outside, and significantly by three Friends who stand to speak. Soon after the children have departed, the first, an elderly man, reads from Psalm 70 without comment, apart from noting that it has a comical quality. A few minutes later, I stand up and (hoping that Friends would recall one or other relevant Quaker texts relating to our belief in the immanence of God) note the irony in the Psalm, given that God was present in the Psalmist all along. After a further five or ten minutes, I count those present, consider the relative uniformity of their/our posture and the clothes they/we wear. Given that we sit in circles, most Friends are in view; I notice that Enid has taken her handbag off her lap and placed it on the floor under her seat. She stands and speaks briefly about Jesus and 'the promise of Christmas', illustrating with personal anecdotes.

Various thoughts pass through my mind before the end of meeting. According to diary entries at that time, I was thinking about the Book of Job. It is impossible to know for certain how others were occupying their time in worship. It is clear, however, that although participants look as if they are doing the same thing, they are not. Participants' comments suggest that they understand and experience meeting for worship in different ways: it is a time for reflection, for prayer, for meditation for contemplation, for winding down, for memories, for making plans, for reading uplifting texts, and so on. Whatever Friends do during meeting, the conclusion is the same: on the hour, two Friends, generally elders, shake hands. On this occasion, I feel a sense of contentment. After a hectic week I am glad of the peace and quiet.

With a certain amount of whispering and stretching, Friends turn to shake hands with their neighbours, before the clerk stands and reads the notices—most of which are indexical ('coded' for insiders) to the extent that newcomers would find them hard to follow. The clerk tells us about forthcoming events, both within the meeting and in the locale. We are informed that this month's collection is for Amnesty International. Quaker acronyms are bandied about. No-one has any other notices and so the clerk invites everyone to adjourn to the Children's Room for tea. Two Friends had left just before the end of meeting in order to prepare. Some stand and make their way out into the concourse, others remain for a while and chat with those around them. Friends continue to talk over tea and biscuits, about family, friends, work, pastimes, Quaker service, and so on. Such talk constitutes a series of ongoing narratives which may continue over months, years, even decades. Quakers are no different from most others in being energetic story-tellers. There is little talk about overtly theological or even broadly religious matters, which may seem odd, given the context.

Virtually all participants stay for tea—those who leave early make their reasons for doing so public: to leave before taking tea requires some kind of an explanation. 'Before' and 'After' meeting are like bookends in that each mirrors the other. Eventually, I say good-bye to Iris, who is the last to leave at 12.50 pm, and tidy up briefly before going through into the warden's flat. After lunch I sit down and reconstruct the morning's events in my notebook. This task takes two or three hours and has become a significant part of my 'after-meeting' ritual.

The Quaker Meeting for worship is subtle, but moving from the general to the specific, the ritual as enacted in (pseudonymous) Dibdenshaw is more subtle still. The ritual I have described would certainly be recognized by all British Quakers as a more or less typical 'version'; it is the same up and down the country. Its performance, however, is local and therefore necessarily different. In trying to understand it as an insider I am attempting to 'do' meeting for worship the 'Dibdenshaw way', to pass as a Dibdenshaw Quaker. As an anthropologist, I am trying to look for ways in which the ritual is similar to others and, at the same time, marking the ways in which it is distinctive. Visitors from other meetings do much the same thing. They know how to 'do the Quaker meeting', but are likely to note and remark on ways in which this one differs from their meeting 'back home'. In this sense, visitors are like anthropologists, also in between—neither insiders nor outsiders. What then defines my position as an insider?

On 'Being a Member'

For Merton (1972), the matter is relatively straightforward: the insider is a member of the group, the outsider is not. I would argue that Merton glosses over a key issue: the definition of membership. I had joined the Society while living in Kent, came to Dibdenshaw as warden in 1989, after having been a member for three years. I was born and brought up in Cardiff, my wife in Gateshead. She had not yet applied for membership and was therefore still an 'attender'. Length of membership at Dibdenshaw varied from one to fifty years. The majority of members were born and brought up in or near the town. Some had long been members of the Society, but transferred to Dibdenshaw after their own meeting, a few miles away, was closed.

My role as warden complicated my relationship with members of the meeting who were my employers (and therefore eager to see me doing a good job) as well as my co-worshippers. As warden I lived, with my family, on the premises, in a house attached to the meeting house; this deepened my involvement in the meeting. I fielded all manner of enquiries, came to know the several groups (Quaker and non-Quaker) who hired our rooms and met members of the meeting more often than those whose visits to the meeting house were limited to Sunday mornings. It was clear to other members of the meeting that I was interested in all things Quaker and that I had read a good deal of Quaker history—an interest I shared with one or two others. Further, I occasionally stood to minister during meeting for worship. After a year or two, when Friends came to know me better, I was nominated for various committees, both at the local and national level: I had both the time and the inclination. Those who sit on national committees, sometimes called 'London Friends', are sometimes thought to develop interests which somehow differ from those whose experience of Quakerism is primarily local.

One's membership of a group, that is one's status as insider/outsider is, to a large extent, an intricate process of negotiation. Membership is multifaceted and the boundaries between aspects of that membership are shifting. My sense of belonging was determined not only by my own perceptions, but also by those of others. Furthermore, being a member is no straightforward guarantee of 'insiderhood'. I was a member, but not a local person. I was involved in Quaker organization at the national level, but was still relatively inexperienced (and therefore not 'seasoned'). My wife attended meeting, but she was not in membership ('only an attender'). I stood to minister, but could hardly be said to be 'an old hand'. We were people 'of the middling sort' and therefore 'typical' Quakers, but younger than the majority of local Friends. I was both insider and outsider—depending on circumstance, and, I would argue, this is true for all members. Of course, Friends define themselves as a group partly by characteristics which they share as individuals and partly on account of differences between themselves and others, which bring their similarities into focus. Boundaries are symbolized in order to make such distinctions as stark as possible (Cohen, 1989). These boundaries are marked in many ways, but especially in and through ritual. Is it one's standpoint in relation to ritual that defines one as insider or outsider?

Quakers Reflect, Too

As an anthropologist of religion, I often wonder about the meaning of ritual—is this what sets me apart as an outsider? Before, during and after my period of fieldwork (rather arbitrarily taken to be those two years when I wrote down my observations), I reflected often on whether meeting for worship might be considered 'ritual'. This may be because of my academic interest in the subject, but it is more likely that this stems from my fascination with the paradoxical nature of Quakerism. When asked why I became a Quaker, I would inevitably comment on my disillusionment with the ritualistic character of other faiths. Yet, meeting for worship clearly includes elements which are shared by rituals described by anthropologists and others. As a Quaker, it has been difficult at times not to write as an apologist. However, if we agree that there can never be a *final* explanation for social phenomena, it is worth reminding ourselves that ritual is not one, but many things. Just as ritual has been interpreted in different ways by anthropologists, so has Quaker worship been characterized variously by participants—sometimes in terms commonly used by anthropologists, sometimes not. Participants and observers alike tend to emphasize those aspects of ritual which strike them as important.

Let me offer a few examples where 'lay' and 'academic' perspectives appear to overlap. I shall start with Victor Turner (1969; 1974; 1982), perhaps the most influential theorist of ritual. Turner contrasts two modes of existence: *societas* (the status system) and *communitas* (the status-free system?). *Communitas* is most obviously manifested during ritual, or at least during one phase of ritual. Like Van Gennep (1960), Turner emphasizes the processual character of ritual, which is best divided into three elements: pre-liminal (or segregation), liminal (separation), and post-liminal (aggregation). *Communitas* is most likely to be generated during the liminal phase and is differentiated from *societas* by Turner by means of binary opposition (*à la* Lévi-Strauss)—by 26 binary oppositions to be precise (Turner, 1969: 106–107). This system of oppositions, or 'tensions', as I would prefer to call them, works well in relation to Quaker worship (Collins, 1998). For instance, here are a few of the most relevant of Turner's opposing pairs (or 'tensions') which, it has been claimed by Quakers, differentiate Quaker worship from what may be said to typify 'the world':

absence of status/status
absence of rank/distinctions of rank
sacredness/secularity
silence/speech
simplicity/complexity
equality/inequality
minimisation of sex differences/maximisation of sex differences

Since the seventeenth century, Quakers have talked explicitly in terms of such oppositions in explaining and justifying their faith and practice; my fieldnotes contain numerous comments made by Friends relating to these distinctions. My reading of Turner led me to reconsider the practice of Quaker worship. It dawned on me one Sunday morning that the hour of worship is but a part of the story, that the ritual was processual, spilling out temporally (and untidily) into a 'before' and 'after'. It was not difficult to map the events of Sunday morning onto Turner's tripartite structure. Intellectually this was very satisfying, but it was only recently that I realized the significance of this analysis for my own religious practice. My role as warden, responsible for the preparation of the meeting house, became, for me, although not for others, of course, a part of the pre-liminal phase of the ritual of worship. The time before meeting no longer seems detached, a mere chaos of arrival and hurried greetings (though it is often still that). Neither is the time spent with Friends after meeting simply a time of idle chatter (although it sometimes still seems little more than that). I have begun to understand the time for tea and biscuits as communion; in discussing this matter with Friends I veer towards the 'ritual criticism' described by Grimes (1988; 1990). Friends have always eschewed such 'outward signs' as irrelevant, but continue to be playful and inventive with their admittedly minimalist liturgy. In this way (and in others), through my anthropological reflections (an outsider's reflections), my religious experience (an insider's experience) has been deepened.

There are many more ways in which we can explain, metaphorize and represent ritual (ritual, according to insiders or outsiders or both, can also be confessional, transformative, playful, moral, emotional, performative, rhythmical, expressive, instrumental, ideological, radical, and so on), but even were we able to consider all these, the conclusion would be the same: 'insiders' and 'outsiders' may or may not agree on what they mean when they use the term 'ritual'. 'Ritual' is a polysemic term which struggles to encompass events, actions and things which are themselves understood to be polysemic. The point is that we should beware of any simple definition of ritual, and we should be aware of the way in which we ourselves are characterizing ritual—it is likely, of necessity, to be a partial account: that is true for both anthropologists and Quakers. We do not model ritual in the same way. Some of the perspectives mentioned above would be acceptable as ways of seeing meeting to some Friends, some would be considered quite unacceptable and wholly missing the point. 'Outsider' accounts are more or less helpful. Sometimes they coincide with 'insider' accounts, sometimes they don't. Each may be plausible, although none is likely to tell the 'whole story'. One's understanding of ritual cannot be a means of determining whether one is an 'insider' or an 'outsider'—Quakers reflect, too. One need not have a degree in anthropology in order to ruminate on Quaker faith and practice—indeed the mode of worship clearly encourages Friends to do just that, as shown occasionally in the content of spoken ministry.

Giddens (1991) has noted that reflexivity is a centrally important characteristic of late modernity. Quakers have been acutely self-aware and self-reflective since the 1650s. Here are just two local examples. The meeting arranged for Derek, a Quaker well known for running interesting courses, to speak to the meeting on the subject of 'community'. This is a popular theme of conferences, retreats, courses, pamphlets, and so forth initiated by Quakers and further suggests a concerted tendency towards reflexivity. He began his introduction by noting the importance of the way in which the meeting room was organized, how the chairs were formed in a circle, no one being higher or set apart from any other, and how this symbolized equality and emphasized the Quaker abhorrence of hierarchy. He went on to suggest the important theological consequences of this arrangement, adding that priests found no place among us, because we had no need of them, believing that God is immanent in everyone. By this time I was hoping he would soon stop in that I would have little else to say in my thesis! As Tony Watling (1999) stated (with regard to his research on ecumenism in Holland): what is the anthropologist left with when his/her informants are capable of this level of analysis—even drawing on those self-same theorists one is drawing on as an academic? How does the anthropologist go beyond such reflection? My feeling remains that it is pointless to try and 'trump' adepts' accounts; the anthropologist can only record them, understand how and why they compare, and set his/her own account alongside them (Collins, 1994).

If the 'outsider' is characterized as the one who reflects on practice, then there are Quakers who are 'outsiders' in relation to Quakerism. This is patently absurd, unless we accept that identities are multiple and not singular and that our perspective may draw on one or more of these identities at any one time. Furthermore, it seems inevitable that any perspective, far from being unitary and straightforward, may be contradictory, ambivalent and ambiguous. The 'insider' is then not easily distinguishable from the 'outsider'—in terms of methodology or epistemology. Both Quakers and anthropologists are given to observation, reflection and discussion. It may be argued that anthropologists have other means at their disposal in gaining a purchase on Quaker ritual: comparison. I will not deal with this at length, but would argue that such claims remain to be proved. Quakers are free to read material on ritual, community, group dynamics, organisation theory, and any other topic tempting to the ethnographer—and some do. At what point does the Quaker become ethnographer? Or do they merely slip from one point on the insider–outsider spectrum from one day to the next? There is, however, a more interesting point to be made here. Increasingly, Friends are not born into the Society, but migrate to it, either from humanism or from other churches. As a result, the majority of Friends have detailed knowledge of at least one other ritual system. Indeed, as I have argued elsewhere, the very identity of Quakerism is founded on a knowledge and rejection of Anglicanism, including its ritual (Collins, 1994; 1995; 1996a).

How else might we separate the 'insider' from the 'outsider'? The theologically inclined reader might be thinking that the distinction between anthropologist and Quaker is surely a matter of faith or belief. The Society of Friends is a non-credal religious organization. In order to be a member, one is not required to subscribe to any particular belief. I have talked with Friends who adhere to a wide variety of belief systems and some to no belief system at all (see also Dandelion, 1996). An anthropologist may hold any of these beliefs or even more than one of them. The 'outsider' is not easily or necessarily distinguishable from the 'insider' in terms of belief.

Perhaps the dichotomy rests on the degree of one's 'ritual commitment' (Humphrey & Laidlaw, 1994)? There are, however, Quakers who attend meeting (or any Quaker event) only once in a blue moon. One member at Dibdenshaw attended a meeting to celebrate the opening of the new meeting house in 1971 and so disliked it that she never returned. Yet, she has retained her membership and considers herself (and is considered by others) to be a Quaker still. The anthropologist may attend every possible meeting and may wish and be permitted to take part in some—as an attender this would be quite possible. Is it not possible that aspects of Quaker ritual might appeal or be 'meaningful' to an anthropologist in ways other than the 'purely' intellectual? It is possible that there are Quakers whose relation to Quaker ritual is entirely intellectualist, wholly rational? Surely, the insider has greater understanding of the nuances of Quaker ritual? This *may* be so, but much depends on the craft of the anthropologist, who might well identify nuances which have hitherto passed unnoticed within the local meeting. Anthropologists, like Quakers, may be more or less astute, more or less aware of their own strengths and weaknesses. What we can be certain of is that we cannot assume that our position *vis-à-vis* the field leads to either insider or outsider knowledge (Griffiths, 1998: 374).

Ontology: The Insider/Outsider Problem as a Fiction

The insider/outsider dichotomy assumes certain things about the self and about society and essentializes both. It implies a unified and unitary self which is largely unchanging and metaphorizes society in a very simplistic way, rather as a series of buildings, each with a single door which serves as both entrance and exit: either one is in or one is out, and if one is in one building, one cannot at the same time be in another. I can say little more about the constitution of society here, except that it is more complex than this metaphor will allow. My view is that society is processual and precipitated in and through the interactions of individuals.

However, I shall introduce an alternative account of the self, a dynamic multiplex self which is dialogic, negotiated in and through social interaction, and therefore dialectically related to society. The self I envisage is a wholly social construct, comprising the narratives one co-constructs during social interaction. These narratives are evident in meeting, sometimes explicitly grounded in Quaker testimonies, but always indexical and bounded by a strong sense of 'the proper' (Collins, 1994; 1995). This suggests that the self is constituted by stories which are necessarily shared by others: a distributed self (Bruner, 1990). From this point of view, self and other are less separate, less easily isolated, the distance between the two is reduced; they are mutually constitutive. From this perspective, the self becomes more dynamic, more apt to change, less monolithic. Its edges become blurred.

The moral valency of storying has long been recognized (for example, fairy tales), although it was Alastair MacIntyre (1985) who showed how intimately related narrative and ethics are. The possibility that storying is constitutive of self has been most strongly argued by contemporary psychologists (Bruner, 1986; Bruner, 1990; Gergen, 1991; Shotter, 1993a; Shotter, 1993b; Harré, 1979). A narrative perspective is taken further in Bakhtin's work (Bakhtin, 1986): our efforts to understand people, relationships and situations (or to resolve moral dilemmas) are acted out internally through the taking on and managing of voices in constructed inner dialogues (one experiments with character and plot, imagining variations in 'endings'—which then become new beginnings). For Bakhtin, utterances and texts (including material culture, such as the interior and exterior of buildings) in the outer world are sites of struggle (I would say 'negotiation') and populated with the voices (stories) of others. Meaning is precipitated by dialogue comprising voices deriving from self and other—it is a 'we experience' (Voloshinov, quoted in Dentith, 1995: 126–143; see also Holquist, 1990: 59–63; de Penter, 1998). I found that the meeting consisted primarily of stories which were braided together by participants during interaction (Collins, 1994; 1996b). It is these narratives which constitute not only individual identity, but also the identity of the group, and therefore a sense of continuity in each case. 'Worship', 'the weekend away', 'community', 'peace', 'children's class', 'business meeting', 'the meeting house', 'family', 'gardening' are a few of the many stories which members of the meeting jointly construct and which partially construct them. Like any other participant, the anthropologist will come, through conversation in particular, to co-construct the stories of meeting, simultaneously weaving his/her self into its fabric.

In epistemological and methodological terms, the insider/outsider dichotomy proves merely unhelpful. I suggest further that the problem posed by the dichotomy is an artifact of a particular ontological position *vis-à-vis* self and society—one which seems less and less plausible. From the standpoint I espouse, the dichotomy disappears. Comprising a multitude of voices, we each become simultaneously insiders and outsiders, and therefore the distinction is largely redundant. The distinction is, however, deeply implicated across a range of discourses, and we should continue with our efforts to understand why this should be so.

Postscript

Both Quakerism and anthropology provide multiple, dialectically related perspectives on the world. In my case, they are voices in intermittent dialogue, each informing and sometimes confusing the other. My fieldwork caused me to take my participation in meeting to another level. Together, Quakerism and anthropology have encouraged me to take the uniqueness of others seriously. Further, I have no doubt that doing anthropology has influenced my faith and practice as a Quaker, while the reverse is equally true. The lack of closure which characterizes the Quaker tradition (Scott, 1980) is similarly present in some contemporary anthropology (Rapport, 1997). Despite their institutional differences, they share—to use a term coined by Wittgenstein (1958)—a 'family resemblance'. Each facilitates a view of the world which celebrates individuality and dwells seriously on the relationship between self and other. Anthropologists and Quakers alike have claimed that we attempt to understand others in order to understand ourselves better. It is likely that having assimilated one (anthropology) I had partially assimilated the other (Quakerism). In assimilating the second (a decade later), I was bounced back again to the first, in an attempt to sustain a dialogue which had already begun, albeit haltingly. It is a dialogue whose premise is that anthropologists have too often tended to create, in Martin Buber's terms, an I-It relationship with those in the field, when they should be actively seeking the I-Thou. I-It knowledge is indirect, mediated through an object, and has a specific content. For Buber, an I-Thou relation lacks a specific content, is mutual, reciprocal and symmetrical, and each partner in the dialogue becomes aware of the other as a subject rather than an object (Buber, 1970).

Acknowledgement

I would like to thank Simon Coleman for his helpful comments on an earlier draft of this paper.

References

Agar, M. *The Professional Stranger.* New York: Academic Press, 1980.
Agassi, J. 'Privileged Access.' *Inquiry* 12, 1969: 420–426.
Bakhtin, M. *Speech Genres and other Late Essays.* Austin: University of Texas Press, 1986.
Bell, C. *Ritual Theory, Ritual Practice.* Oxford: Oxford U. P., 1992.
Boon, J. *Other Tribes, Other Scribes.* Cambridge: Cambridge U. P., 1982.

Bruner, J. *Actual Minds, Possible Worlds*. Cambridge, Massachusetts: Harvard U. P., 1986.

Bruner, J. *Acts of Meaning*. Cambridge, Massachusetts: Harvard U. P., 1990.

Buber, M. *I and Thou*. New York: Scribners, 1970.

Clifford, J. & Marcus, G. M., eds. *Writing Culture: The Poetics and Politics of Ethnography*. Berkeley: University of California. Press, 1986.

Cohen, A. P. *Whalsay: Symbol, Segment and Boundary in a Shetland Island Community*. Manchester: Manchester U. P., 1987.

Cohen, A. P. *The Symbolic Construction of Community*. London: Routledge, 1989 (originally published in 1985 by Ellis Horwood, Chichester).

Collins, P. J. *The Sense of the Meeting: An Anthropology of Vernacular Quakerism*. Unpublished PhD thesis, Manchester University, 1994.

Collins, P. J. 'The Meeting House and Its Meanings.' *Friends Quarterly* 30, 1995: 194–207.

Collins, P. J. "'Plaining': The Social and Cognitive Practice of Symbolisation in the Religious Society of Friends (Quakers)." *Journal of Contemporary Religion* 11 (3), 1996a: 277–288.

Collins, P. J. "Auto/Biography, Narrative and the Quaker Meeting." *Auto/Biography* 4 (2/3), 1996b: 27–39.

Collins, P. J. "Quaker Worship: An Anthropological Perspective." *Worship* 72 (6), 1998: 501–515.

Dandelion, P. *A Sociological Analysis of the Theology of Quakers*. Lampeter: Edward Mellen Press, 1996.

Dentith, S. *Bakhtinian Thought*. London: Routledge, 1995.

De Penter, J. "The Dialogics of Narrative Identity." In Bell, M. M. & Gardiner, M., eds. *Bakhtin and the Human Sciences*. London: Sage, 1998: 30–48.

Ellis, C. & Bochner, A. P., eds. *Composing Ethnography: Alternative Forms of Qualitative Writing*. London: Sage, 1996.

Ellis, C. & Flaherty, M. G., eds. *Investigating Subjectivity*. London: Sage, 1992.

Evans-Pritchard, E. E. *The Nuer*. Oxford: Clarendon Press, 1940.

Firth, R. *We, the Tikopia*. Beacon Press, 1963 (first published in 1936).

Geertz, C. *The Interpretation of Cultures*. New York: Basic Books, 1973.

Geertz, C. *Works and Lives: The Anthropologist as Author*. Cambridge: Polity, 1988.

Gergen, K. *The Saturated Self: Dilemmas of Identity in Everyday Life*. New York: Basic Books, 1991.

Giddens, A. *Modernity and Self-identity*. Cambridge: Polity Press, 1991.

Griffiths, A. I. "Insider/Outsider: Epistemological Privilege and Mothering Work." *Human Studies* 21, 1998: 361–376.

Grimes, R. L."Ritual Criticism and Reflexive Fieldwork." *Journal of Ritual Studies* 2 (2), 1988: 217–239.

Grimes, R. L. *Ritual Criticism: Case Studies in its Practice, Essays on its Theory*. Columbia: University of South Carolina, 1990.

Harré, R. *Social Being*. Oxford: Blackwell, 1979.

Headland, T. N., Pike, K. & Harris, M., eds. *Emics and Etics: The Insider/Outsider Debate*. London: Sage, 1990.

Holquist, M. *Dialogism: Bakhtin and his World*. London: Routledge, 1990.

Humphrey C. & Laidlaw, J. *The Archetypal Actions of Ritual*. Oxford: Clarendon, 1994.

Lakoff, G. & Johnson, M. *Metaphors We Live By*. Chicago: Chicago U. P., 1980.

Lévi-Strauss, C. *Tristes Tropiques*. Harmondsworth: Penguin, 1976.

MacIntyre, A. *After Virtue*. London: Duckworth, 1985 (2nd ed.).

Malinowski, B. *Argonauts of the Western Pacific*. New York: Dutton, 1922.

Malinowski, B. *A Diary in the Strict Sense of the Term*. London: Routledge & Kegan Paul, 1967.

Merton, R. K. "Insiders and Outsiders: A Chapter in the Sociology of Knowledge." *American Journal of Sociology* 78, 1972: 9–47.

Okely, J. *The Traveller-Gypsies*. Cambridge: Cambridge U. P., 1983.

Quaker Faith and Practice: The Book of Discipline of the Yearly Meeting of the Religious Society of Friends (Quakers) in Britain. London: Britain Yearly Meeting, 1995.

Rapport, N. J. *Diverse World-views in an English Village*. Edinburgh: Edinburgh U. P., 1993.

Rapport, N. J. *Transcendent Individuality: Towards a Literary and Liberal Anthropology*. London: Routledge, 1997.

Scott, J. *What Canst Thou Say: Towards a Quaker Theology*. Swarthmore Lecture. London: Quaker Home Service, 1980.

Shotter, J. *Cultural Politics of Everyday Life*. Buckingham: Open U. P., 1993a.

Shotter, J. *Conversational Realities*. London: Sage, 1993b.

Soskice, J. M. *Metaphor and Religious Language*. Oxford: Oxford U. P., 1985.

Steier, F., ed. *Research and Reflexivity*. London: Sage, 1991.

Strathern, M. *Kinship at the Core*. Cambridge: Cambridge U. P., 1981.

Stringer, M. D. *On the Perception of Worship: The Ethnography of Worship in Four Christian Congregations in Manchester*. Birmingham: University of Birmingham Press, 1999.

Turner, V. *The Ritual Process*. Chicago: Aldine de Gruyter, 1969.

Turner, V. *Dramas, Fields and Metaphors: Symbolic Action in Human Society*. Ithaca, New York: Cornell U. P., 1974.

Turner, V. *From Ritual to Theatre: The Human Seriousness of Play*. New York: Performing Arts Journal Publications, 1982.

Van Gennep, A. *The Rites of Passage*. London: Routledge & Kegan Paul, 1960 (first published in 1908).

Van Maanen, J. *Tales of the Field: On Writing Ethnography*. Chicago: University of Chicago Press, 1988.

Van Maanen, J., ed. *Representation in Ethnography*. London: Sage, 1995.

Watling, T. *Negotiating Religious Pluralism: Ecumenism and the Development of Religious Identities in the Netherlands*. Unpublished PhD thesis, University of London, 1999.

Wittgenstein, L. *Philosophical Investigations*. Oxford: Blackwell, 1958.

6 "Going Native in Reverse": The Insider as Researcher in British Wicca

JO PEARSON

Introduction

Since its inception in the 1950s and continuing into the 1990s, modern witchcraft has attracted increasing public attention.[1] Once misunderstood,[2] it has become a relatively acceptable spiritual alternative within the plurality of modern religiosity.[3] Drawing on pagan traditions of the past, images of the witch, and the occult revival of the *fin de siècle*, modern witchcraft presents itself as a modern-day mystery religion (Wicca), a form of feminist/Goddess spirituality (feminist witchcraft), the survival of ancient rural wisdom (hedgewitchcraft) and a means by which magic is returned to an otherwise disenchanted world. Publications on the subject of modern witchcraft increase seemingly year by year, and the academic study of witchcraft and Paganism is becoming more popular.[4] Yet, the emergence of modern witchcraft into relative popularity since the late 1970s and 1980s[5] has engendered diverse manifestations of what is often simply called 'the Craft'.[6]

This chapter begins by outlining the three main types of witchcraft which have emerged over the past 50 years. It then concentrates on Wicca as the focus for researching initiatory religion as an 'insider'. Some problems associated with the study of such religions are addressed in a critical examination of earlier research by Tanya Luhrmann. The chapter closes with an assessment of the insider/outsider position suggesting that, rather than being essentially problematic, such a position can in fact be advantageous to the researcher, the research, and the researched community.

Contemporary Forms of Witchcraft: Three Types

Wicca has developed into a number of contemporary forms since the 1950s, some of which call themselves a variation of 'Wicca', and some of which identify themselves as a type of 'witchcraft'. From these, three main types have emerged—Wicca, feminist witchcraft, and hedgewitchcraft. These three different entities are often conflated into a mythically normative 'Wicca' or 'witchcraft', which is generalized across a broad spectrum. Due to the inherent problems of such generalizations, it may be useful to present an 'ideal typology' of witchcraft in the 1990s, firstly in order to avoid confusion, and secondly in order to specify the focus of this chapter.

Wicca

In the 1950s, Wicca emerged in Britain as a highly ritualistic, nature venerating, polytheistic, magical and religious system, which made use of Eastern techniques, but operated within a predominantly western framework. It arose from the cultural impulses of the *fin de siécle*, in particular from the occult revival of the 1880s onwards. Various threads were gradually gathered together and woven into Wicca in the 1940s by Gerald Gardner.

Wicca became more widely known in the 1950s with the publication of Gardner's books, *Witchcraft Today* (1954) and *The Meaning of Witchcraft* (1959), and in the early 1960s, it was exported to North America. Gardner died in 1964, but his tradition of Gardnerian Wicca was firmly established, much to the annoyance of those who practised Traditional and Hereditary witchcraft, which they believed to be a witchcraft religion older than Gardner's Wicca.[7] Another current was injected into this stream in the 1960s, as Alex Sanders brought a stronger application of high ritual magic to his branch of Wicca.

Alexandrian and Gardnerian Wiccans are those with a provable line of descent, by initiation from Gerald Gardner, Alex and Maxine Sanders, or both. Gardnerian witches trace their initiatory lines back to Gerald Gardner and practise a form of Wicca subtly different from that of Alexandrian Wicca. Alexandrians trace their initiatory lineage back to the more recent influential figure of Alex Sanders. Due to increased dialogue between Gardnerian and Alexandrian Wicca, many practices are in fact a synthesis of the two traditions, and an increasing number of witches are initiated jointly or separately into both traditions, thus tracing their lineage back to both Gardner and Sanders.

Thus, today, many Wiccans are initiates of both Gardnerian and Alexandrian Wicca. The differences between the two traditions have been played down, and the similarities and synthesis are emphasized to such an extent that some Wiccans claim that there is no difference between them. While others retain a 'pure' Gardnerian or Alexandrian practice, a great deal of ritualizing and socializing occurs between practitioners of both traditions.

Both traditions have influenced each other, and both regard themselves as so similar that we can now talk of 'Alexandrian and Gardnerian Wicca' in one breath, or conflate the two and refer to them as 'Alexandrian/Gardnerian', especially given the number of Wiccans who are initiates of the two traditions combined. It is the Alexandrian, Gardnerian, and combined Alexandrian/Gardnerian traditions of Wicca on which this chapter specifically concentrates.

Feminist Witchcraft

The development and movement of Wicca beyond its traditional boundaries took place largely in North America in the late 1970s and 1980s, at a time when the New Age Movement was becoming conscious of itself as a movement and when feminist spirituality was emerging (see e.g. Hanegraaff, 1998: 85–87). This should draw our attention to obvious parallels between the three movements. All three are, for instance, regarded as having their roots in the counter-culture of the 1960s and as having developed interdependently. An example of the development of new forms of witchcraft will suffice to illustrate this point. Wicca, as it was traditionally practised in Britain, was exported to the United States by Raymond Buckland in the 1960s where, according to Orion (1995: 143), it was transformed into a "very different kind of religion".[8] In particular, Wicca was adapted by the women's spirituality movement, resulting in the development of Pagan Goddess spirituality and feminist witchcraft traditions, such as Dianic and Reclaiming witchcraft. This "mutant 'Feminist Witchcraft'", according to Salomonsen (1996: 32), developed, as female witches gradually took part in the Women's Movement and "in some cases met, in other cases helped create, the Goddess Movement" (ibid: 32; Bonewits, 1989: 110). The Goddess Movement, however, has not adopted witchcraft, but has been inspired by the use of ritual expression in witchcraft.[9] Wicca and feminist/Goddess spirituality thus blend into each other, and it is predominantly this blurring of distinctions between the original British Wicca and North American feminist witchcraft into a normative, generally applied (mis)understanding of Wicca/witchcraft which has been the reason for misrepresentative categorization.

Yet, the distinctly feminist branch of witchcraft has little in common with Alexandrian and Gardnerian Wicca in Britain beyond an initial framework of rituals centred around the seasonal changes of the year. Feminist witchcraft, for example, explicitly emphasizes the Goddess as representative of divinity, attempts to maintain an explicitly non-hierarchical organization inherited from the feminist consciousness movement (in which women rotate leadership and make collective decisions), and engages in political activism after the feminist saying "the personal is political is spiritual" (Culpepper 1978: 222). Alexandrian and Gardnerian Wicca, however, emphasize both gods and goddesses as representative of divinity, allow a 'hierarchy of experience' (implicit in their organization in covens led by a High Priestess and/or High Priest and the structure of three degrees of initiation), and tend to maintain a distance between spirituality and politics. Whereas Alexandrian and Gardnerian Wicca can be considered one entity, feminist witchcraft is an altogether different entity, consciously distinct from its non-feminist kin.

In order to distinguish between these two currents, I refer to Alexandrian and Gardnerian 'Wicca' and to feminist 'witchcraft'. This distinction partly reflects the terminology used by practitioners. On the one hand, Wiccans use the term 'Wicca' to denote a mystery religion involving a process of initiation and rigorous training within a cosmos polarized between male and female forces, all of which is an inheritance from the magical secret societies from which Wicca is descended. The term is also used in order to differentiate between the anthropological study of 'primitive', tribal witchcraft[10] and the Wiccan religion of Western, literate, post-industrial society (re)invented by Gerald Gardner in Britain in the 1940s and developed since that time into its contemporary forms. On the other hand, feminist witches prefer the term 'witchcraft', using it to describe a religious practice based upon the human (female) witch becoming empowered through interaction with the Goddess as divine counterpart of the witch, an empowerment which is sought in order to provide personal liberation for the individual woman and thus sustain women in their struggle against patriarchy. Feminist witchcraft is thus located within the wider feminist spirituality and Goddess movements, making use of a constructed image based on a feminist reading of the witchcraft persecutions of the sixteenth and seventeenth centuries and on the myth of matriarchy, both of which are preferred alternatives to a legacy from secret societies, which are regarded as a predominantly male preserve, and Gerald Gardner as founding father.

Hedgewitchcraft

The third strand of witchcraft is Hedgewitchcraft. Hedgewitches are usually solitary practitioners, and as such operate with no hierarchy or organizational structure,[11] do not necessarily regard witchcraft as a religion, and therefore may, or may not, honour gods and goddesses. Where witchcraft is seen as religious practice, a ritual of self-dedication to a particular god and/or goddess may be performed rather than an initiation. Hedgewitches perceive

Wicca as the organized form of witchcraft, operating almost as an institutionalized religion; in order to distance themselves from it, they identify themselves as witches, hedgewitches, ditch witches or green witches rather than as Wiccan. They have little in common with Wiccan history[12] or the myths of feminist witchcraft, but rather regard themselves as the modern version of the 'cunning man' or the 'wise woman'. The heritage of hedgewitches is drawn from the lore of the cunning folk, who were believed to be the wise people in particular rural locations, to whom people would turn for healing, midwifery, fertility spells, charms and blessings. Magic and spells used in this tradition tend to be natural, based on a knowledge of herbalism, the phases of the moon, and the seasonal cycle of the earth.

In outlining these three types of witchcraft, my aim has been to dispel the idea of witchcraft/Wicca as a monolith and to provide some of the distinguishing features of the different types. For the remainder of this chapter, I shall, however, focus on Wicca, explaining some of the problems which can occur in the study of such a religion and suggesting ways in which these might be mitigated. In so doing, my emphasis turns to the status of insider and outsider in initiatory systems, and the consequent advantages and disadvantages of the researcher's position as insider/outsider.

Tanya Luhrmann and the Study of British Wicca

In 1983, Tanya Luhrmann began fieldwork among witches in London; her book, *Persuasions of the Witch's Craft* ([1989], 1994), became the first academic study of Wicca as practised in Britain. Indeed, until December 1999, when it was joined by Ronald Hutton's *The Triumph of the Moon: A History of Modern Pagan Witchcraft*, it was the only published academic monograph on British Wicca. Thus, to date, Luhrmann's work, unfortunately, remains definitive within academia. I say 'unfortunately' because there are a number of problems with her work. Firstly, her study is limited largely to one Wiccan coven in London and to witches practising in the London area, yet, the subtitle of her book, *Ritual Magic in Contemporary England*, suggests a representative study of Wiccan magical practice in the whole of England. Her study is, to my mind, limited in scope and based on a small, unrepresentative sample: capital cities are rarely representative of a nation.

Secondly, while Luhrmann argues that the paradigms of magic presented in anthropological work among primitive societies is inadequate to interpret magical practices in literate, post-industrial western society, she fails to question her own premise that western magicians in the 1980s must *fool* themselves into believing in magic in order to retain their rational stance in their everyday lives. In contrast to earlier North American sociological studies, her inquiry was not based on questions of social deviancy, but instead set out to consider why people become involved in the occult and whether one has to be, or whether one becomes, 'irrational' in order to 'believe' in magic. However, in following this argument, Luhrmann perpetuated the reductionist approach used to portray the occult, magic, witchcraft, paganism—indeed, even religion—as irrational.

Assuming that magic is a non-conformist, irrational mode of interpretation which requires a complex social and mental initiation process in order to be appropriated, Luhrmann developed the notion of 'interpretive drift'. This "slow, often unacknowledged shift in someone's manner of interpreting events as they become involved in a particular activity" (Luhrmann, 1989: 340) is used to explain people's acceptance of magic and magical practice.

Although applied to the magicians and witches she studied, 'interpretive drift' does not, however, seem to apply to Luhrmann herself, a 'rational' scholar who, as a modern, successfully socialized social scientist, is apparently immune to irrational concepts, such as religion, witchcraft, and magic. Although she was initiated into a coven and welcomed at a variety of rituals, Luhrmann stresses, "I am no witch, no wizard, though I have been initiated as though I were", and points out, "I never have, and do not now 'believe' in magic" (ibid: 18, 19). Like Michael Faber (1993), Luhrmann retreats to a position which reduces Wicca and magical practice to a childish, regressive state, in which "these witches were recreating a childhood world, enchanting adulthood" (Luhrmann, 1989: 19). In so doing, Luhrmann ignores the fact that magic has existed as part of human life experience for millennia, and instead reduces reality to empirical daily life by which the reality of any religious view of the world is invalidated. The consequence is that witchcraft (and indeed, religion) becomes 'something else', becomes 'other', and is devalued.

The American anthropologist Katherine Ewing has criticized this reductive and analytical approach to religion, which Luhrmann adopted, and its implicit methodological premises. Ewing claims that

[t]hough [Luhrmann's] research strategy involved becoming initiated into several practising groups, her research did not lead her to question her own premises about rationality. She assumed that belief entails a move from a stance of rationality to an acceptance of the irrational, an assumption that, it could be argued, is embedded within the atheistic hegemonic discourse in which anthropology participates. (Ewing, 1994: 573)

Ewing reminds us that a scholar who takes belief seriously 'unfortunately' runs the risk of 'going native', one of the few taboos remaining in anthropology, but Ewing stresses that the opposite stance is problematic—if we refuse to acknowledge that the people studied may know something about the human condition that might also be personally valid for the anthropologist.

This is the major problem with which this chapter is concerned; it is a problem for which Luhrmann has been severely criticized. The problem concerns the ambiguity of the insider/outsider position and the ethical position of the researcher, not only with regard to the community s/he is researching, but also with regard to future researchers and the academic community whom s/he is representing. For although Luhrmann experienced the benefits of participation as an insider, she is thought by some to have misrepresented herself to other participants or to have denied her own experience in her ethnography. In either case, Ewing suggests, "*the effect of her denial is to make her claims of respect for the people she worked with sound somewhat hollow*" (Ewing, 1994: 573, my emphasis).

Studying Wicca—Access and Limitations

Among the Wiccan community in Britain, Luhrmann is regarded by some as a 'pretender' who was initiated into Wicca on false pretences, was unethical in her research, and misrepresented Wicca in her book. Certainly, as I have indicated, Luhrmann portrays witches as somewhat childish and irrational, a portrayal which I have found—in my own fieldwork—to be a misrepresentation. However, I cannot claim to know whether the accusations against Luhrmann are true, although Luhrmann herself says, "I was honest about my enterprise, but my intention was to fit in, to dispel outsider status, and *I was rather relieved when people forgot what I had so carefully told them*" (Luhrmann, 1989: 18, my emphasis).

Some scholars have criticized British Wiccans for being 'naive' (Salomonsen, 1996: 56), for forgetting that an anthropologist is always on duty and for feeling 'jilted'[13] when Luhrmann finished her study and moved on. Such comments do not take into account the underlying trust inherent in initiatory Wiccan covens in Britain. One of my contacts, who was an initiate of one of the London covens which accepted Luhrmann as a visitor at rituals, explained that she had felt that Luhrmann operated covertly and that she had used information given in trust, i.e. in a circle.[14] A generally accepted 'rule'[15] in British Wicca is that things said in a circle between participants in ritual are not to be repeated outside; therefore, it is hard to accuse witches of being 'naïve'. Since Luhrmann had been initiated and was known to be studying Wicca *in the field*, it was not unreasonable of Wiccans to expect her to honour commonly observed rules and to be capable of drawing a line between acceptable and unacceptable behaviour. It was hardly surprising that when I began my fieldwork in 1994, eleven years after Luhrmann started her fieldwork, I found Wiccans still feeling they could not trust anyone studying Wicca; one priestess even asked me, 'You're not going to do another Tanya on us, are you?' It is quite obvious, but nevertheless worth pointing out, that the effects of previous research in a particular field on later researchers can be extremely negative.

Breach of trust by a researcher in an initiatory religion cannot, to my mind, be excused by accusing the researched community of naïveté. This is particularly so when working in religions which regard themselves as secret, initiatory mystery traditions. Luhrmann asserts that she was initiated 'as though she were' a witch. She must therefore have taken vows of secrecy at her initiation and, as Vivianne Crowley reminds us in the introduction to her volume *Wicca: The Old Religion in the New Millennium*, "[t]he words of the oath of the first initiation bind us to secrecy" (Crowley, 1996: x).

Without a doubt, in conducting the first academic study of British Wicca, Luhrmann undermined what could have become a trusting relationship between Wiccans and researchers, and made it more difficult for those following after her. It has taken considerable effort to rebuild that relationship, which could have been avoided, if Luhrmann had, as Sarah Pike points out,

> dealt more completely with the ambiguities and tensions that accompanied her role as participant-observer. She discusses what she shares with the London magicians and yet disavows an identity as a magician or witch. Such disclaimers are problematic when studying within one's own culture... More clarity on her part about the nature of her ambiguous role as insider/outsider would have been helpful. (Pike, 1996: 366)

Such ambiguities are made all the more explicit when one is studying a group of people who make themselves inaccessible through veils of secrecy. The self-styled mystery religion of Wicca, with three levels of initiation, is therefore not easy to investigate from the position of an 'outsider'. A barrier must be crossed in order to study Wicca as a religion in any level of depth and without misrepresenting its practitioners. Luhrmann crossed that barrier and was initiated into at least four groups, one of which was a Wiccan coven; but the barrier was crossed as part of an intellectual process, and she remained an outsider to the extent that she was, allegedly, able to disregard her initiation vows, break the trust of those who accepted her into their homes and rituals, and act unethically. How does the researcher enter such a field and undertake effective fieldwork with integrity, without dishonouring the mode of entry (initiation) and the trust of his/her research community?

The 'Insider/Outsider' Dichotomy

Since Luhrmann herself failed to address these concerns in her research on witchcraft and has been criticized for this failure, we cannot ourselves neglect to grapple with the ambiguous insider/outsider role. I have myself crossed the same boundary as Luhrmann, but with one difference—my initiation into Wicca was not part of an intellectual process related to my doctoral research, but a genuine initiation into a religion which I had been personally involved in, albeit as a pre-initiate, for some eighteen months previously. During those months, I began to study on the Wicca Correspondence Course, attend Pagan events, and make contacts with initiated Wiccans. It was not until twelve months later that I registered as a PhD student in the Department of Religious Studies at Lancaster University.

Therefore, I do not consider myself to have broken the anthropological taboo against 'going native', for I was a 'native' already. The situation has, in fact, been quite the opposite, one of "insider going outsider, going native in reverse" (Puttick, 1997: 6). Rather than being an outsider who has become intensely involved in my field of research to such an extent that I became part of it, I have instead come from inside my field of research to employ an insider/outsider position which would allow me to study Wicca as scientifically as possible on a foundation of thorough knowledge. Nevertheless, the ambiguities remain. Could I, as an insider, maintain the required objective stance deemed necessary to produce an effective study?

The 'insider as researcher' position is becoming increasingly common, as Elizabeth Puttick points out, and must therefore be considered within the academy. As a former member of the Osho movement, Puttick has first-hand experience of this process and is worth quoting at some length. She says,

> this is now becoming an increasingly common situation, resulting in the blurring of boundaries between the subjects and objects of study. As new religions are becoming more integrated into mainstream society, they appeal more than ever to ... academics, who may therefore cross the line out of personal interest. At the same time members of NRMs are becoming less anti-intellectual, perceiving the value of certain academic

disciplines for understanding religion, and joining the ranks of academia as students and teachers. This trend presents a challenge to traditional notions of objectivity and the subject/object duality which are the basis of scientific methodology. (Puttick, 1997: 6)

She goes on to explain Weber's methodology of *verstehen*, which values primarily an understanding of the inner experience and interpretation of practitioners, since "only if he [*sic*] can gain some apprehension of what it means to be a believer can he say anything useful about the religious movement he studies; and yet, in gaining that understanding, he must not actually become a believer" (Weber, 1982: 13, cited in Puttick, 1997: 6). Even here, the bias is still towards the outsider position and we must therefore question whether one can truly be an outsider and gain any understanding of the practitioners' stance in an esoteric mystery tradition, such as Wicca, which requires initiation as the means of entry.

I have already mentioned the vows of secrecy which form part of the first initiation in Wicca. It is, to my mind, a serious breach of trust if one then breaks one's oath in order to fit a pre-ordained academic code. We must, it seems, ask ourselves whether such codes are any longer viable, given the increasing popularity of alternative spirituality. If one follows the established rule of maintaining distance in order to produce quantitative studies of a sociological nature, one risks basing such studies on a profound lack of understanding of the religious community itself. On the other hand, if one involves oneself in a religious community to produce qualitative studies, one risks neglecting to provide any empirical data through which the community being researched may be contextualized. It seems far more appropriate to combine the two approaches, so that quantitative material is informed by a solid bedrock of depth understanding, and qualitative material adequately framed and contextualized by empirical data.[16]

We return to my original question: could I, as an insider, maintain the required objective stance deemed necessary to produce an effective study? Firstly, we must make the point that objectivity as an absolute cannot exist— research, especially research which involves people, will always have some effect on the researcher, and will always be filtered by the researcher's own subjective views. It is therefore necessary to apply a rigorous self-reflexivity in order to bracket off personal beliefs and values, *whether one is an 'insider' or an 'outsider'* to the religious community one is researching (cf. Puttick, 1997: 6).

It was not an easy decision to 'come out', as it were, as an insider. Yet, the necessity for me as a researcher to situate myself with reference to my object of study became increasingly clear. Given my knowledge about Wicca as a mystery religion, it seemed all too obvious that I must be an initiate in order to have gained this knowledge, and it therefore seemed impossible to pretend to be anything else. I concur with Puttick's belief that "to admit one's personal position is more valid and illuminating that hiding behind the defence of scientific objectivity, which is anyway unobtainable" (Puttick, 1997: 8). In addition, it is a fact in religious studies that there are some religions which can be studied whether one is 'inside' or 'outside' that tradition. It is perhaps less clear that there are some religions where this is not the case. Therefore, I cannot follow Luhrmann's disclaimer and say that 'I am not a witch though I have been initiated as though I were', for such disclaimers—to my mind— reveal a profound lack of respect for both the religion and the discipline of academic study as well as bring into question the integrity of the researcher. As Ninian Smart has asserted, if one "visits a village simply to get material for a doctorate, without consideration of the villagers as fellow human beings with their own sensitivities and concerns, that is arrogant and heartless" (Smart, 1997: 6).

I would maintain that the insider perspective is at least as valuable as that of the outsider; Peter Berger points out that "one's own faith and the experience brought on by this faith will actually constitute 'data' or 'evidence' upon which inductive reflection can take place" (Berger, 1979: 141). However, if the two perspectives can be combined, perhaps we can move towards a study of religion which provides a depth of understanding which is both ethical and informative, and which denies the value of neither the religious community nor that of the academy.

I have attempted to portray the research relationship diagramatically in order to outline the negotiation of the insider/outsider position (see Fig. 1).[17]

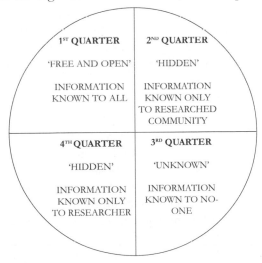

Figure 1 The Insider/Outsider Position

The first quarter is 'free and open', representing what is known to both the religious community and to the researcher, what is common knowledge, although it may be inaccurate.[18] The third quarter represents what is known neither to the researcher nor to the researched community. The second and fourth quarters represent, respectively, what is known only to the researched community and what is known only to the researcher—those areas which are likely to be, and indeed may even remain, hidden realms. It is in the interface between the second and fourth quarters that the relationship between the researcher and researched community is negotiated, and where the research proper takes place.

In my use of the word 'hidden', I am concerned chiefly with knowledge which is 'hidden' due to lack of expertise or experience, particularly at the beginning of a study, rather than implying that things are deliberately hidden by either the researcher or the researched community. Although the latter scenario can sometimes be the case, resulting in a possible 'stalemate' or stagnation of the research, the aim of this diagram is to explore a rather more fluid scenario, whereby those 'hidden' sections *on both sides* become less predominant as the research progresses and, consequently, the 'free and open' section is expanded in a mutually beneficial and respectful manner.

There are obvious similarities between my diagram and the Johari Window, developed by Professors Joseph Luft and Harrington Ingham (Johari is a combination of the authors' first names, 'Jo' and 'Hari') to map four states of awareness. The 'public' state represents what I know of myself and what the public knows of me; the 'secret' state represents what I know of myself, which the public does not know of me; the 'blind' state represents what the public knows of me, which I do not know of myself; and the 'unknown' state represents what neither I nor the public knows of me.[19] If we combine the Johari Window with my diagram, we can perhaps consider our own 'blind', 'secret', and 'unknown' states, and perhaps attain a greater state of awareness of our motives as researchers.

To take Wicca as an example, the first quarter could represent Wicca as a Pagan religion, a generally known 'fact' about the researched community, which the researcher also knows. The third quarter, on the other hand, could represent the secrets of the ancient mystery religions upon which Wicca draws, but which have not been revealed during the course of history and are therefore known neither to the researcher nor to the researched community. The second quarter could represent the differences between the variety of Wiccan and witchcraft traditions and the ongoing differentiation between Wicca and Paganism, which might be 'hidden' to the researcher, at least at the beginning of the research period. The fourth and final quarter, on the other hand, could represent the different theories and categories of religion, which may be hidden from the researched community, simply because the community does not know of them.

In leaving aside the first and third quarters, which deal with what is widely acknowledged and what is unlikely ever to be known, we come to the crux of the research, the 'grey areas'. Here, the researcher and the researched community engage in a dialectic relationship in which the researcher aims to learn about the community (second quarter) within the framework of his/her own reference points (fourth quarter), while the community finds out about its own context within that wider frame of reference and aims to maintain its integrity within it.[20] In initiatory religions, such as Wicca, this relationship can become exceedingly strained, as the researched community also attempts to maintain its 'mysteries' or secrets in the face of investigation. While the information offered through such a relationship can assist in discarding incorrect perceptions among outsiders (resulting from lack of familiarity with Wicca), it may also, as Wouter Hanegraaff warns in a general sense, "unveil aspects of the religion which are unknown and surprising (and not necessarily welcome) to the believers themselves" (Hanegraaff, 1998: 6).

Conclusion

The insider-as-researcher position is becoming increasingly common and increasingly recognized by the academy. For example, Jacob Needleman, has suggested, with regard to the study of esoteric spirituality, that "scholars need to allow the seekers *within themselves* to exist; and seekers after esoteric knowledge must, for their part, allow within themselves the validity of the outward, analytical, or critical mind" (Needleman & Faivre, 1992: xxix). In terms of the diagram presented above, if the researcher is an 'insider' and thus has one foot in the second quarter and the other in the fourth, the tension between the two can be impossible to manage; it is, however, also possible that, if the researcher is a member of the researched community, s/he can act as a bridge between the two. In so doing, the researcher may be able not only to maintain a deep understanding of the community, but also to retain an 'objective' stance through the application of theory and the adoption of a relevant methodology which allows for both distance *and* involvement. The researcher thus acts as both insider *and* outsider, embodying the resulting tension in a positive manner which enables constant reflexivity in the movement from inside to outside the community, and back. In so doing, the three accessible 'quarters' are opened up to the researcher and a more holistic study of the community can be undertaken.

Notes

1   The 1990s in particular have witnessed an increase in public attention through the medium of television, where 'The Wicca Man' was included in a Channel 4 series on alternative spirituality, *Desperately Seeking Something* (broadcast 25.11.96) and in the Everyman programme *Pagans' Progress*, broadcast on BBC 1 (30.11.97).

2   I refer here specifically to the misconstrual of modern witchcraft as Satanism resulting from the theological notion introduced in the sixteenth century that "the essence of witchcraft was adherence to the Devil" (Thomas, 1991: 534). This misunderstanding still persists, and came to light most recently in the ritual abuse cases of the late 1980s and early 1990s.

3   In particular, the acceptance of Wicca as an alternative form of religiosity in the modern world is evident in the inclusion of Wiccans at Interfaith meetings.

4   See, for example, the collected volumes edited by Harvey and Hardman (1996), Lewis (1996), and Pearson *et al.* (1998). Undergraduate courses which include the study of Paganism and Wicca have been taught at Bath Spa University College, Bristol, King's College, Lampeter, Lancaster, and Winchester. Postgraduate research on Wicca and Paganism is being conducted at all of the above institutions, as well as, for example, at Cheltenham and Gloucester College of Higher Education, Goldsmith's College, and the London School of Economics.

5   Salomonsen (1996: 42) reports that 1979 is "the year referred to by many of my informants when 'it' all happened: the Goddess movement burst forth in full bloom. The new 'gospel' was being spread through a number of important books and conferences." These publications include Christ & Plaskow, 1979; Stone, 1976; Goldenberg, 1979; Daly, 1978; Adler, 1979; and Starhawk, 1979.

6   A term which I avoid here, as 'the Craft' is also used to denote Freemasonry and Druidry.

7   No evidence has yet been produced to prove the existence of pre-Gardnerian Wicca, but the claims have often been vehement. Doreen Valiente notes that "the real traditional witches, I have been told, were furious at the behaviour of Gerald Gardner in 'popularizing' the Old Religion and regarded such enterprises as the opening of his museum on the Isle of Man as a disaster" (Valiente, 1989: 85). She further states that she thinks it was Robert Cochrane, who claimed to be a Hereditary witch, who "invented the word 'Gardnerian'—originally as a term of abuse" (ibid: 122), and that Cochrane "frequently expressed hatred of 'Gardnerians' … [and] relished the prospect of having what he called 'a Night of the Long Knives' with the Gardnerians" (ibid: 129). Valiente produces references to newspaper articles which back up her recollections of division and denigration between traditional and Gardnerian witches in the 1960s (ibid: 130–132).

8   Orion (1995: 143) lists several differences, including a less formal and hierarchical ritual style which is more inventive and celebratory, Native American influences, such as shamanism and drumming, the superimposition of psychotherapy onto Wicca, and the application of Wicca to political activism.

9   Salomonsen (1996: 33) further points out that the Goddess Movement does not associate itself with the occult, magical tradition or with Paganism; "[a]lthough Neopagan men (and women) may worship the Goddess, women in the Goddess Movement do not regard them as feminists".

10 I use here as specific examples Evans-Pritchard, 1976, and Ginzburg, 1992.

11 Although the burgeoning interest in hedgewitchcraft led to the formation of the Association of Solitary Hedgewitches (ASH) in 1994, it operates as a contact organization only. Solitary hedgewitches can use the association to make contact with each other in order to share experiences and ideas.

12 Hutton states that cunning folk are "increasingly significant as role models now that the individual practice of witchcraft is coming into ever greater vogue, but they have little relation to the essentially communal character of mid-twentieth century paganism" (Hutton 1996: 6–7).

13 Comment by Chas Clifton (clifton@uscolo.edu), February 1999. E-mail contribution to the Nature Religion Scholars discussion group (natrel-l@uscolo.edu).

14 In 1995, when I was involved in organizing the conference *Nature Religion Today: Paganism, Shamanism and Esotericism in the 1990s*, a colleague suggested inviting Tanya Luhrmann. When I mentioned this to my contact she told me that, if Luhrmann attended the conference, British Wiccans would not support the venture.

15 Wicca does not have any formalized rules as such. However, there are commonly accepted and observed rules within the religion, this being one of them.

16 Hanegraaff (1995) presents an extensive argument for the importance of empirical data in the study of religion, while emphasizing the requirement that the researcher maintains respect for the world view of believers which "encompasses an empirically perceptible one *and* one or more meta-empirical realms" (Hanegraaff, 1995: 101). See also Puttick (1997: 9) who states that "we are accountable to the multi-level complexity of 'truth' to present as complete and comprehensive an interpretation as possible in the context of broader social and spiritual trends".

17 I am grateful to Derek Reinhard who, after chairing a paper I presented on this subject at the Association of University Departments of Theology and Religious Studies (AUDTRS) conference in 1999, pointed out the similarities between my diagram and the Johari Window.

18 Inaccurate 'facts' which are known by both the community and the researcher are likely to be stereotypes, such as the 'common knowledge' that all witches are female and have black cats, or that all witches are devil worshippers.

19 For further information, see Luft & Ingham, 1955.

20 Cf. Jan G. Platvoet (1983: 6) who says that "methods of collecting data and interpreting them have a hermeneutical setting: they are operated in a two-way framework of interpretation intimately linked to the person of the investigator and necessarily involving his or her subjectivities in their operation".

References

Adler, M. *Drawing Down the Moon: Witches, Druids, Goddess-Worshippers, and other Pagans in America Today.* Boston: Beacon Press, 1979.

Berger, P. *The Heretical Imperative: Contemporary Possibilities of Religious Affirmation.* New York: Anchor Press (Doubleday), 1979.

Bonewits, I. *Real Magic.* York Beach, Maine: Samuel Weiser, 1989 (1st ed. published in 1971).

Christ, C. & Plaskow, J., eds. *Womanspirit Rising: A Feminist Reader in Religion.* San Francisco: Harper & Row, 1979.

Crowley, V. *Wicca: The Old Religion in the New Millennium.* London: Thorsons, 1996.

Culpepper, E. "The Spiritual Movement of Radical Feminist Consciousness." Needleman, J. & Baker, G., eds. *Understanding the New Religions.* New York: Seabury Press, 1978: 220–234.

Daly, M. *Gyn/Ecology: The Metaethics of Radical Feminism.* London: The Women's Press, 1978.

Evans-Pritchard, E. E. *Witchcraft, Oracles and Magic Among the Azande.* Oxford: Clarendon Press, 1976.

Ewing, K. P. "Dreams from a Saint: Anthropological Atheism and the Temptation to Believe." *American Anthropologist* 96 (3), 1994: 571–583.

Faber, M. *Witchcraft and Psychoanalysis.* Rutherford: Fairleigh Dickinson U. P., 1993.

Gardner, G. B. *Witchcraft Today.* London: Rider, 1954.

Gardner, G. B. *The Meaning of Witchcraft.* London: Aquarian Press, 1959.

Ginzburg, C. *Ecstasies: Deciphering the Witches' Sabbat.* New York: Penguin, 1992.

Goldenberg, N. *Changing of the Gods: Feminism and the End of Traditional Religions.* Boston: Beacon Press, 1979.

Hanegraaff, W. J. *New Age Religion and Western Culture: Esotericism in the Mirror of Secular Thought.* New York: SUNY, 1998.

Hanegraaff, W. J. "Empirical Method and the Study of Esotericism." *Method and Theory in the Study of Religion* 7 (2), 1995: 99–129.

Harvey, G. "The Authority of Intimacy in Paganism and Goddess Spirituality." *Diskus* 4 (1) 1996: 34–48.

Harvey, G. & Hardman, C. *Paganism Today: Wiccans, Druids, the Goddess and Ancient Earth Traditions for the Twenty-First Century.* London: Thorsons, 1996.

Hutton, R. "The Roots of Modern Paganism." In Harvey, G. & Hardman, C., eds. *Paganism Today: Wiccans, Druids, the Goddess and Ancient Earth Traditions for the Twenty-First Century.* London: Thorsons, 1996: 3–15.

Lewis, J. R. *Magical Religion and Modern Witchcraft.* New York: SUNY, 1996.

Luft, J. & Ingham, H. *The Johari Window: A Graphic Model for Interpersonal Relations.* California: University of California Western Training Laboratory, 1955.

Luhrmann, T. M. *Persuasions of the Witches' Craft: Ritual Magic in Contemporary England.* Basingstoke: Picador, 1994 (1st ed. published in 1989).

Needleman, J. & Baker, G., eds. *Understanding the New Religions.* New York: Seabury Press, 1978.

Needleman, J. & Faivre, A., eds. *Modern Esoteric Spirituality*. London: SCM Press, 1992.

Orion, L. L. *Never Again the Burning Times: Paganism Revived*. Prospect Heights, Illinois: Waveland Press, 1995.

Pearson, J., Roberts, R. H. & Samuel, G. eds. *Nature Religion Today: Paganism in the Modern World*. Edinburgh: Edinburgh U. P., 1998.

Pike, S. M. "Rationalizing the Margins: A Review of Legitimation and Ethnographic Practice in Scholarly Research on Neo-Paganism." In Lewis, J. R., ed. *Magical Religion and Modern Witchcraft*. New York: SUNY, 1996: 353–372.

Platvoet, J. G. *Comparing Religions: A Limitative Approach*. The Hague, Paris, New York: Mouton, 1983.

Puttick, E. *Women in New Religions: In Search of Community, Sexuality and Spiritual Power*. London: Macmillan, 1997.

Salomonsen, J. *"I am a Witch—a Healer and a Bender": An Expression of Women's Religiosity in Contemporary USA*. Unpublished PhD dissertation, University of Oslo, 1996.

Smart, N. *Dimensions of the Sacred: An Anatomy of the World's Beliefs*. London: Fontana Press, 1997.

Starhawk. *The Spiral Dance: A Rebirth of the Ancient Religion of the Great Goddess*. San Francisco: HarperCollins, 1979.

Stone, M. *When God was a Woman*. New York: Harcourt Brace Jovanovich, 1976.

Thomas, K. *Religion and the Decline of Magic*. Harmondsworth: Penguin, 1991 (1st ed. published in 1971).

Valiente, D. *The Rebirth of Witchcraft*. Washington: Phoenix Publishing, 1989.

7   The Insider/Outsider Problem in the Study of New Religious Movements

ELISABETH ARWECK

Introduction

This essay is not so much concerned with the study of ritual or religious practice in religions or religious groups, nor is this essay about theorizing faith, if theorizing is used in the sense of developing a theory about a particular faith or about the way in which a particular faith might be understood. What I hope to offer by way of theorizing concerns the varying perspectives about religious groups (in particular new religious movements)—both from the inside and from the outside—and the way in which these different perspectives influence accounts *by* religious groups and *about* religious groups. I would like to present some reflections on the various types of internal and external accounts and on the interaction which takes place or which may take place in the construction of these accounts.

New Religious Movements: Definitions and Perspectives

The kinds of religious groups that I am dealing with are generally referred to as 'New Religious Movements' or NRMs. In some contexts, they are also referred to as 'cults'. Examples of such groups and movements include the Unification Church (the 'Moonies'), the Hare Krishna movement (ISKCON—International Society for Krishna Consciousness), the Brahma Kumaris, the Osho movement or Rajneesh Foundation, Scientology (officially known as the Church of Scientology), Sahaj Yoga, Transcendental Meditation, etc. I will not enter here into a debate or discussion of the definition of the terms 'NRMs' and 'cults', except to indicate briefly what kinds of groups we mean when we use these terms.[1]

New Religious Movements emerged as a phenomenon in the Western societies in the late 1960s and early 1970s. I broadly adhere to the concept of

NRMs as defined by Peter Clarke, according to whose definition, those religious groups or movements are regarded as NRMs which have emerged in North America and Europe since the Second World War (see e.g. Clarke, 1997). The foundation of some of the movements may go back before that time; for example, the beginnings of Sōka Gakkai, a Japanese new religious movement with which Helen Waterhouse's essay in this volume is concerned, go back to 1930 when it was founded by Tsunesaburo Makiguchi and Josei Toda,[2] Divine Light Mission (now known as Elan Vital) was founded in the 1930s in India by Shri Hans Ji Maharaj,[3] and Rastafarianism has its beginnings in the Back-to-Africa movement which started with Marcus Garvey at the beginning of the 20th century.[4] The New Age movement has (at least some of) its spiritual roots in the Transcendentalist Movement, Theosophy and New Thought, movements which originated in America in the late 19th century.[5] The important point about NRMs is that they *came to prominence* in North America and Western Europe since the Second World War.

The term 'New Religious Movements' is generally used by academics and it is their preferred term for referring to this phenomenon. There are a number of reasons for this, but the main reason—which is important for the purpose of this essay—is that the term 'NRM' is considered neutral and value-free, while the term 'cult' is generally used in popular parlance where it has assumed negative connotations, especially when used in combination with pejorative adjectives, such as 'destructive' or 'bizarre'.

The category of NRM is not a 'neat' one, in the sense that academics agree entirely about what should and should not be considered a New Religious Movement. For example, some include the People's Temple in this category, some do not.[6] Some consider Scientology an NRM, others treat it as a form of magic or a 'manipulationist sect' (Wilson, 1970) or a modern, 'secular religion' (Wilson, 1990).[7] Further, some NRMs did not start as NRMs. For example, Scientology had a precursor, Dianetics, a therapy for removing 'engrams' (see footnote 7). Another example is *est* (Erhard Seminar Training) which also started as a therapy in the early 1970s, founded by Werner Erhard; it is replaced by The Forum which includes a number of courses (on topics, such as productivity, empowerment, relationships) which are organized by The Centres Network (see Barker, 1989: 170).

The terminology and the usage of categories and definitions are important with regard to the perceptions which are associated with NRMs. Such perceptions both shape and are in turn shaped by the perspective of the person speaking or writing about them. For example, a journalist would take a different perspective compared to an academic, even if they were both to write an article for a newspaper about the subject.

A Chorus of Voices

When I started studying NRMs in Western Europe in the early 1980s, I soon realized that I needed to do more than simply become familiar with whatever relevant literature was available. I became acutely aware that the *provenance* and the agenda of some of the writings revealed themselves only after very careful scrutiny of the texts and after careful examination of the context from which such texts arose. Information about the publishers, the background of the author(s), clues about the author's (authors') agenda or affiliation with an organization, etc. were important details which needed to be taken into account. This realization led me to the concept of 'contaminated writings', by which I meant writings which had an agenda which was not immediately recognizable.

The implication of this realization is that texts and documents need to be looked at in the particular context in which they are embedded and from which they arise. This also entails the necessity to examine and assess the importance of the documents in that context, namely, to ascertain details about the person(s) who is (are) speaking (in the case of NRMs, is a grassroots member speaking or a spokesperson for the group or someone in a leadership position?), the reasons for which documents are created (regarding NRMs, some documents are created for internal use, some are directed towards an audience outside the group), the response which documents wish to elicit (for example, a document may have been created in order to provide information, to comment on, or correct, the statement of a third party, or to solicit support from sympathetic quarters), and the response which documents actually elicit. The last point has also been consequential for academic work on NRMs. For example, in late 1990, a group of German academics[8] prepared a paper on Scientology (REMID, 1990) which was intended for enquirers, but the document was appropriated by Scientology for its own purposes and circulated widely (see Arweck, 1999). Another instance in which the assessment of an NRM by academics was consequential occurred in the immediate aftermath of the sarin attack on the Tokyo underground in 1995. After the attack, but before it was established that Aum Shinrikyo had committed this act of violence, two American researchers visited the movement in Japan and expressed their concern regarding the rights of religious movements and fears of government repression of religion (see Reader, 1995).

Such issues concern the question of how accessible information is, how information is created, for what purpose it is created, how it is distributed, and to which institutions it is distributed. These are questions which are central to the sociology and philosophy of knowledge, but they are highly relevant for the study of NRMs. A situation in which such considerations played a significant role occurred in early 1993, during the confrontation between the state authorities—the BATF (Bureau of Alcohol and Tobacco and Firearms) and the FBI—and the Branch Davidians at Waco, Texas. David Koresh, the leader of the Branch Davidians, promised to leave the compound at Mt. Carmel after completing a manuscript on the Seven Seals of the Book of Revelations. Koresh had produced texts on this topic earlier—in fact, these had been studied by two academics, Dr Philip Arnold and Dr James Tabor. Careful scrutiny of these texts could have given the authorities clues about Koresh's thinking and about the way they could have led the negotiations during the siege in order to achieve a non-violent outcome. Instead, they thought it unlikely that Koresh would complete the manuscript and therefore they thought that he would never leave Mt. Carmel. Besides, as Koresh had broken previous promises to leave the compound, his credibility was undermined in the eyes of the authorities. The implication is that the siege at Waco could have had a different outcome,[9] if the negotiators had taken Koresh's texts into consideration.[10]

I have spoken earlier about 'contaminated writings' with reference to writings with an 'undeclared' or 'hidden' agenda. Peter Berger also uses the notion of 'contamination', but he uses it in a different sense—he speaks of 'cognitive contamination'. Berger explains that in a pluralistic world, plausibility structures are only temporary and when we are exposed to other cultures or communities, 'cognitive contamination' takes place, as plausibility structures are reviewed and revised according to the cultural aspects to which we are exposed and which we may include in existing plausibility structures (see Berger, 1992: 38–40).[11]

There is, however, an important aspect to 'cognitive contamination' in my view, which Berger does not point out: it can only take place, if we are *willing* to be exposed to other cultures and communities, listen to what their representatives have to say, refer their values and beliefs back to our own values and beliefs, and thus have our own culture scrutinized and questioned. In other words, for 'cognitive contamination' to take place, a certain amount of openness to the 'other' is required. I would argue that those studying NRMs or religion in general have this openness and the willingness to expose themselves to religious values and beliefs which they may not necessarily share with those who hold them. It is said sometimes that in a sociologist of religion lurks a religionist *manqué*. I have no doubt that students of religion bring certain predispositions and affinities to the subject and it may well be that the openness which I mentioned is the lowest common denominator or one of these predispositions. Berger's notion of 'cognitive contamination' could be helpful in exploring and understanding the extent to which accounts are 'negotiated' between the various parties which participate in the debate of NRMs.

There are political ('political' in a general, not party political sense) aspects involved in the process of creating texts and documents as well as in the relationships between organizations and groups concerned with the study of NRMs or the existence of NRMs. I have come to consider the range of institutions and organizations which are involved in the debate of NRMs as a variety of voices. (see Arweck, 1999: 33–35)

Which organizations form part of this chorus of voices? There are the movements themselves, the media, the 'anti-cult movement',[12] former members of NRMs (ex-members or apostates), various institutions and agencies of the state or public authorities, the churches, legal representatives, therapists and counsellors of various kinds, and finally the academics studying NRMs as well as related social groups and topics.

Again, the categories mentioned are not 'neat' in the sense that each would represent a distinct type of organization or institution; each of these categories comprises a *range* of different groups and organizations, which—for the sake of the argument—are subsumed under a heading; NRMs are often discussed in a way which indicates that they could all be lumped together as one type, while in fact, they represent a wide array of different groups and movements. If we speak of 'type', it would be in terms of Weber's notion of the 'ideal type'—a theoretical construct which describes a set of criteria informed both by empirical and theoretical concerns; 'the ideal type' represents a category under which those NRMs can be subsumed which respond to the greatest number of criteria, but any one NRM in a particular category will never fulfil *all* the criteria.[13] This applies equally to the category of 'anti-cult movement': the term 'anti-cult movement' is a label which is used for a variety of organizations and groups, and this diversity is to some extent acknowledged in the distinction between 'secular anti-cult movement' and 'religious counter-cult movement' (see e.g. Introvigne, 1995; see also Arweck, 1999). The category of 'former member' includes those who simply leave an NRM to carry on with their lives and those who leave to become engaged in various levels of campaigning against the movements of which they were members. Regarding NRMs, there is a somewhat self-contradictory platitude among those who study NRMs: it says that the only generalization one can make about NRMs is that one cannot generalize.

However, given the range of voices of which I have spoken, there is also a range of agendas, attitudes, and interests associated with them. There are also differences with regard to the political weight which each of these voices carries; some voices may be heard over and above other voices. I have come to see these different voices as engaged in a contest: they are competing *with* one another, they are competing *among* one another, they are forming alliances with one another, and they are striving for legitimation. (see Arweck, 1999: 33–35)

The various groups and organizations engaged in the debate of NRMs have constructed accounts about NRMs. These can be, *prima facie*, subsumed under two headings: accounts emanating from within a movement (they reflect the insider perspective) and accounts which take the view from without (they reflect the outsider perspective). Eileen Barker's paper on the "Scientific Study of Religion: You must be Joking!"[14] speaks of primary accounts and secondary accounts (Barker, 1995).

Examples of primary constructions or representations of the insider perspective include accounts which come from within the movement, such as texts produced for PR purposes, accounts by grassroots members, or accounts by those in leadership positions. All these accounts are influenced by a variety of factors, including geography, chronology, demography.

As to geography, NRMs have been compared with international companies, as their branches are scattered across the world. The experience of a member of the Hare Krishna movement in India would, for example, be different from that of a Hare Krishna member in the United States. There are also variations within countries: the experience of a member located on the East coast of the US would be different from that of a member located on the West coast.

Regarding chronology, NRMs have—since their emergence in the 1960s and 1970s—undergone notable changes and have developed in various ways. With the passage of time, the age range in the membership may change, because of changes in the recruitment strategies or because of a second generation of members growing up. The ways in which funds are raised and managed may change. The leadership structures can change, with new structures being set in place or new structures becoming necessary, for example after the death of the founder or leader. Such factors will have an effect on the movement's growth and composition. There may be changes in the way in which a group deals with defection, etc. (see Barker, 1991). To use the example of the Hare Krishna movement again: the account of a member's experience in the 1960s would be different compared with say, that of the account of a member's experience in the 1980s or 1990s.

With regard to demography and length of membership, a young member, who may be a second generation member, would have a different perspective compared with that of an older member who joined in the early years of the movement. Therefore, a long-standing member is bound to provide an account which varies from that of a newly recruited member.

Examples of secondary constructions or representations of the outsider perspective include accounts by former members, parents and relatives affected by NRM membership, the media, legal experts, politicians, therapists or counsellors, 'anti-cult' groups, and, of course, social scientists and academic researchers.

It would seem obvious that the insider accounts and the outsider accounts differ, depending on who is speaking, depending on the purpose for which accounts are produced, or depending on the agenda which is pursued by the person(s) producing the account.

For example, academic accounts can be produced at various levels: when presenting research data in a paper within an academic forum or in an academic publication, when acting as expert witness in a legal context, or taking part in a panel discussion at a media event, etc. The purpose determines the angle which the account takes in the given context and the emphasis which is placed on certain aspects.

In most cases, the purpose or the agenda is explicit and generally understood by participants: PR representatives of NRMs want to show their movement in a good light, the media want 'good stories', solicitors and barristers want to win their clients' cases, the ACM groups are 'fighting' 'cults' and want to restore children to their parents, politicians want to win votes, etc. The 'agenda' of academics would seem to consist in serving the furtherance of knowledge and insight through the application of 'scientific' methods, and therefore, most academics working in this area are likely to subscribe to notions, such as taking an 'objective' approach, using rigorous research methods, such as building theories on evidence gathered in field research, not pre-empting results by making data fit hypotheses, assessing the varying accounts from inside and outside, which includes balancing one against the other as well as against the evidence in the field and thus come to an account which can stand up to the scrutiny of one's peers. The ideals of the academic approach include values, which are expressed in terms, such as value free judgement, neutrality, detachment, setting aside preconceptions and prejudices, etc. These ideals require an awareness of personal attitudes and preconceived ideas which may influence the gathering and interpretation of field data. Ideally, such ideas should be set aside or bracketed off, although in practice, this may not be (and is not) always easy or possible.[15]

However, the categories of primary and secondary accounts to which I have referred may seem plausible and straightforward, but often they are not—they are not as neat and clearly compartmentalized as one might assume or as one might wish them to be.

There are areas where insider and outsider perspectives overlap or where the secondary account is the result of 'negotiation' between insider and outsider views, where—in Berger's words—'cognitive contamination' may have influenced the construction of the secondary account. I would like to offer some comments on areas where I see an overlap between the academic (the outsider) account and the NRM (the insider) account.

Affinities, Sympathies, and Agendas in Academic Research

Research in the field (participant observation) brings researchers in contact with people, 'real' people; studying them means that researchers are spending time with them, sharing activities, and learning about their ways—after all, that is the purpose of fieldwork and participant observation. For this purpose, social scientists use the Weberian concept of *verstehen*. This concept can be described as sympathetic empathy; it includes an attitude of openness which was mentioned earlier; it also includes the ability to look at beliefs and practices as they are perceived by a practitioner and thus gain an understanding of them, without actually becoming a practitioner oneself. The concept of *verstehen* is very useful, but potentially problematic: it is useful for furthering insight into, and appreciation of, another faith and another way of life which is based on religious priorities; it is potentially problematic when sympathetic empathy turns into empathetic sympathy, in cases where the academic observer gets so close to the representatives of the faith s/he studies that a certain amount of detachment is lost or—as the saying goes— that the researcher goes native. This has consequences for the way in which the researcher handles the data which s/he has collected and interprets his/her material. There are, of course, various degrees to which a researcher's detachment can be weakened.

A researcher's detachment may not just be weakened through the contact with a particular group through research. A researcher may bring affinities or personal sympathies to his/her research about a religious group s/he is studying or with some beliefs or practices or attitudes to which the group adheres, the researcher may be a practitioner of some kind her/himself— such sympathies or affinities could have been the very reason why a researcher embarked on the study of the group in question in the first place. For example, the academic study of neo-paganism has expanded in recent years because of certain affinities which some academics have brought to the topic. Jo Pearson's contribution to this volume is a case in point. Another example is the New Age movement: in his book on this movement, Paul Heelas expresses some sympathies with New Age thought towards the end of the book (Heelas, 1996). A French PhD student told me that his academic interest in NRMs stems from his connection with a group which is mainly active in France. A recent book on methods and findings in *American Buddhism*

(Williams & Queen, 1999) includes an essay which refers to the researcher of Buddhism *qua* practitioner of Buddhism (see Prebish, 1999).

Instances of academic affinities or sympathies can be observed when researchers adopt an agenda with regard to NRMs, for example, when they feel that their work should present a 'corrective' view. It could be that an academic feels strongly that a particular group is portrayed in a consistently negative way in the media, a picture which may not be borne out by the researcher's data. S/he may edit his/her material so that only positive aspects of the group are included in an article or a publication or the researcher may speak on behalf of a group as an expert witness. Such support is sometimes solicited by NRMs. For example, when The Family (formerly the Children of God) was accused of child abuse in France, Spain and other countries, it appealed to the academic community for help.[16] Some academics supplied affidavits and similar statements. (see Arweck, 1999: 30)

Another area which is relevant for the academic study of NRMs are accounts which are negotiated between NRM representatives and academic researchers. It has happened that a researcher produced an account about a particular group and that the group did not agree with what s/he said. When a group does not agree with (at least some of) the researcher's findings, it contests (some) statements in the researcher's account.

This has consequences with regard to the co-operation on which researchers rely for their field research and participant observation. Whoever has carried out field research knows to what extent a researcher feels indebted to his/her informants and to what extent s/he feels a sense of obligation towards those who have facilitated the research. Such feelings arise both from the personal contact with individuals and from considerations which are associated with standards of professional conduct. One would not wish to misrepresent anyone, break confidentiality, interfere with internal matters, or alienate the group one has studied. There are considerations related to professional ethics, for example, informants have the right to have a say,[17] one would not want to forfeit further research among the particular group, and one does not want to risk other unwanted consequences, such as the possibility of a law suit (see also Homan, 1991). The latter consideration has been quite pertinent with regard to NRMs, as some of them have proved extremely litigious with regard to statements published about them. For example, Paul Rose—he was the MP for Manchester Blackley in the mid-1970s and instrumental in setting up the first 'anti-cult' group in Britain—fought a libel action brought against him by the Unification Church, as did the *Daily Mail* in 1980. (see Arweck, 1999: 63) The Rajneesh group in Cologne (Germany) went to court over statements which were published in a public report. VPM (*Verein zur Förderung der psychologischen Menschenkenntnis*), a group founded in Zurich in 1986, whose teachings are based on the work of Friedrich Liebling, took the author of a report (Hemminger, 1991) to court, which contained statements with which VPM did not agree.

Contested statements in secondary accounts can occur before publication, as in the case of Roy Wallis's book *The Road to Total Freedom*, which was published in 1976 (Wallis, 1976). Roy Wallis started his study of NRMs by researching the Church of Scientology in the 1970s. When he had completed his manuscript for the book, he submitted it to Scientology leaders for comment. He was mindful of the organization's right to have a say, but also mindful of any potential lawsuits. He found himself between the choice of on the one hand exercising his academic freedom—the freedom of speech—and possibly incurring prosecution as a result, and on the other hand consulting the movement and possibly having to sacrifice some of his findings. In the end, both sides struck a compromise by negotiating which passages in the book had to be edited to the satisfaction of both. There were about 100 passages in the manuscript which were edited. (see Wallis, 1977)

The important point for me about the compromise of the final version is that the kind of negotiation which went on between Roy Wallis and Scientology is not obvious for those who read his book. If one looks at *The Road to Total Freedom*, one cannot tell where the corrections occurred and there is no indication which particular passages were edited prior to publication. If Wallis had not written about the methodological difficulties which he encountered during his research (Wallis, 1977), we would not know that the negotiations had taken place at all. (see Arweck, 1999: 93)

Interestingly, when Wallis published his account of "The Moral Career of the Research Project" (Wallis, 1977), Scientology requested the right to reply, on the grounds that the readers of the collection of essays would then get the full picture. Thus, Wallis's account is counter-balanced by a rejoinder written by a representative of the Church of Scientology (see Gaiman, 1977). Scientology demanded the right to reply in order to present a 'corrective view' to the perspective offered by Wallis. This kind of 'talking back'[18] and the request for having the right to reply illustrate the clash between insider and outsider perspective and illustrate that the boundaries between the two perspectives can be blurred. (see Arweck, 1999: 93)

For those who may object that Wallis's case goes back to the 1970s, let me add three further examples. The first relates to an article in *The Guardian* on the Friends of the Western Buddhist Order (FWBO) in late October 1997. The journalist who wrote the article, Madelaine Bunting, had made a point of involving the Communications Officer of the FWBO while preparing the text. *The Guardian* also made space for a response to the article by giving voice to a senior member of FWBO, whose reply was printed in early November

1997. However, during a discussion between the journalist and the Communications Officer of the FWBO during a day seminar in late November 1997,[19] it became clear that the FWBO were not happy with the article by *The Guardian* journalist, while Madelaine Bunting felt strongly that sufficient concessions had been made to the group during the preparation stage. (see Arweck, 1999: 94)

The second example is even more recent and occurred in the context of editing the *Journal of Contemporary Religion*. It concerns a response to an article about a particular group, which was published in the *Journal*. For reasons of confidentiality, I shall not mention any names. The group in question pointed to some factual errors and felt misrepresented by some of the statements in the article. It therefore submitted a response in which it sought to rectify the errors and to present a 'corrective view' which was intended to counterbalance the article. The group wished to have a voice in the academic discussion about its affairs and wished to 'talk back'.

The response was treated as a submission to *Journal* and thus submitted to the referee process: two independent reviewers were asked to comment on the text sent to them. This process is anonymous, so that neither the author(s) know the identity of the reviewers nor do the reviewers know who the author(s) is (are) or even what the *provenance* of the submission is. Predictably, both referees recognized the agenda of the response and both pointed out that the response showed the clash between insider and outsider perspective, or in the terms used in social anthropology, that it was related to the emic–etic discussion.

The last example concerns the Bruderhof.[20] It resorted to action rather than words, when it took issue with a critical paper which was published in 1997 (Rubin, 1997) as part of a collection of essays on the topic of 'harmful religion' (see Osborn & Walker, 1997). Instead of seeking redress through the right of reply, the group bought the entire print run of the book and therefore effectively withdrew it from circulation. (see Arweck, 1999: 96)

NRM Members Qua Academics

Another area of overlap occurs in cases where members of NRMs have gone through academic programmes and thus combine the role of member with that of academic. The question here is not whether NRM members (or members of any religious group) can study their own groups—there are obviously advantages as well as disadvantages. One of the issues which is relevant in this context is that it may not always be obvious in which capacity such a person is speaking, *qua* member or *qua* academic, if it is at all possible to draw a line between the two. There are other questions which one might raise in this context (and these are also relevant for the issues mentioned above, namely sympathies or affinities on the part of academics), such as whether religious affiliations should be declared, whether it is possible to be a 'good' academic as well as a 'good' religionist (provided, of course, we know what we mean by 'good' academic and 'good' religionist), where the line should be drawn between the two, or how close (or distant) research object/subject and researcher should be.

In the 1980s, the question of whether academics should attend NRM-sponsored conferences raised vigorous discussion and debate.[21] It is true that this debate has receded into the background, but the methodological issues associated with the debate, such as the closeness of research subject and researcher, legitimation of movements, etc., have in my view not been 'solved'. These issues appear again and again in different guises: for example, when (non-academic) representatives of NRMs attend academic conferences to make presentations;[22] when members of NRMs attend academic conferences *qua* academics; when NRMs organize academic conferences, either in their own right or in conjunction with established academics; when academic conferences include a programme of rituals and practices associated with a particular group or movement; when research opportunities are offered to academics by NRMs.

Apparent Academic Sympathies

Regarding method and methodology in the study of NRMs, there are instances where the (scrupulous) application of research methods and the subsequent results make academics *appear* to be sympathetic towards NRMs, when in fact they simply carry out research and report their findings. This occurs, for example, when academics adopt a certain language: in the case of NRMs, simply not using the term 'cult' indicates to some participants in the debate that an academic must be 'sympathetic' to such groups. The usage of some terminology is sometimes seen as an indication of the attitude of the speaker. NRMs themselves do not like to be referred to as 'cults', just as those engaged in the 'anti-cult movement' reject that label and prefer to be referred to as 'cult-monitoring' or 'cult-observing' groups. The situation is not helped by the fact that some sections of the academic community do use the term 'cult'. There are, therefore, political aspects involved in using the term 'cult', a topic which Richardson and Dillon have addressed (see Dillon & Richardson, 1994). Another example illustrates the importance of the way in which language and terminology are used. Researchers who have described the teachings and rituals of a particular group by including some of the terminology current inside a group (as does Helen Waterhouse in her essay in this volume, when she provides an account of the experience of ritual in Sōka Gakkai) have found that their audience assumed them to be members or at least spokespersons for the group, while their aim was to describe and record accurately what they found in the field, treating particular words as 'technical terms'. For example, in Mahikari—a Japanese NRM which has members in Western Europe, including Britain—initiated members wear a kind of 'amulet', referred to as *omitama*. The members believe that the wearer of the *omitama* can radiate 'True Light' and that s/he is protected, blessed and continually purified. Mahikari members do not want the *omitama* to be referred to as an 'amulet' and they feel misrepresented when that happens. However, an academic using this term and other terms relating to specific rituals and beliefs in Mahikari was considered to be a member when she gave a talk about the group at an academic conference.[23]

As part of my doctoral research I interviewed a handful of academics working in the field of NRMs about the methodology involved in the study of NRMs. One of them commented that with respect to NRMs, researchers are faced with a situation which requires them to be able to understand them and talk about them with that understanding, without however sounding or behaving like one of them. (see Arweck, interview material) In my view, this applies especially to cases when academics are asked to provide information about NRMs for a third party, such as a law court or public institution, although it applies to the way academics represent their research in general.

It seems to me that the role of the academic here is the kind of role that professional mediators and translators play: they need to have an understanding of both sides without siding with either party and they need to explain to the parties involved what it is that makes the other side 'tick', without prejudice or interference. It is a fine line to tread and often a difficult balance to strike, especially when personal considerations are involved. However, I believe that the very fact that the account is academic and secondary makes it different (and *should* make it different) in nature and essence from an internal account. Bryan Wilson has spoken of the sociologist of religion as a person who is deeply interested in religion and hopefully widely informed about it, while at the same time s/he is a person who is not—and deliberately not—a religiously-committed person, at least as long as s/he is practising sociology. Wilson has compared the role of the researcher to that of the photographer: s/he *takes* pictures of what he finds, but s/he is not *in* the picture him/herself. This metaphor is good illustration of the researcher's detachment, the professional nature of his/her commitment, his/her sympathetic relationship with his/her respondents, and the point where his/her set of values meets those of the respondents. (see Wilson, 1982: 25–26).

Notes

1   For a detailed discussion of definitions and terminology, see Arweck, 1999: 36–52.
2   For an introduction to Sōka Gakkai's beliefs and practices from an insider's perspective, see Causton, 1988; for a sociological studies of Sōka Gakkai, see e.g. Wilson & Dobbelaere, 1994, and Machacek & Wilson, 2000.
3   A study of the movement in the US in the 1970s is provided by Downton, 1979. To my knowledge, this group has not received much attention from academics in recent years, which would have resulted in published work.
4   Studies of Rastafarianism are provided by Cashmore, 1979, and Clarke, 1986.
5   The literature on New Age is substantial and well-nigh impossible to survey. For example, Heelas, 1996; Hanegraaff, 1996, and York, 1995, provide a general treatment of the topic.
6   The People's Temple formed under the leadership of Jim Jones in the US in the 1970s; its beliefs have drawn on the Bible and Christian teachings. With increasing fears of persecution, the group moved to a remote location in Guyana where it could operate as a self-sufficient community without interference from outside. However, when Congressman Leo Ryan went to Guyana in 1978 to investigate concerns from parents and relatives, the People's Temple felt threatened, interpreting his arrival as evidence for renewed persecution by US authorities. This triggered what is known as the Jonestown tragedy, the 'mass suicide' of over 900 people, among them 260 children. In her book on Jonestown, Mary McCormick Maaga makes a cogent contribution to the question of whether the People's Temple should be categorized as an NRM. She argues that a membership shift occurred in the People's Temple when it relocated to California, resulting in three groups within a single movement (see McCormick Maaga, 1998: Chpt. 5).
7   Scientology was founded in 1954 by L. Ron Hubbard. Briefly, it holds—among other beliefs—that people have to be treated or undergo 'auditing' (with the help of an instrument, called the 'E-meter') in order to erase 'engrams'—these have been recorded on to parts of the mind and interfere with the optimal functioning of the mind and body. A person who is free of 'engrams' is a 'clear'. (see Barker, 1989: 173)
8   The group is known as REMID which stands for *Religionswissenschaftlicher Medien–und Informationsdienst e.V.*, which was set up in early 1989. One of its principal aims is to provide better information about religions and religious movements for the public and to gather such information by using the approach of *Religionswissenschaft*. (see Arweck, 1999: 21–22)

9 Almost 90 members of the Branch Davidians, including David Koresh, died in a fire which destroyed the compound of the group at Mt. Carmel.

10 In September 1993, Dr Nancy Ammerman submitted a report to the Justice and Treasury Departments, in which she provides an assessment of the advice which the agencies involved in the situation had sought and received (see Ammerman, 1993). Substantial parts of the report are included in Ammerman, 1995.

11 I am indebted to Mrs Bernice Martin for drawing my attention to this aspect of Berger's work.

12 Like the term 'cult', the term 'anti-cult movement' is problematic. I am using it as a technical term, as an umbrella term which designates groups—often parents' organizations—which are critical of NRMs and their practices and whose *raison d'être* consists in counteracting NRMs and their activities, in particular their recruitment strategies and their efforts to insert themselves in the wider society. For a more extensive discussion of such groups, see Arweck, 1999.

13 There have been a number of attempts to develop typologies for NRMs, for example, Roy Wallis's classification of world-affirming, world-rejecting, and world-accommodating groups (see e.g. Wallis, 1984) or Jim Beckford's approach of looking at the way in which NRMs are inserted in their host societies (see Beckford, 1985). For an overview of existing typologies, see Arweck, 1999: 81–84.

14 The paper was first given as the presidential address to the Annual Meeting of the Society for the Scientific Study of Religion in November 1993 and published, in slightly revised form, in the *Journal for Scientific Study of Religion* in 1995 (see Barker, 1995).

15 For a more detailed discussion of the 'scientific' approach of the sociology of religion, see e.g. Wilson, 1982: Chpt. 1.

16 Circulars were addressed to members of the SISR (International Society for the Study of Religion) in late 1993 (see Arweck, 1999: 30).

17 This is one of the areas with which Homan deals at length in his book on *The Ethics of Social Research* (see Homan, 1991).

18 The expression 'talking back' is used by Bernice Martin to describe the contest of truth claims between researchers and researched in the NRM context (see Martin, 1981; see also Arweck, 1999: 50–52).

19 The seminar was organized by INFORM in London and focused on the media and NRMs.

20 The Bruderhof (also known as the Society of Brothers) is a Christian community which was founded by Eberhard Arnold in the 1920s in Germany. There are c. 2,200 members in America and England who live in settlements or *hofs* and support themselves by producing toys. (see e.g. Rubin, 1997; Whitworth, 1975) Given the working definition of NRMs cited above, the Bruderhof would not—strictly speaking—fall into the category of NRM. However, its action is

mentioned here as an example of the way in which religious groups outside the mainstream have 'talked back' and responded to criticism from outside the group.

21 In 1983, an issue of *Sociological Analysis* was devoted to this issue (Vol. 44, No. 3, 1983).

22 The first conference of this kind in my experience was the conference organized in 1993 at the LSE in London, where a member of an NRM imposed his agenda on the conference, despite express directives that conference participants were to subscribe to the rules of standard academic discourse.

23 I am indebted to Dr Louella Matsunaga for drawing my attention to this point.

References

Ammerman, N. T. *Report to the Justice and Treasury Departments Regarding Law Enforcement Interaction with the Branch Davidians in Waco, Texas.* 1993.

Ammerman, N. T. "Waco, Federal Law Enforcement, and Scholars of Religion." In Wright, S. A. *Armageddon in Waco: Critical Perspectives on the Branch Davidian Conflict.* Chicago: University of Chicago Press, 1995: 282–296.

Arweck, E. *Responses to New Religious Movements in Britain and Germany, with Special Reference to the Anti-Cult Movement and the Churches.* PhD thesis, King's College London, 1999.

Barker, E. *New Religious Movements: A Practical Introduction.* London: HMSO, 1989.

Barker, E. 'Changes in New Religious Movements.' In Fuss, M. *New Religious Movements. Vol. II.* Rome: International Federation of Catholic Universities, Center for Coordination of Research, 1991: 759–781.

Barker, E. "Presidential Address: The Scientific Study of Religion? You Must be Joking!" *Journal for the Scientific Study of Religion* 34 (3), 1995: 287–310.

Beckford, J. A. *Cult Controversies: The Societal Response to the New Religious Movements.* London: Tavistock, 1985.

Berger, P. L. *A Far Glory: The Quest for Faith in an Age of Credulity.* New York, London: Anchor Books, Doubleday, 1992.

Cashmore, E. *Rastaman: The Rastafarian Movement in England.* London: George Allen & Unwin, 1979 (1st ed.), 1983 (2nd ed.).

Causton, R. *Nichiren Shōshū Buddhism: An Introduction.* London: Rider, 1988.

Clarke, P. B. *Black Paradise: The Rastafarian Movement.* Wellingborough, Northants.: Aquarian Press, 1986.

Clarke, P. B. "Introduction: Change and Variety in New Religious Movements in Western Europe, c. 1960 to the Present." In Arweck. E. & Clarke, P. B. *New Religious Movements in Western Europe: An Annotated Bibliography.* Westport, CT: Greenwood Press, 1997: xxvii–xliii.

Dillon, J. & Richardson, J. T. "The 'Cult' Concept: A Politics of

Representation Analysis." *Syzygy* 3 (3–4), 1994: 185–197.

Downton, J. V. *Sacred Journies: The Conversion of Young Americans to Divine Light Mission.* New York: Columbia U. P., 1979.

Gaiman, D. "Appendix: A Scientologist's Comment." In Bell, C. & Newby, H., eds. *Doing Sociological Research.* London: Allen & Unwin, 1977: 168–169.

Hanegraaff, W. *New Age Religion and Western Culture.* Leiden: Brill, 1996.

Heelas, P. *The New Age Movement: The Celebration of the Self and the Sacralization of Modernity.* Oxford: Blackwell, 1996.

Hemminger, H. *Verein zur Förderung der Psychologischen Menschenkenntnis (VPM, IPM, GFPM).* Vienna: Referat für Weltanschauungsfragen, 1991.

Homan, R. *The Ethics of Social Research.* London, New York: Longman, 1991.

Introvigne, M. "The Secular Anti-Cult and the Religious Counter-Cult Movement: Strange Bedfellows or Future Enemies?" In Towler, R., ed. *New Religions and the New Europe.* Aarhus: Aarhus U. P., 1995: 32–54.

Machacek, D. & Wilson, B., eds. *Global Citizens: The Sōka Gakkai Movement in the World.* Oxford: Oxford U. P., 2000.

McCormick Maaga, M. *Hearing the Voices of Jonestown.* New York: Syracuse U. P., 1998.

Martin, B. "Whose Knowledge? Methodological Problems and Procedures Arising from Sociology's Rediscovery of Religion." In Vassallo, M., ed. *Youth in Perspective: Methodological Problems and Alternatives in the Study of Youth.* Malta: The Euro-Arab Social Research Group, 1981: 85–114.

Osborn, L. & Walker, A., eds. *Harmful Religion: An Exploration of Religious Abuse.* London: SPCK. 1997.

Prebish, C. S. "The Academic Study of Buddhism in America: A Silent Sangha." In Williams, D. R. & Queen, C. S., eds. *American Buddhism: Methods and Findings in Recent Scholarship.* Richmond, Surrey: Curzon Press, 1999: 183–214.

Reader, I. "Aum Affair Intensifies Japan's Religious Crisis: An Analysis." *Religion Watch* 10 (9), 1995: 1–2.

REMID. "Stellungnahme zur gegenwärtigen Auseinandersetzung um die Scientology-Kirche [Statement Regarding the Current Controversy about the Church of Scientology]." Marburg: REMID, 1990.

Rubin, J. H. "The Other Side of Joy: Harmful Religion in an Anabaptist Community." In Osborn, L. & Walker, A., eds. *Harmful Religion: An Exploration of Religious Abuse.* London: SPCK. 1997: 81–98.

Wallis, R. *The Road to Total Freedom: A Sociological Analysis of Scientology.* London: Heinemann, 1976.

Wallis, R. "The Moral Career of the Research Project." In Bell, C. & Newby, H., eds. *Doing Sociological Research.* London: Allen & Unwin, 1977: 149–167.

Wallis, R. *The Elementary Forms of the New Religious Life.* London: Routledge & Kegan Paul, 1984.

Whitworth, J. M. *God's Blueprints: A Sociological Study of Three Utopian Sects.* London: Routledge & Kegan Paul, 1975.

Williams, D. R. & Queen, C. S., eds. *American Buddhism: Methods and Findings in Recent Scholarship*. Richmond, Surrey: Curzon Press, 1999.

Wilson, B. R. *Religious Sects: A Sociological Study*. London: Weidenfels & Nicolson, 1970.

Wilson, B. R. *Religion in Sociological Perspective*. Oxford: Oxford U. P., 1982.

Wilson, B. R. *The Social Dimensions of Sectarianism: Sects and New Religious Movements in Contemporary Society*. Oxford: Clarendon Press, 1990.

Wilson, B. R. & Dobbelaere, Karel. *A Time to Chant: The Sōka Gakkai Buddhists in Britain*. Oxford: Clarendon Press, 1994.

Wright, S. A. *Armageddon in Waco: Critical Perspectives on the Branch Davidian Conflict*. Chicago: University of Chicago Press, 1995.

York, M.. *The Emerging Network: A Sociology of the New Age and Neo-Pagan Movement*. Lanham, ML: Rowman & Littlefield, 1995.

8 Quaker Ethnographers: A Reflexive Approach

ELEANOR NESBITT

Introduction

The decision to focus this chapter on the relationship between being a Quaker and being an ethnographer arises from my own experience. For 30 years, I have attended Meeting for Worship in the Religious Society of Friends (Quakers) and for the past 20 years, I have conducted and reported field studies of faith communities in the British Midlands.[1] During this period, I became aware of six other Quaker ethnographers (hereafter QEs), of whom four are women. My intention is to examine the significance of ethnographers' personal religious contexts or associated worldviews for their studies of faith communities or the religiosity of individuals and to draw attention to this dimension of reflexivity in field studies more generally.

I take reflexivity to mean the recognition that both researcher and researched inhabit a shared cultural space and that neither can be quite the same after the fieldwork encounter. By ethnography I mean a distinct approach and method—that of social anthropology, and in particular observation (with more or less participation) and interviews (ranging from structured to unstructured). Since quantitative sociological or psychological study may have an ethnographic dimension, the tendency to dichotomize quantitative and qualitative approaches is both unhelpful and unrealistic (Brannen, 1992). An ethnographic approach is sometimes characterized by an awareness of multiple interactions between the fieldworker and 'the field'. This is in contra-distinction to any positivist attempt to reduce inter-influence of this kind to a minimum or in contra-distinction to any assumption—or even assertion—that the methodology eliminates the possibility of the researcher affecting the field.

'Quaker ethnographer' is not a term that was chosen or agreed to by all the seven practitioners whose experience is the basis of this article (apart from myself, these include the persons mentioned in the Acknowledgements at the end of this article). Pam Lunn, for example, identified what she was engaged in as "an interdisciplinary narrative study of lives". However, the designation is tenable, as we are all members of Britain Yearly Meeting of the Religious Society of Friends and have also, to varying degrees, adopted an ethnographic approach to our field studies. For example, for data collection and for the construction of theory, Dandelion acknowledges the necessity of adopting a qualitative approach to supplement the quantitative (Dandelion, 1996: 31). Moreover, all seven QEs have focused their enquiry either wholly or in part on (a) communities defined primarily by their faith tradition, (b) religious belief and practice, or (c) (in the case of Lunn) on the religiosity of individuals. It may be objected that British Quakers need to be understood in sociological terms as members of a particular social class and that a reflexive approach needs to concentrate on the sociological factors implicit in being a Quaker, rather than simply on the fact of being a Quaker. However, in this chapter I propose to operate with the category of Quaker, allowing readers to deconstruct it as they will.

I shall draw both on interviews, conducted during 1998 (including one conducted by e-mail, one by telephone, and one self-administered and taped), with five of the seven QEs and on the published writings of four QEs. From these I shall consider the explicit statements of inter-influence rather than attempting a wider, more speculative analysis of their texts. As I reflect on the process of producing this chapter, I endeavour to involve and distance my own experience. I do this in part by identifying points from my reflections that have appeared in two British Quaker publications, *The Friend* and *Quaker Monthly,* on the relationship between being a Quaker and encountering people of faith (Nesbitt, 1980; 1987) and then carrying out ethnographic studies of them (Nesbitt, 1993a; 1994; 1997). This method faintly echoes Kim Knott's use of quotations from her "methodological autobiography" which she had taped and transcribed (Knott, 1995).

How Ethnographers Situate Themselves: Religio-Ethnic Group

Although the researcher's gender is the single factor to have received most discussion (see e.g. Knott, 1995; Papanek, 1964; Shaw, 1999 on the 'gendering of religious studies'), the contribution of any researcher's religio-ethnic background (including white post-Christian non-alignment with any single tradition) to the experience which s/he brings to the field encounter has received less attention. Individual ethnographers do routinely preface their reports of religio-ethnic groups by statements about the researcher's ethnicity and religion. Heilman suggests the advantages and disadvantages of being not only an Orthodox Jew, but also a member of the particular congregation that he was studying (Heilman, 1973), and Kalsi, a Ramgarhia Sikh in Yorkshire, records his privileged access to data on the local Sikh community as a long-standing member (Kalsi, 1992: 5). Bhachu has shared her thoughts on the implications both of being a woman and of researching her own (London East African Sikh) community (Bhachu, 1987), and both Papanek (1964) and Saifullah-Khan (1974) reflect upon being women who are outside the religio-ethnic community that they are studying. However, researchers do not generally relate their own ideological position or spiritual journey to the fieldwork experience, although several religious studies scholars have shared insights into the synergy between their personal faith and their academic exploration (see e.g. Eck, 1993; O'Flaherty, 1999).

When field workers define themselves as insiders or outsiders, this does not always reflect the more complex reality of identity and belonging. Raj criticizes over-easy distinctions between 'insiders' and 'outsiders' and, as a Canadian Hindu Punjabi researching London (UK) Hindu Punjabis, identifies her own position as that of an "uncomfortable insider" (Raj, 1997: 54–58). Chaudhry, a Pakistani Muslim who came from Pakistan to research Pakistani Muslims in California, provides a moving insight into the "tensions and contradictions informing the research process" through three vignettes (Chaudhry, 1997: 441). These she reconstructed from field notes and her reflective journal; they point to the uncomfortableness of her insider/outsider status, as a member of the same religio-ethnic group, but one whose worldview had been differently formed. Smith (a Maori researching Maoris) reminds us that insider research involves painful complexities (e.g. of disillusionment) for the insider researcher (Smith, 1999: 139). In his foreword to Myerhoff's study of the Jewish elderly in Southern California, Victor Turner gives the title "thrice-born" to anthropologists who return to their "nation of birth", declaring that "our discipline's long-term program has always included the movement of return, the purified look at ourselves" (Turner, 1978: xiii). However, as Raj and Chaudhry have suggested, other members of the ethnographer's religio-ethnic group (even if s/he can be sure whom this includes) are not unproblematically her/his 'nation of birth'. Distances—geographical, social and generational—between individuals and clusters of individuals complicate talk of insider and outsider.

Moreover, the ethnographer's relationship with the belief, practice or religiosity of those encountered in the field may shift over time. This serves to challenge further the insider/outsider dichotomy. Some ethnographers have described such shifts, including the internalization of the beliefs of others or ways of expressing these, and so "going native" (Barker, 1987). The ethnographer's participation may involve performing/undergoing ritual or other activity and reflecting upon the extent to which this involvement differs from that of the full insider. For example, Brown ponders her experience of Vodou (Brown, 1991: 11) and Kenna records the effect of a pilgrimage to a miracle-working icon on her subsequent academic interests (Kenna, 1992: 158).

Situating Quaker Ethnographers

Citing Heilman (1973) as an example of overt research by an insider, Dandelion provides a useful four-fold typology of insider research. This makes a distinction between insider research as covert or overt and between being an insider to the particular group or to its wider context. He identifies the advantages and constraints of insider research and finally considers the ethical implications (Dandelion, 1996: 37–50). Tentatively applying Dandelion's typology to the work of the QEs, however, challenges such a schema.

Of the seven QEs, two were overt insiders to the wider context (the Society of Friends) and to particular groups (local meetings) that they studied (Collins, 1994; Dandelion, 1996); two have made case studies of individuals from a range of Christian/post-Christian backgrounds—one examining the 'nurture' of young people, including Quakers (Jackson & Nesbitt, 1992), the other examining life story (Lunn, 1994). The transmission and adaptation of Sikh culture provided a focus for one QE (Nesbitt, 2000a). Three QEs have studied Hindus (chiefly in Britain). Of the three, one (myself) became—in an important respect—part of a Hindu community, Punjabi Hindus, and more specifically Brahmins, in Coventry—by marriage during the fieldwork period. The foci of the Hindu studies have included children's 'nurture' as Hindus (Jackson & Nesbitt, 1993), issues in religious identity (Nesbitt, 1991; 1998), the Hindu temple community in Leeds (Knott, 1986a), processes of adaptation (Knott, 1991), the Hare Krishna movement (Knott, 1986b) and death, dying and bereavement (Firth, 1991; 1993a; 1993b; 1996; 1997; 1999a; 1999b). One QE (who had earlier become a Muslim while retaining her membership of the Society of Friends) has studied Pakistani Muslims in Pakistan, the Netherlands and Britain, with particular attention to issues of health (Imtiaz & Johnson, 1993) and multi-lingual strategies of adaptation in the diaspora (Imtiaz, 1998). Evidently, Dandelion's typology provides a useful framework but, even on the basis of the scant information provided above, the experience of individual ethnographers does not always 'fit' comfortably, since their roles and degree of involvement change.

In relation to specific studies, some QEs were insiders to the group or to the group's wider context, and all can be described as insiders to the context of faith: as Quakers, all are ready to affirm (as well as debate what is meant by) a spiritual dimension to life. In her interview, Knott singled out 'insider/outsider' and 'scholar/devotee' issues as being of particular interest to her. She used the word 'believer' (indicating quotation marks by her intonation) for an 'insider to the context', not to the denominational or faith community to which particular local groups belonged, but to the much wider context of faith, the context of people who perceive their experience as in some sense religious. Knott states: "Being a 'believer' as well as a scholar means I'm personally situated in that debate... I'm not neutral. I use myself as a means of reflecting on them." (Knott, interview, 1998)

Acknowledging the Implications of One's Religious Location

In her introduction to Hinduism, Knott situates herself in relation to the tradition by mentioning that not only is she related to the colonizers of India, but "additionally I am a Quaker by religion, not a Hindu: what I have written is not intentionally influenced by my own religious identity" (Knott, 1998: 5). She seems to acknowledge the importance for readers to know that she is not Hindu, rather than to claim any particular relevance for being Quaker, as compared with being, say, Methodist or Buddhist. However, she also admits to the possibility of her own religious allegiance unintentionally influencing her account of Hinduism. Paul Heelas, on the other hand, who was not one of the QEs interviewed, regards his Quaker upbringing as making him almost an insider to the New Age Movement. Consequently, he commences "My background", the opening section of his introduction to the New Age Movement, with the statement that "brought up a Quaker—one of the most 'New Agey' forms of Christianity—I was a part-time participant of the counter-culture of the later 1960s and earlier 1970s" (Heelas, 1996: 10). For Heelas, it appears appropriate to declare his Quaker upbringing as part of his credentials for undertaking an exploration of the New Age movement. The reader is thus allowed to know that the writer has the benefit not only of academic distancing from the field, but of experiential closeness.

Reflexive awareness requires of the student of belief and practice in any faith community an ongoing interrogation of her/his cultural conditioning and religious/ideological stance and alertness to inter-influence between these and the field. Reflection on my experience and attention to what other QEs have said suggested the following questions: do being a Quaker and being an ethnographer involve (or develop) similar attitudes and skills? (Or, as Lunn suggested in her interview, is it simply that Quakerism appeals to the sort of person who is also drawn towards field studies, especially of religious communities?) What is the significance for the conduct of field studies of being perceived as a Quaker? What are the implications of being a Quaker for researching Quakers? These questions will be explored in the following sections.

Do Being a Quaker and Being an Ethnographer Involve/Develop Similar Attitudes?

> I'm doing the sort of research I'm doing because I'm already the sort of person I am ... and I'm a member of the Society of Friends because I am who I am and can be this among Friends. The relationship between me and the research and the relationship between me and being a member are similar and not necessarily reinforcing. (Lunn, interview, 1998)

Whether or not the relationship between the two is reinforcing, it is to some degree compatible and I shall therefore examine some documented Quaker tendencies regarding their relevance to ethnographic approaches. Quakers take a positive view towards openness to the insights of others, including those of 'other' faiths; the Quaker response to individuals and communities has characteristically included a readiness to listen and to learn from them. Indeed, it is likely that some Friends have joined the Society, partly because of this very openness (Nesbitt, 1997: 11). This makes Quakerism attractive to the ethnographer whose project is to interpret and represent religio-ethnically diverse individuals and communities. Firth stated: "I found Christians from other denominations have problems with other faiths—especially Anglicans and any evangelicals who took the Bible literally." (Firth, interview, 1998)

As Dandelion (1996: 12 and passim) elaborates, acceptance that in everyone there is 'that of God' is a widespread, almost defining Quaker understanding. What this phrase means is debatable in theological terms (see e.g. Allum, 1998: 10)—it can be understood as pantheism, panentheism, an affirmation of 'that of good' (rather than God), and so on. What is, however, clear is that the acceptance that there is 'that of God' in every other person, confirms the QE in paying receptive attention to those of any faith or none, regardless of age, culture, politics, or socio-economic group.

Collins avoids 'God language' altogether in pointing to a shared approach to understanding and interpreting human behaviour, when he says that "In a way being an anthropologist and being a Quaker mesh quite well in relation to ways of life and thought—in each case one is given to respect the individuality of every person whilst expecting supra-individual 'forces' to impinge on those individuals' thoughts and feelings, sense of well-being etc." (personal communication, 1998).

In my own case, Quaker tradition provided resources for resolving perceived conflicts between the demands of being a Quaker and being an ethnographer. For example, when fieldwork required me to work on Sundays, as participant observer in Christian congregations, the specific Quaker attitude to the sabbath that no one day is more hallowed than the rest of the week helped offset my sadness at being unable to attend Meeting for Worship. The QEs observed also that their social and ethical concerns—for example, the promotion of greater understanding between groups in a mixed society— accord with conducting ethnographic studies of different communities in which faith/religiosity are a focus. Further, the QEs overarching and specific aims might mould the research questions and the envisioned outcome of the research. Knott remarked that

> Peace and social justice resonate with me in other areas that I'm involved in... It's more to do with engaged work—meaning engaged with people, about things that other people are interested in, that have importance NOW. I couldn't have worked on mediaeval theology. (Knott, interview, 1998)

Not only in the conduct of fieldwork, but also in reporting it, Knott sensed a depth and context implicit in her Quaker vision. Thus the communication of her findings is more than an academic exercise:

> I think of all my writing, whether it's specifically about ethnography or about religion in general—I think of it as in a way as a kind of meditation—well this sounds too precious, a way of working out both my ideas and my outreach—a funny way of putting it—to my readers, wherever they're situated personally, so it's a conversation I'm trying to have. (Knott, interview, 1998)

Certainly, some QEs are convinced that their research writing has a purpose beyond academia. Through her published and oral presentations of her field study of Hindus in 'Westmouth', Firth sought to lessen the anguish of dying and bereavement for families and individuals by sensitizing and informing members of the medical and caring professions (Firth, 1993a; 1993b; 1996; 1999a; 1999b). Similarly, in 1993, reflecting on being a Quaker and a researcher in religious studies, I expressed the view that

... a major objective of my field work was to use my observations to make teachers and others sensitively aware of the rich and varied experience of the children with whom they come into contact. Another aim is to introduce pupils to the ideas and experiences of children from a wide range of backgrounds, and to help them to empathise imaginatively with them. I hope that these intentions are in keeping with Friends' expectations of education and with their concern for better community relations in our society. (Nesbitt, 1993a: 160)[2]

Clearly, the attitudes of QEs as Quakers may cohere as a social vision which further motivates and contextualizes their work.

Do Being a Quaker and Being an Ethnographer Involve/Develop Similar Skills?

Referring to an earlier interpretation of Quaker practice (Bauman, 1983), Collins suggests that reflexivity (in the sense of continuous reflection on their Quakerism) is intrinsic to being a Quaker:

If one is to be true to Quakerism a properly reflexive approach is necessary. Bauman (1983, *passim*) clearly indicates how Quakers have themselves been reflective of their faith and practice from the very beginning... In order to do justice to the reflexive self-determination which characterises Friends' praxis I have attempted to maintain a reflexive methodology in the text. (Collins, 1994: 38)

Another Quaker characteristic, identified in a recent study by Homan and Dandelion (1997), is acute awareness of the slipperiness of words. The Quaker tendency to "occupy themselves with the scrupulous negotiation and definition of aspects to belief" (ibid: 205) predisposes Quakers to be ethnographers rather than the subjects of ethnographic investigation.

The defining debates of interpretative anthropology also speak to a Quaker (or post-modern Quaker) condition: living—as many Quakers do—with ambiguity about whether to be Quaker is to be Christian or not, while questioning definitions and boundaries as well as being aware of the uneasy relationship between culture, heritage, creed, and personal insights. As inheritors of a dissenting tradition, it is possible that the Quakerism of the QEs inclines them to distrust and question dominant discourses, to avoid reification or the over-hasty equation of Clifford Geertz's concepts of experience near and experience distant (Geertz, 1983: 57).

In addition to the reflexive character of Quaker tradition and its fostering of alertness to challenge terms and definitions, QEs experience listening as central to both their Quaker and ethnographic practice. Listening "pattern[s] Quaker spirituality" (Loring, 1997: 2) and is, of course, a prerequisite of ethnographic research (as I emphasize in an exploration of principles for researching the religious lives of children in Nesbitt, 2000b). Indeed, 'participant observation' (which stresses the aspect of watching) necessarily involves participant listening.

Listening is a layered and diverse means of response and Loring eloquently articulates the scope of Quaker listening:

> By listening I mean the widest kind of prayerful, discerning attentiveness to the Source intimated within us, evidenced through others... This kind of listening is not simply auditory. It may be visual, kinesthetic, intuitive or visceral as well... Quaker practice ... is also a holograph, with the element of listening patterning all its parts. (Loring, 1997: 2–3)

When 'listening' in Meeting for Worship, Quakers experience silence as a medium, no less than the words, rather than as an absence. This differs from the ethnographer's listening in much the same way as vocal ministry (spoken contributions to Meeting for Worship) does from 'normal' conversation or indeed the ethnographic interview. QEs suggest that Quaker listening benefits ethnographic listening. Karima Imtiaz spoke of both Meeting and the ethnographic interview as requiring the suspense of one's own feelings or wish to intervene and noted how "concentrated" the listening is in Meeting for Worship and meeting for business (Imtiaz, interview, 1998). In my experience, I recorded that "this listening is complex: we register the verbal content of the spoken ministry and respectfully reflect on its layers of meaning, and we are also alert to the speaker's tone" (Nesbitt, 1997: 13).

An essential aspect of Quaker listening in Meeting is the acceptance of silence between oral contributions and indeed a valuing of silence, even above words, for mediating meaning and uniting the gathering. While discourse analysis has generally concentrated more on the verbal elements of discourse than the spaces between the words, Davies's study of ministry in a Quaker meeting recognizes silence as a key rule of the discourse, the fact that "members recognise one another by keeping to the (linguistic) rules of ... silence, by doing being silent together" (Davies, 1988: 132).

For Knott, the Quaker way of silence, together with doing a part-time counselling course, opened up the possibilities of the 'space' in interviews that is empty of words:

> Being a Friend gives me another way of thinking about being a religious studies researcher. When I was a researcher and not a Friend, although listening without interrupting was very important ... when I'd thought about silence in other ways that gave me another way of thinking about the space between the researcher and the 'respondent'. (Knott, interview, 1998)

QEs did not suggest that interviews adopt the silence that characterizes Meetings, but the interviewers' ease with silence and valuing of it had the potential to influence their conduct of interviews.

Resistance/Tensions Arising from Being a Quaker

So far it appears that QEs have experienced their Quakerism and their ethnography as mutually affirming and that they regard their Quakerism as a resource for their professional activities. However, some also voiced tensions. Imtiaz mentioned her increasing awareness of the opportunities and drawbacks of research. While she hoped that her research in a transnational Muslim *tariqat* (Sufi order) would further her spiritual development, the fact of being paid to do the research also troubled her. As a Quaker who is also a Muslim, she expressed the tension which she felt between the demands of being an ethnographer in certain worship situations and the imperative to be there as a worshipper. Firth "had difficulty with the tension between being a support/friend during a bereavement, while still being a researcher" (Firth, personal communication, 1998).

My experience of fieldwork has at times made me acutely aware of the incompatibility of some Quaker assumptions, priorities and commitments with those of communities in which I became immersed through fieldwork. The flatly plain and the competitively lavish, the egalitarian and the hierarchical (including the worship of spiritual luminaries), gendered and gender-free roles—these are some of the polarities which I experienced not only intellectually, but also existentially, as an ethnographer who is also a part of a Hindu community. Adopting the role of non-judgmental reporter (rather than activist for change) sometimes smacked of irresponsibility. At the same time, my assumptions about Quaker principles and practice, such as those implied earlier in this paragraph, received jolts.

Quaker Ethnography of Quakers

For QEs researching in Quaker settings, the tensions may result from being an insider to the group. Dandelion looks at practical consequences of being a Quaker for his research and the ethical implications of insider research (Dandelion, 1996: 136ff); regarding my brief study of 'religious nurture', in my preparative meeting (of which I was then an elder), I experienced role confusion in the sense of facing conflicting priorities. For the QE whose Meeting for Worship is 'data', there is the question whether participant observation in worship can be worship. The QE feels unable to worship because of the imperative to listen and watch, to record, and not to 'centre down'. ('Centring down' refers to the Quaker practice in Meeting for Worship and means allowing one's thoughts to become stiller and more consciously receptive to spiritual guidance.) A different listening (observing, recalling and analyzing) pushes at the attentive receptivity with which one has become comfortable as a 'worshipper' in Meeting.

In addition to the tension for the QE researching Quaker worship, Collins reports some of the strain affecting relationships in the Meeting:

> I have talked about 'tensions' but 'resonances' might be a better word in that 'tensions' too easily conjures up negative qualities. In studying Quakers, balancing the roles of academic and adept was challenging— and sometimes exhausting (my PhD turned out to be more contentious —for one or two Friends—than I could possibly have anticipated). (Collins, personal communication, 1998)

In conducting an ethnographic study of Quakers, the QE's perception of the group to which s/he belongs designedly sharpens and thus changes. Collins detected among Friends a "possible unifying resource", not in the peace testimony or in affirming the inner light, but in "plaining", a process, he argues, whereby Quakers continually define themselves *vis-à-vis* others in terms of their plainness (Collins, 1994; 1996a). Dandelion's research contributed to his identifying "the Quaker double-culture (the liberal belief system and conservative organisational structure)" (Dandelion, 1996: 283). Reflecting on Bowman's distinction of official and folk or popular religion (Bowman, 1992), I became more intent on "listen[ing] out for actual presuppositions and values" (Nesbitt, 1997: 12).

Collins's research involved a distancing of himself (as ethnographer) from himself (as Quaker, and indeed the warden of the Meeting House). In reporting his fieldwork he uses the third person, using the pseudonym Simon

(Collins, 1994). The reality, as he later presents it, is a composite of reflection, refraction and juxtaposition:

> I have re-presented aspects of my auto/biography through the interpretive lenses of two traditions. In the context of my auto/biography, Quakerism and anthropology co-exist as corresponding frameworks for understanding the world. As a Quaker, I perpetually reflect that tradition back in on itself; as an anthropologist, I refract and then juxtapose facets of Quakerism against other traditions. Each process realizes a multiplication of meanings which bear on subsequent attempts at interpretation—both Quakerly and anthropological. (Collins, 1996b: 37)

The Significance of Being Perceived to Be a Quaker

When researching Quakers, the QE's relationships are affected by the fact that other Quakers perceive her/him as a Quaker, even forgetting that s/he is also conducting research. For the QE who is relating to research participants who are not Quakers, there may be an initial decision to be made—whether or not to identify oneself as Quaker. Being perceived as Quaker may be more advantageous in some situations than others. Pam Lunn reports benefits:

> Being a Quaker has been an interesting and mostly useful position to come from because of vague and undefined public perceptions of Quakers as generally nice/good/liberal/accepting/moral/vaguely religious ... i.e. respectable and acceptable. (Lunn, interview, 1998)

Of course, reaction depends on what the 'subject' thinks a Quaker is, especially in relation to Christian belief. Lunn continues:

> Everyone talked freely—e.g. black women talking about what literature says they won't talk to white women about. One Catholic did say it'd have been more difficult if I'd not been 'Christian'. (She assumed I was Christian because I was Quaker...) (Lunn, interview, 1998)

However, Lunn noticed that

> Two or three Catholic women ... were constrained by my being non-Catholic, because of their perception of what I'd understand and so what it was interesting or safe to talk about. They differ strongly from all my other interviews. (Lunn, interview, 1998)

Similarly, when studying the nurture of Christian children across 13 denominations, I sensed that by identifying myself as a Quaker, I put myself into the category of a potential convert for members of some congregations and experienced the disapproval of a Greek Orthodox parent who understood Quakerism as a heresy at three historical and theological removes from the true (Orthodox) faith. When researching among Hindus and Sikhs, my being a Quaker was irrelevant. Subjects located others as *gora* (white) or non-*gora*, as Asian (a term widely used in Britain for all people of South Asian, i.e. Indian sub-continental ancestry) or *apna* (from one's particular South Asian community, e.g. a Hindu Punjabi). Knowledge that I was married to a Punjabi Hindu was more relevant than that I belonged to a particular church. At a time when Khalistani separatists suspected a conspiracy between Hindus, academics and the Indian government to undermine the claims of Sikhs to be a distinct community, one politicized Sikh father was suspicious of my motivation.

Freilich (1977) uses the phrase 'marginal natives' for anthropologists, participants who are also observers, always on the edges of their fieldwork community. Quakers are (and by some members of Christian churches are perceived to be) marginal to the theological 'mainstream' (those churches sharing a core of Trinitarian doctrine). This sense of Quakers' marginality may also be pertinent in understanding how others relate to the QE in the field, although the widespread ignorance of what the term 'Quaker' means must not be overlooked.

Quakers, Ethnography and Interfaith Understanding

Academic studies of faith communities other than one's own are one element in a growing concern for organized inter-faith encounter. For the QE, as a member of a Society which is committed to inter-faith understanding, such fieldwork is part of a socially and theologically driven enterprise. Of course, the commitment to deepen understanding between members of different faith communities is not peculiar to Quakers. Barton (1986) and Bowen (1988) exemplify field studies by an Anglican priest and a United Reformed Church minister, respectively, whose academic and pastoral careers have been largely dedicated to inter-faith understanding. However, it is arguable that the character of a faith community contributes in specific ways to encounter and dialogue. For instance, marginality to the theological mainstream characterizes Quakerism, and I have suggested the value of being marginal, as "this borderline position can render the role of intermediary between those of different persuasions and faiths easier than for more doctrinally defined traditions" (Nesbitt, 1987: 225).

Moreover, Quakers experience their traditional emphasis on openness to the light, from whatever quarter it comes, and respect for other faith traditions, coupled with their relish for freedom from doctrinal shackles, as enabling in inter-faith encounter (Nesbitt, 1987). To quote Firth:

> Being part of [another church's committee for inter-faith relations] made me realise the handicap of orthodoxy, the evangelical sub-text of X began to irritate me—the subtext of so many people. I think I've always felt this since I was a child—offended on behalf of Jews and Muslims. (Firth, interview, 1998)

Naturally, fieldwork involves the ethnographer in drawing comparisons between communities. To an understanding and interpretation of the religiosity and faith tradition of others, the QE brings a specifically Quaker reference point. My reflection on my immersion in Sikh studies (Nesbitt, 1980) included awareness of resemblance (e.g. on the part of 'founders' a reformist critique of contemporary religious institutions) and difference (e.g. the tenth Guru's affirmation that when all other means have failed, it is right to draw the sword and Quakers' peace testimony[3]) between our traditions. Had my community of faith and its emphases been other, my experience of Sikh communities would have been filtered differently.

At the same time, it was my exposure to ethnographic literature and thinking (as well as the experience of living in a Hindu family), which encouraged me to urge other Quakers to note and question the filter of western concepts/terms. I urged them to see what was familiar (e.g. the Society of Friends, Christianity) in a new light by looking at it through, say, the Indic conceptual filter of *dharma* and *sanskar* (formative cultural influences) (Nesbitt, 1994: 205–209).

Fieldwork and the Ethnographer's Spiritual Journey

So far I have used terms, such as 'religious context' and 'religious positioning', terms as inherently static as 'standpoint' (Denzin, 1997: 221), 'stance', 'lifeworld' and 'worldview'. Do such terms do justice to what is dynamic and interactive? In her rich reflection on "Women Researching, Women Researched", Knott records:

> It was at this time that I began to gratefully acknowledge the personal growth that came as a result of fieldwork, where I had previously

tended to see the impact on my personal feelings as a sign of my weakness. (Knott, 1995: 205)

She found that she was not alone:

One [woman researcher] saw her research with older women as 'not just an intellectual journey, but a personal journey as well'. Another said, 'I get a lot out of doing interviews. They can challenge you and make you think about your own philosophy.' (ibid)

Clearly, the terms 'growth' and 'journey' convey a sense of movement (progression?), change and the richness of experience which eludes more static terms. 'Spiritual journey' is a metaphor which allows for both theistic and non-theistic conjectures and convictions. 'Spiritual' in this usage encompasses 'religious', without carrying the latter's connotation of discrete faith communities or institutional weight, but with an emphasis on individual experience at depth.

Knott articulates the role of her fieldwork immersion in Hinduism in a journey which brought her to membership of the Society of Friends:

I started out as a non-religious person ... when I was starting ethnography I was not a religious individual. I never attended anything. I was honed by Hindu temple worship. That's where I got all my experience of religious practice. So my context for coming to Quakerism is entirely through Hindu religious practice and Hindu and Buddhist religious ideas. (Knott, interview, 1998)

O'Flaherty's discussion of 'the approach from the head to the heart' in the experience of scholars of religion (O'Flaherty, 1999: 344) is illustrated by Knott's awareness that one particular dimension of the Hindu tradition, North Indian *bhakti* (devotion to a personal God in the tradition of the saint-poets), provided her with insight which went deeper than academic insight:

My scholarly perspective on Hinduism is really focused in the area of North Indian Vaishnavism ... if I was to read the *bhakti* poets, that's a part of my religious persona... I'd never use phrases like 'Quaker Buddhist' or whatever, but it would be impossible for me to deny that *bhakti*, particularly North Indian *bhakti*, has been an important spiritual resource for me. (Knott, interview, 1998)

It was her research on a particularly evangelical strand of the Hindu tradition, the International Society for Krishna Consciousness (ISKCON), which helped precipitate her commitment to a particular (Quaker) tradition:

> That invitation that the Hare Krishna movement gave to me to pay more attention to my spiritual journey was certainly part of what brought me to Quakerism. Why Quakerism? That was to do with my temperament and character. It could have been anything, couldn't it? But the invitation to think afresh about my spiritual journey moved me forward ... (Knott, interview, 1998)

The challenge of her involvement in a community that was active in proselytizing had a transformative impact on her own spiritual journey. Consistent with a widely-held South Asian view that one cannot (or should not) escape one's family roots and conditioning, Knott explained that 'I needed something which in terms of culture and tradition was part of my people' (Knott, interview, 1998).

Firth's experience also suggests the appropriateness of the metaphor of the journey. She moved from the United Reformed Church to the Society of Friends during the period of her long academic involvement with a local Hindu community. Far from being non-religious, her experience from childhood was steeped in religion—her parents were missionaries in India. She "grew up in a household in which theology was discussed all the time", her school friends in Pune were Parsi, Jewish and Hindu; two other important influences were her father's love of Hindu and Buddhist philosophy, which she "subsequently studied academically, and learning Buddhist meditation at a retreat that was run by that remarkable eclectic Parsi, Firoza Mehta" (Firth, personal communication, 1998).

For Firth, too, ethnographic research—combined with other inter-faith activity—was a factor and possibly a catalyst in her journey towards Quakerism:

> Researching contributed to my becoming a Quaker. I started research in 1982 and became a Friend 1991-2... There were a variety of factors— the fact of being involved in interfaith dialogue contributed to this. (Firth, interview, 1998).

The fieldwork of individual QEs, and reflection upon it, continue to feed into their worship and thinking as Quakers. Knott describes her own "gift to Meeting":

Everyone in the Meeting brings something different to the Meeting by virtue of their religious journey. I mean some people in my Meeting have a fantastic knowledge of the Bible, which I don't have, I bring something about a whole range of other religions ... sometimes if I feel called to minister then that background may emerge in what I say. (Knott, interview, 1998)

In my case, a mantra or devotional music from fieldwork in Hindu congregations has on occasion helped focus my thoughts during meeting for worship. Occasionally, fieldwork has provided inspiration for spoken ministry. The experience of being a participant observer in worship situations— including Quaker Meetings for Worship—has sharpened my critical awareness of what occurs during Meeting and the characteristic features of spoken ministry (participants' oral contributions). Shifts in my thinking (arising from reflection upon 'experience–near' concepts, such as *sanskar*) exemplify what Jackson calls edification: "pondering on the issues and questions raised by ... the activity of grasping another's way of life" (Jackson, 1997: 130).

Conclusion

The experience of some Quakers engaged in field studies of religiously defined communities or the religiosity of individuals suggests that the ethnographer's (largely overlooked) religious context or commitment does demand attention in discussions of reflexivity. It is this, I have suggested, that contributes to some ethnographers' decisions to engage in particular ethnographic studies, and it may affect their approach to the fieldwork encounter—for example, in the Quaker case, by placing value on listening. Where studies of religious belief and practice are concerned, ethnographers who identify with one or more communities of faith (or who acknowledge a spiritual dimension to their experience) are insiders to the context. Although analytically the distinction remains useful, any polarization of insider and outsider is problematic, and the QEs illustrate how various the ethnographer's relationship to the focus community can be. As Knott especially reveals, the ethnographer is on a journey, with shifting insights and patterns of allegiance over time—Dandelion's useful typology needs to accommodate this. Certainly, the experience of the QEs suggests that Evans-Pritchard's dismissive dictum that "the study of anthropology probably affects faith little" is questionable (Evans-Pritchard, 1962: 171).[4]

Certain elements of Quakerism appear to be pertinent to ethnographic studies: I have suggested that these elements include an affirmation of silence and listening, the marginality to mainstream Christian tradition, together with a fundamental and pervasive openness to other faiths and a distrust of terminology, especially of theological formulae. The fact that for Quakers, their beliefs are, in Dandelion's analysis, less conservative than their practices, potentially differentiates the QE's interaction with faith communities in the field from that of an ethnographer whose faith community holds more defined or conservative beliefs. Discussion of reflexivity will need to recognize the inter-influence between the ethnographic enterprise and the fieldworker's specific religious context/worldview, including the secular or non-theistic. In some cases, the experience of the small sample of QEs suggests, it is appropriate to recognize the research as a dynamic or a catalyst, a factor in the ethnographer's personal growth and spiritual journey. However, the fact that the majority of the QEs are women raises the question, for a future exploration, of how discussions of reflexivity are to relate spiritual journey with gender and feminist perspectives.

Acknowledgements

I gratefully acknowledge Ben Pink Dandelion (one of the QEs) and *The Journal of Quaker Studies* for permission to use an article which appeared in 1999 (Nesbitt, 1999). I would like to thank Roger Homan for the original suggestion and the other QEs, Peter Collins, Shirley Firth, Karima [formerly Sharon] Imtiaz, Kim Knott, and Pam Lunn, for generously sharing their experience.

Notes

1 These studies have focused on the transmission and adaptation of religious tradition in several Christian, Hindu and Sikh communities. See, for example, Jackson & Nesbitt, 1992; Nesbitt, 1993b; Jackson & Nesbitt, 1993; Nesbitt, 1991; Nesbitt, 1998; and Nesbitt, 2000a.
2 In 1996, the Warwick Religions and Education Research Unit, for which I work, won the Templeton Award "for promoting tolerance and understanding through ethnographic research on children and associated curriculum work".
3 Guru Gobind Singh's statement is in Zafarnama, a letter to Emperor Aurangzeb. "Peace testimony" refers to a stance expressed in successive exhortations to eschew war, currently distilled in *Quaker Faith and Practice* (1995: 1.02.31).
4 This quotation comes from his Aquinas Lecture 1959 on "Religion and the

Anthropologists", in which he also observed that "the attitude of ... social anthropologists in particular, towards religious faith and practice ... has been for the most part bleakly hostile" (Evans-Pritchard, 1962: 155) and that of the Christian minority of anthropologists, "a considerable proportion are Catholics" (ibid).

References

Allum, J. "That of God in Everyone?" *The Friend* 156, 28 August, 1998: 9–10.

Barker, E. 'Brahmins Don't Eat Mushrooms: Participant Observation and the New Religions.' *LSE Quarterly*, June 1987: 127–152.

Barton, S. *The Bengali Muslims of Bradford: A Study of their Observance of Islam with Special Reference to the Functions of the Mosque and the Work of the Imams.* Leeds: University of Leeds, 1986.

Bauman, R. *Let Your Words Be Few: Symbolism of Speaking and Silence among Seventeenth Century Quakers.* Cambridge: Cambridge U. P., 1983.

Bhachu, P. "The Resocialisation of an Anthropologist: Fieldwork within One's Own Community." In Epstein, S., ed. *Female Ethnographers: Researchers Working within their own Communities.* Delhi: Hindustan Publishing Corporation, 1987.

Bowen, D. *The Sathya Sai Baba Community in Bradford: Its Origin and Development, Religious Beliefs and Practices.* Leeds: Community Religions Project, University of Leeds, 1988.

Bowman. M. "Phenomenology, Fieldwork and Folk Religion." Occasional Papers 6. British Association for the Study of Religions, 1992.

Brannen, J., ed. *Mixing Methods: Qualitative and Quantitative Research.* Aldershot: Avebury, 1992.

Brown, K. M. *Mama Lola: A Vodou Priestess in Brooklyn.* Berkeley: University of California Press, 1991.

Chaudhry, L. N. "Researching 'My People', Researching Myself: Fragments of a Reflexive Tale." *Qualitative Studies in Education* 10 (4), 1997: 441–453.

Collins, P. J. *The Sense of the Meeting: An Anthropology of Vernacular Quakerism.* Unpublished PhD Thesis, Manchester University, 1994.

Collins, P. "'Plaining': The Social and Cognitive Practice of Symbolisation in the Religious Society of Friends (Quakers)." *Journal of Contemporary Religion* 11 (3), 1996a: 277–288.

Collins, P. "Narrative, Auto/Biography and the Quaker Meeting." *Auto/Biography* 213 (4), 1996b: 27–39.

Dandelion, P. *A Sociological Analysis of the Theology of Quakers.* Lampeter: Edwin Mellen, 1996.

Davies, A. "Talking in Silence: Ministry in Quaker Meetings." In Coupland, N., ed. *Styles of Discourse.* Beckenham: Croom Helm, 1988: 105–137.

Denzin, N. K. *Interpretive Ethnography: Ethnographic Practices for the 21st Century.* London: Sage, 1997.

Eck, D. L. *Encountering God: A Spiritual Journey from Bozeman to Banaras*. Boston: Beacon, 1993.

Evans-Pritchard, E. E. *Social Anthropology and Other Essays*. New York: Free Press of Glencoe, 1962.

Firth, S. "Changing Patterns in Hindu Death Rituals in Britain." In Killingley, D.; Menski, W., & Firth, S. *Hindu Ritual and Society*. Newcastle: S. Y. Killingley, 1991: 52–84.

Firth, S. "Hindu and Sikh Approaches to Death" and "Cross Cultural Perspectives on Bereavement." In Dickinson, D. & Johnson, M., eds. *Death, Dying and Bereavement: A Reader*. London: Sage, 1993a: 26–32; 254–261.

Firth, S. "Cultural Issues in Terminal Care." In Clarke, D., ed. *The Future for Palliative Care: Issues of Policy and Practice*. Milton Keynes: Open U. P., 1993b: 99–110.

Firth, S. "The Good Death: Attitudes of British Hindus." In Jupp, P. & Howarth, G., eds. *Contemporary Issues in the Sociology of Death, Dying and Disposal*. London: Macmillan, 1996: 96–110.

Firth, S. *Dying, Death and Bereavement in a British Hindu Community*. Leuven: Peeters, 1997.

Firth, S. "Hindu Widows in Britain: Continuity and Change." In Barot, R., Fenton, S. *et al.*, eds. *Ethnicity, Gender and Social Change*. London: Macmillan, 1999a: 99–113.

Firth, S. "Spirituality and Ageing in British Hindus, Sikhs and Muslims." In Jewell, A., ed. *Ageing and Spirituality*. London: Jessica Kingsley, 1999b: 158–174.

Freilich. M., ed. *Marginal Natives at Work: Anthropologists in the Field*. New York: Wiley, 1977.

Geertz, C. *Local Knowledge*. New York: Basic Books, 1983.

Heelas, P. *The New Age Movement: The Celebration of the Self and the Sacralization of Modernity*. Oxford: Blackwell, 1996.

Heilman, S. C. *Synagogue Life: A Study in Symbolic Interaction*. London: University of Chicago Press, 1973.

Homan, R. E. & Dandelion, P. "The Religious Basis of Resistance and Non-Response: A Methodological Note." *Journal of Contemporary Religion* 12 (2), 1997: 205–214.

Imtiaz, S. *A Comparative Study of Multilingual Pakistanis in Amsterdam and Birmingham*. Unpublished PhD Thesis, Centre for Research in Ethnic Relations, University of Warwick, 1998.

Imtiaz, S. & Johnson, M. D. R. *Healthcare Provision in the Kashmiri Population of Peterborough: An Initial Investigation of Issues of Concern*. Peterborough: North West Anglia Health Authority, 1993.

Jackson, R. *Religious Education: An Interpretive Approach*. London: Hodder, 1997.

Jackson, R. & Nesbitt, E. "The Diversity of Experience in the Religious Upbringing of Children from Christian Families in Britain." *British Journal of Religious Education* 15 (1), 1992: 19–38.

Jackson, R. & Nesbitt, E. *Hindu Children in Britain*. Stoke on Trent: Trentham, 1993.

Kalsi, S. *The Evolution of a Sikh Community in Britain: Religious and Social Change among the Sikhs of Leeds and Bradford*. Leeds: Community Religions Project, University of Leeds, 1992.

Kenna, M. E. "Changing Places and Altered Perspectives: Research on a Greek Island in the 1960s and the 1980s." In Okely, J. & Callaway, H., eds. *Anthropology and Autobiography*. London: Routledge, 1992.

Knott, K. *Hinduism in Leeds: A Study of Religious Practices in the Indian Community and in Hindu Related Groups*. Monograph Series. Leeds: Community Religions Project, University of Leeds, 1986a.

Knott, K. *My Sweet Lord: The Hare Krishna Movement*. Wellingborough: Aquarian Press, 1986b.

Knott, K. "Bound to Change? The Religions of South Asians in Britain." In Vertovec, S., ed. *Oxford University Papers on India: The Modern Western Diaspora*. Delhi: Oxford U. P., 1991: 86–111.

Knott, K. "Women Researching, Women Researched: Gender as an Issue in the Empirical Study of Religion." In King, U., ed. *Religion and Gender*. Oxford: Blackwell, 1995: 199–218.

Knott, K. *Hinduism: A Very Short Introduction*. Oxford: Oxford U. P., 1998.

Loring, P. *Listening Spirituality. Vol 1: Personal Spiritual Practices among Friends*. Washington: Openings Press, 1997.

Lunn, P. "Inner Selves Outer Lives: Class, Religion and Interiority, and their Interaction with Gender Ideology and Attitude to Feminism in Two Groups of Women Adult Education Students." MA Dissertation in Interdisciplinary Women's Studies, Centre for Study of Women and Gender, University of Warwick, 1994.

Nesbitt, E. "Out of a Single Fire: Sikhs and Quakers." *Quaker Monthly* 59 (April), 1980: 75–78.

Nesbitt, E. "That of God." *Friends Quarterly* 24 (5), January 1987: 221–227.

Nesbitt, E. *"My Dad's Hindu, My Mum's Side are Sikhs": Issues in Religious Identity*. Charlbury: National Foundation for Arts Education, 1991.

Nesbitt, E. "On Being a Quaker and a Researcher in Religious Studies." *Quaker Monthly* 72 (August), 1993a: 160–162.

Nesbitt, E. "Transmission of Christian Tradition in an Ethnically Diverse Society." In Barot, R., ed. *Religion and Ethnicity: Minorities and Social Change in the Metropolis*. Kampen: Kok Pharos, 1993b: 156–169.

Nesbitt, E. "Living with Other Faiths: Reflecting [on] our own Sanskars." *Quaker Monthly* 73 (October), 1994: 205–209.

Nesbitt, E. "Of Faiths and Cultures." *The Friend* 155 (22), 1997: 11–14.

Nesbitt, E. "British, Asian and Hindu: Identity, Self-Narration and the Ethnographic Interview." *Journal of Beliefs and Values* 19 (2), 1998: 189–200.

Nesbitt, E. *The Religious Lives of Sikh Children*. Leeds: Community Religions Project, University of Leeds, 2000a.

Nesbitt, E. "Researching Children's Perspectives on their Experience of Religion." In Lewis, A. & Lindsay, G., eds. *Researching Children's Perspectives*. Buckingham: Open U. P., 2000b: 135–149.

Nesbitt, E. & Kaur, G. *Guru Nanak*. Norwich: Religious and Moral Education Press, 1999.

O'Flaherty, W. D. "The Uses and Misuses of Other People's Myths." In McCutcheon, R. T., ed. *The Insider/Outsider Problem in the Study of Religion: A Reader.* London: Cassell, 1999: 331–349.

Papanek, H. "The Woman Fieldworker in a Purdah Society." *Human Organisation* 23, 1964: 160–163.

Quaker Faith and Practice: The Book of Discipline of the Yearly Meeting of the Religious Society of Friends (Quakers) in Britain. London: The Religious Society of Friends (Quakers) in Britain, 1995.

Raj, D. S. *Shifting Culture in the Global Terrain: Cultural Identity Construction among Hindu Punjabis in London.* Unpublished PhD Thesis, University of Cambridge, 1997.

Saifullah-Khan, V. *Pakistani Villagers in a British City (The World of the Mirpuri Villager in Bradford and in his Village of Origin).* Unpublished PhD Thesis, University of Bradford, 1974.

Shaw, R. "Feminist Anthropology and the Gendering of Religious Studies." In McCutcheon, R., ed. *The Insider/Outsider Problem in the Study of Religion: A Reader.* London: Cassell, 1999: 104–113.

Smith, L. T. *Decolonizing Methodologies: Research and Indigenous Peoples.* London: Zed, 1999.

Turner, V. "Foreword." In Myerhoff, B. *Number Our Days.* New York: Simon & Schuster, 1978: xiii–xvii.

9   Epilogue: The Ethnographer and the Quest for Meanings

LOWELL W. LIVEZEY

The Religion in Urban America Program

How many times while reading the splendid essays of this volume was I thrown back for comparison and contrast with the ethnographic research of the Religion in Urban America Program in Chicago, which I have directed since 1992. While our Chicago project is addressed to the entire life of the religious congregation—defined broadly to include synagogues, mosques, temples, and other religious assemblies as well as churches—ritual is central in every case, not only reflecting the importance of worship in religious practice, but the ubiquitous tendency of religious groups to ritualize their collective activities. Therefore, like the authors of this volume, my colleagues and I have spent a great deal of our time participating in and observing rituals. And like the authors in this volume, we have repeatedly found ourselves coping with the reality that we simultaneously shared a great deal with the groups we were studying, yet differed from them in ways that made insider access difficult to secure and insider insight difficult, if not impossible to attain. Both projects exemplify what I might call the 'ethnographic condition', which is the constant need to negotiate and re-negotiate one's status, seeking just the right measure of member-like acceptance, while preserving critical distance sufficient for 'scientific' discernment and honest reporting.

I vividly recall attending morning worship at the Carter Temple Christian Methodist Episcopal (CME) Church in Chicago's Chatham neighborhood, an area accurately described as the 'bastion of the black middle class'. Carter Temple's relatively new, elegant, 1,000-seat sanctuary was packed with well-dressed African Americans and two white folks—my wife and me. Outsiders? Well, yes, we certainly were not and had never been members of this church, or of the larger 'black church in America', the collection of denominations and independent congregations that scholars like C. Eric Lincoln have called "the cultural womb of the black community" (Lincoln & Mamiya, 1990: 8).

Nor could we have been members of the black community itself, constituted in America as perhaps nowhere else, except South Africa, by the involuntary racial boundary that is the deepest fault-line of our culture. Yet the hymns of John and Charles Wesley struck a responsive chord with me: although I had been raised in a rural Methodist church, I had rarely heard these hymns in the modern, liberal, urban churches to which, for theological and ideological reasons, I have belonged as an adult. Within seconds I was belting out the hymns with a near-primordial zeal, no need to look at the hymnal, no need to read the notes, so instantly at home was I in the musicology of this black church. And there was much in the service to reinforce this sense of home-coming: the evangelical style, the frequent biblical references, the 'family' metaphors, especially of 'brother' and 'sister' as honorary titles for people of recognized authority and leadership, the warmth with which we were welcomed into the service. So I was a *participant* observer: no problem finding common ground; the danger for me was being "engulfed" (see Pollner & Emerson, 1983: 252).

But then we were outsiders again. "For our scripture today I'll be reading, as we always do at Carter Temple, from the *African Heritage Bible*", the pastor intoned. "Other churches may think Jesus and his disciples were white, and the Holy Land is north of the Red Sea. But at Carter Temple we know that was the invention of European scholars. Hear now the words of our Lord Jesus Christ, the Son of God and a man of color, who shares our African heritage. Sure, Jesus came to save white folks too; but you listen now, *he is one of us*." Carter Temple is a special kind of black church, one that celebrates its blackness and constructs that as central to its *religious* identity, an essential part of the faith. Therefore, just before the sermon on this 'Black Male Emphasis Sunday' (the third Sunday of every month), there was a special ritual of recognition and prayer for the men and boys of the church. The ritual identified all the men and boys of the church as role models for the entire black community, and reaffirmed Carter Temple's mission "to reclaim the black man to his proper role and status in the family, the church, and the community"—thus addressing one of the major social problems of the day. I watched as the men and boys—perhaps 300 of them—moved from the pews and choir loft to join hands around the sanctuary, the pastor noting their achievements in school, business, and professions, and thanking God for their deliverance from the drugs, crime, unemployment, violence, family decay, and the "Eurocentric individualism" that undermines community and isolates black men. I discreetly jotted some notes in the margin of the bulletin, feeling really glad to be able to witness the ritual, conducted in my own language with familiar religious and social symbolism, identifying with the men as adult males and as Christians, and even to think about how their "black Jesus" may have meaning for them, something like my memories of the picture of the blue-eyed shepherd Jesus in my grandparents farmhouse. I did not have to be black, I thought, to have access to *their meanings* in this ritual; indeed, the distance of racial difference might actually help me understand those meanings and interpret them to my readers.

But I was not permitted to stay at this distance. The lady behind me touched my shoulder gently and motioned that I should join the line encircling the sanctuary. Did she think I was a light-complexion African American, I wondered? Another turned to me with a similar gesture. Soon the pastor (who knew the purpose of my visit) looked at me: "Professor Livezey! *Brother* Livezey, won't you please join us? You a *black man* today. You at Carter Temple!" So there I was, an insider again—transported across the deep chasm of race into one of the central rituals by which this church both invokes its heritage and socially constructs its religious identity. My outsider-based claims to objectivity were attenuated; my ties to the blue-eyed Jesus and the white Methodist farmers of my past were eclipsed by the black community and its Afrocentric theology, as I clasped hands and bowed in prayer with the men and boys of Carter Temple CME Church.

This is but one homely, if poignant example of the ethnographic condition that is portrayed, propounded, and examined throughout this book: that as field researchers we are almost always both insiders and outsiders, albeit in a variety of respects and dimensions, in different degrees, and in a partly-negotiated balance between the two. Our circumstances and subjects are diverse in ways more obvious even than the rich variety of groups and rituals discussed in this book. We have conducted ethnographic case studies of some 60 congregations in the Chicago metropolitan region, so we have the opportunity, as these authors did at their conference and the readers of this volume now do, to reflect on each congregation and on the methodological problems of studying it, in the bright light of comparison and with the supportive scrutiny of colleagues. As a result of a very generous grant from the Lilly Endowment, Inc., a major foundation based in Indianapolis, Indiana, we were able to include a dozen senior scholars and as many student assistants in the field research as well as in the data analysis and writing. The intent was to take a fresh look at the field historically known as 'urban ministry', but to refrain from privileging ministries of service to the poor and political action on their behalf that had more or less constituted the urban ministry paradigm. Rather we were to look comprehensively at the life and work of churches and other religious groups in urban areas, and to attempt to discern how their many ministries and other activities—from philanthropy to worship, from social action to religious education—contributed to the quality of urban life. The inclusion of 'other religious groups' was also a major innovation, given the post-1960s influx of immigrants from Asia, South Asia, Africa, and Latin America and the multiplicity of religious faiths and organizations they brought with them. The first book based on this research, *Public Religion and Urban Transformation* (Livezey, 2000), argues that cultural innovation and the social construction of cultural material are important means by which congregations address urban issues, such as racism, poverty, violence, and the loss of community.

The fact that we had sufficient funds to support a large research team not only enabled us to cover a comparatively large number of congregations, but also to deploy researchers who had differing dimensions and degrees of insider status in particular congregations selected as case studies—a point to be discussed further below. Moreover, our team sustained an invigorating discourse alongside the field research, and this in turn helped us establish some of the critical distance that is often hard to establish in the field. However, in the end, ethnography is ineluctably an individual undertaking, and often a lonely one at that. As I read the foregoing chapters, I found myself identifying with author after author, in different respects, and with the authors as a group.

While it is occasionally suggested in these essays that the insider/outsider distinction itself is unhelpful, for example by Peter Collins (on the grounds that it is based on a faulty ontology), their overall import is to explore the dimensions and consequences of being both, and to consider how to make the most of that unavoidable condition. In so doing, these authors, like my colleagues and I in Chicago, are continuing the work of the more self-reflective ethnographers who, at least since the 1930s, have been devoted to not only doing the work, but developing the method. For although, as Martin Stringer argues so cogently in his introduction, the peculiarly interior dimensions of worship and the ineffable aspects of faith pose unique challenges to ethnography, the insider/outsider problem is inherent in field research by its very nature. As Geertz noted in "From the Native's Point of View", "[t]he formulations have been various: 'inside' versus 'outside', or 'first person' versus 'third person' descriptions; 'phenomenological' versus 'objectivist', or 'cognitive' versus 'behavioral' theories; or perhaps most commonly 'emic' versus 'etic' analyses… " (Geertz, 1983: 65). These were all formulations of the same problem, namely, how to gain access to the *meanings* of one's subjects, 'to see things from the native's point of view', and to know and be able to explain that one does so, even though one is not, and does not wish to identify fully with, a subject. One had to be intimate, but also scientific. Geertz was, of course, writing (in 1983) in a summary fashion on the basis of decades of methodological development. More than half a century had passed since Malinowski had left his colleagues at camp to stay the night in his subjects' village. And a half century had passed since University of Chicago sociologist Robert Park (1968) recruited Nels Anderson, a hobo, to become a graduate student, conduct field research on hobos, and eventually write the classic ethnographic study, *The Hobo* (Anderson, 1923). A scientific outsider, Malinowski had to gain entry, acceptance, rapport in an alien culture; in contrast, a 'natural insider', Anderson had to acquire at Chicago the disciplines of distance and objectivity to transcend the 'point of view' of his own culture and that of the hobos he studied. I doubt if any of this book's authors are as completely outside the culture of the group being studied as Malinowski was; only Peter Collins and perhaps Eleanor Nesbitt are natural insiders like Anderson. Most of us work closer to the middle of the spectrum, more like Beatrice Potter (later Beatrice Webb) who, as a co-worker with Charles Booth, assumed the unlikely role of seamstress to experience sweatshop conditions in turn of the century East London, nevertheless shared the English language (if not the accent), the city, the female sex, etc., with her subjects (Emerson, 1983: 6). Like her, most of the authors of this book struggle with the in-between. In retrospect, Geertz's famous essay was a kind of constructive progress report on decades of work on the problems which the authors of this book are still attempting to address.

Partial Vision of the Social Scientist

In the Religion in Urban America Program we assumed that both insiders and outsiders have 'blinders' as well as insights. We therefore created a diverse research team so that much of the field study could be done in pairs. Each of the partners, one a relative insider and one a relative outsider, would be an initial check against omission and distortion by the other. For example, a Protestant and a Catholic worked together on a Catholic parish; a Christian and a Jew on a synagogue; a Mexican-American graduate assistant worked with a Jewish senior scholar to study both Catholic and Protestant churches in a Latino neighborhood, an Indian Hindu scholar studied her own temple in a team with a Christian, and also worked with Christians in studying Protestant churches; a Muslim graduate student worked with Christians in the studies of the mosques. Because religious culture is rarely devoid of racial and ethnic content, we tried to make our teams inter-racial as well as inter-religious. Working with me in the study of Carter Temple, for example, was a graduate research assistant who was a black woman—not the racial outsider that I was, but quite outside the sub-group of men and boys who comprised such a central symbol in the particular ritual reported above. To reap the benefits of this team-based strategy, it was necessary to spend a good deal of time debriefing—reading each others notes, discussing them with each other and with other members of the project. To make this possible, of course, required not only a generous grant; it took a decision to include a large number of part-time people who were willing to work collegially, yielding a portion of their scholarly autonomy in recognition that even the most insightful vision is partial.

We also instituted a formal procedure of sharing our findings with representatives of the groups we studied, and inviting their feedback, both at mid-course and just before the conclusion of field research. This was a reflection of the view that all perception is partial. Thus, the people in the congregations were not just observed subjects and informants, but critics of our conclusions and interpretations. We were always clear that they did not have a veto or any form of control. They were honored by our promise to reconsider every point they criticized; to investigate and consider every piece of evidence they felt we had ignored or misconstrued; and to talk with them as long as they wished about points of disagreement. This was not quite the formal 'negotiation' of the content of the product that Jo Pearson describes; perhaps it is more comparable to the kind of persuasive interaction suggested by Peter Collins. In any event, it was for us an important way of ensuring that total insiders, i.e. long-standing members and clergy, would have a say, not only as sources of detail, but as evaluators at the final stages of interpretation.

All of this is rooted in an epistemology very similar to that offered by Elisabeth Arweck, in which no single 'voice' has the capacity for the whole truth, but in which every voice is a potential source of fact and insight, and in which valid conclusions and adequate interpretation are more likely, when the multiple voices are sensitively heard and considered. Thus the same epistemology that undergirds the use of multiple sources of data (not all insiders are alike, as Helen Waterhouse points out, and some may have an axe to grind), also undergirds the employment of multiple observers with different distances from the boundaries. Obviously, individual scholars can do good ethnographic research (we cannot always be part of a team), but that is more because, rather than in spite of, the fact that we are simultaneously both insiders and outsiders. Since neither we nor our subjects are omniscient, even about our immediate circumstances, I believe it is in fact an advantage to be neither insider nor outsider, but a bit of both. To the extent that we are only one or the other, like Malinowski or Nels Anderson, we must—like Beatrice Potter—*become* the other as well. If we can build multiple perspectives into our research project, whether through team research in the field, sharing at conferences, or other forms of collegial discourse, we are blessed.

The Field Researcher's Negotiated Status

The essays in this volume continue the quest for identifying the kinds of relationships between observer and observed, between research scholar and research subject, that foster discernment of meanings as expressed and experienced by the subjects, perhaps best expressed in the Weberian notion of *verstehen*, which is explicitly invoked by several of the authors. While this locates the discussion within a conventional methodological frame, it does seem to me that without explicitly stating the point, evidence builds throughout the volume that the role of the observer and the observer's relationship with the observed are—and ought to be—constantly in flux, always being re-invented. Moreover, this re-invention is never the sole action of the researcher, but some sort of negotiation or collaboration between the researcher and the subjects. As Melvin Pollner and Robert M. Emerson have put it, the researcher's position is not "given or obtained once and for all but rather one which is continually reproduced, threatened, and preserved through the particularities of interaction" (Pollner & Emerson, 1983: 236). While the essays tend to focus on the indicators and extent of the researcher's insider or outsider status as well as the consequences of that status, the presentation of evidence almost always discloses a process of dynamic interaction in which the terms of relationship are mutually established. We learned, for example, about some of the elements which Pollner and Emerson call the 'dynamics of inclusion', such as the researcher performing work useful to the group (Helen Waterhouse, Peter Collins), being a formal member (Jo Pearson) or prospective recruit (Mathew Guest, Helen Waterhouse, Elisabeth Arweck), being an intimate with some of the members (Peter Collins, Jo Pearson). And we saw some of their strategies for keeping distance, for avoiding 'engulfment', including various statements of limited commitment or non-commitment, being 'up front' about the research purpose, as distinguished from personal spiritual quest, and so on. It is interesting, for example, to compare Jo Pearson's account of her involvement in British Wicca with a brief quote, used by Pollner and Emerson, from Evans-Pritchard:

> The Azande were talking about witchcraft daily… any communication was well-nigh impossible unless one took witchcraft for granted… If I wanted to go hunting or on a journey, for instance, no one would willingly accompany me unless I was willing to produce a verdict of the poison oracle that all would be well, that witchcraft did not threaten our project; and one goes on arranging one's affairs, organizing one's life in harmony with the lives of one's hosts, whose companionship one seeks and without which one would sink into disoriented craziness, one must eventually give way, or at any rate at least partially give way. If one must

act as if one believed, one ends in believing, or half believing as one acts. (Evans-Pritchard, 1976: 244, cited in Pollner & Emerson, 1983: 250)

Perhaps because she was already an initiated member, Pearson does not report tension between her initial beliefs and those she is expected by her subjects to affirm. However, like Evans-Pritchard, she depends on a scholarly community external to the subject group as part of the project of discernment and interpretation, and she has to negotiate a *modus operandi* within the group that evokes their co-operation on a project not their own.

The Aims of the Research Should Affect the Negotiation

Another important consideration in negotiating one's insider/outsider status has to do with the broader aims of the particular research project. For example, Eleanor Nesbitt's review of the several studies by Quaker ethnographers helpfully notes that some of the studies investigate religious communities, others focus on the beliefs and practices, and practices that groups define as religious, and yet others examine the religious beliefs and practices of individuals. Although the other essays of this book do not provide much information about the larger aims of the projects they discuss, I think Nesbitt's distinctions have important methodological consequences. This is not to deny the essential analytic goal of discerning meanings as expressed, experienced, and understood by the subjects: *verstehen*, by whatever name, is still the gold standard. However, when an organization or a formal group—a church or synagogue or coven—is the unit of study, it is insufficient (although essential) for the researcher to get inside the minds of the members, to see the group from the members' points of view, to grasp *their* meanings. The formal organizational entity has a public status that is independent of its members' perceptions. This is most obvious when one considers the possibility that the members of a secret cult may have been duped by their charismatic leader. However, the importance of the point lies not in cases, such as secret organizations with misguided or mischievous leaders, but in the fact that organizations have public as well as internal roles, institutional as well as psychological dynamics, historical as well as contemporary stories. Thus for the adequate analysis of an organization, the interior meanings experienced by subjects and expressed among themselves are data to be combined, compared, and contrasted with other data from other sources and obtained by other methods. For purposes of incorporating other sources and methods, the 'outsider' has the comparative advantage— the skills, the contacts, the temperament.

The essays in this volume seem to be concerned with the study of the groups that practise rituals and participate in their meanings, with only Martin Stringer's introduction focusing strictly on the study of ritual as such. Martin Stringer is, of course, quite clear, as he is in *On the Perception of Worship* (Stringer, 1999), that ritual usually occurs within the context of an organization and that the organization affects both the ritual and the perception of it. He is, however, quite disciplined in his analytic focus on the meanings as experienced by the worshippers, on the dynamics of their construction and expression, and on the epistemological problems of discerning and verifying those meanings. The other essays, those examining the research activities of their authors, seem to be, in differing degrees, more organizational in their focus, more 'sociological', and thus—appropriately— more eclectic in their methods. As a result, they demonstrate more clearly the value of the outsider role.

This observation is perhaps too obviously that of the outsider—the view from the Religion in Urban America Program, where we are unabashedly focused on the congregation and its multi-faceted interaction with its neighborhood and city. Yet I think that our project illustrates why ethnographic method is often essential to the integrity of research, even when it is not the only method and when its central purpose—access to the interior meanings of subjects—is not the only aim. At a time in American public life when both government and the media increasingly expect religion to save our cities and our families from decline, the tendency of both politicians and journalists is to portray religious organizations in terms of their external activities and the findings of positivist social science. While the members' points of view are not the whole truth, it is neither fair to them nor adequate social science to ignore those views completely. Ethnographic research is thus an essential bulwark against both injustice to religious people and faulty science in the understanding of the public contribution of religion.

The Relevance of Gender, Race, and Class

Finally, the researcher's status and negotiated position as insider and outsider is necessarily affected by the different ways in which religious organizations and rituals incorporate racial, ethnic, gender-based, and class-based cultural material. I mentioned earlier that our research team in Chicago was selected to be diverse, not only religiously, but racially, ethnically, and in terms of gender and academic discipline, reflecting the view that the insider/outsider problem is reflected in all of these categories. That religious groups are regularly constituted along racial, ethnic, and class lines is a fact that could not be ignored by scholars of American religion since the publication in 1929 of Richard Niebuhr's *The Social Sources of Denominationalism* (Niebuhr, 1929). Three quarters of a century after the appearance of Niebuhr's book, denominations have become much more ethnically diverse, but congregations are still not only ethnically homogeneous, but construct and conduct rituals so as to incorporate their ethnic culture. A Roman Catholic parish in a Polish neighborhood conducts several Sunday masses in Polish and venerates Our Lady of Czestochowa, while in a nearby community of Mexican immigrants, the Roman Catholic church offers mass in Spanish, serenades La Señora de Guadalupe to the music of a mariachi band, and organizes Christian Base Communities on the Latin American model. The white priest in a nearby black Roman Catholic church preaches 'like a black Baptist' and the choir sings urban Gospel music to piano and drums. Therefore, one cannot be an insider simply by virtue of Catholic baptism and membership, and faithful religious practice (see Wedam, 2000; Hurtig, 2000).

The congregations discussed in this book differ markedly from those in our Chicago study. I believe only the Hindu groups studied by Eleanor Nesbitt are comprised primarily of people who are non-white and non-British. Thus it was relatively easy to limit the insider/outsider consideration to the religious dimension, although—as several authors point out—one might be an adherent to the faith, but not a member of the particular congregation, a member of the religion, but not of the particular denomination, a member, but not a long-term member, and so on. Some authors were also self-conscious about the inherent outsider-ness of being an academic in a non-academic setting. Conversely, some noted non-religious similarities between themselves and their subjects that tended to foster entry and acceptance. For the most part, however, the authors of the essays were able to abstract the religious dimension of the insider/outsider problem from the other categories of inclusion and exclusion, and indeed from the non-religious dimensions of group identity and boundary definition. In some respects, this is a great convenience, being able to focus in a pure way on the religious dimension, which was of primary interest. Yet it is also a burden, tending to obscure the ways in which the group's religious identity may incorporate racial, ethnic, or class-based cultural material. How can I, as a white, middle-class, well-educated Chicago Christian take realistic account of my *insider* status in a Buddhist temple which is made up of mainly white, middle-class, well-educated, Chicago converts to Buddhism? It seems to me that the problem of 'engulfment', of how to establish critical distance, is especially acute in situations where the terms of likeness and inclusion are taken for granted, and where they are adjacent to the central analytical field. At Carter Temple, for example, I was quite aware that the *African Heritage Bible* and the painting of 'The Last Supper' with African figures were assimilations of black culture with a more traditional manifestation of Christian culture. However, would I have been equally aware, prior to studying Carter Temple, that the blue-eyed Jesus of my youth was an assimilation of European culture with the Christian story? As an ethnographer, hearing the scripture read from, say, the New International Version, in a predominantly white church, would I have recorded a note like 'Eurocentric translation'? One hopes so, but I doubt it. We have to admit that is difficult to note the salient characteristics of the familiar and the expected. That seems to me to have been one of the challenges facing the ethnographers who have written for this book. Whether or not they were outsiders to the religion they studied, they were mostly insiders to the culture in which the religion was embedded. Thus the negotiation of an epistemologically sound relationship to their subjects was a formidable challenge, but one that shows how being an outsider in multiple ways can be a source not only of tension, but of insight.

References

Anderson, N. *The Hobo.* Chicago: University of Chicago Press, 1923.

Emerson, R. M., ed. *Contemporary Field Research: A Collection of Readings.* Berkeley, CA: University of California Press, 1983.

Geertz, C. *Local Knowledge: Further Essays in Interpretive Anthropology.* New York: Basic Books, 1983.

Hurtig, J. "Hispanic Immigrant Churches and the Construction of Ethnicity." In *Public Religion and Urban Transformation: Faith in the City.* Livezey, L. W., ed. New York: New York U. P., 2000: 29–56.

Lincoln, C. E. & Mamiya, L. H. *The Black Church in the African American Experience.* Durham, NC: Duke U. P., 1990.

Livezey, L. W., ed. *Public Religion and Urban Transformation: Faith in the City.* New York: New York U. P., 2000.

Niebuhr, H. R. *The Social Sources of Denominationalism.* New York: World, 1929.

Park, R. E. "The City as Social Laboratory." In Smith, T. V. & White, L. D., eds. *Chicago: An Experiment in Social Science Research.* Chicago: University of Chicago Press, 1968.

Pollner, M., & Emerson, R. "The Dynamics of Inclusion and Distance in Fieldwork Relations." In Emerson, R. M., ed. *Contemporary Field Research.* Boston: Little Brown & Co., 1983: 235–252.

Stringer, M. D. *On the Perception of Worship.* Birmingham: University of Birmingham Press, 1999.

Wedam, E. "'God Doesn't Ask What Language I Pray In': Community and Culture on Chicago's Southwest Side." In Livezey, L. W., ed. *Public Religion and Urban Transformation: Faith in the City.* New York: New York U. P., 2000: 107–132.

List of contributors

Elisabeth Arweck completed her PhD in 1999 on the social responses to New Religious Movements in Britain and Germany at King's College London, University of London. She is the Co-Editor of the *Journal of Contemporary Religion* and Convenor of the BSA Sociology of Religion Study Group (2000–2003). She published, with Peter Clarke, *New Religious Movements in Western Europe: An Annotated Bibliography* (Greenwood Press, 1997) and contributed to *Dialog und Unterscheidung: Religionen und neue religiése Bewegungen im Gespräch* (Berlin, 2000) as well as to *Religion in the Modern World* (Routledge, 2001).

Peter J. Collins is Lecturer on Social Anthropology in the Department of Anthropology at the University of Durham. His doctoral research was concerned with British Quakerism on which he has published widely since, with contributions in *Quaker Studies, Journal of Contemporary Religion*, and *Celibacy, Culture and Society* (University of Wisconsin Press, 2001). His currents interests include lay understandings of stress and the narrative constructiion of lives.

Mathew Guest studied theology at the University of Nottingham. After spending a year doing research at the University of Durham, he moved to Lancaster to begin a PhD on the transformations of contemporary evangelicalism within the context of an ethnographic community study based in the north of England.

Lowell W. Livezey has directed the Religion in Urban America Program (RUAP) at the University of Illinois, Chicago, since 1992. He is the editor of *Public Religion and Urban Transformation* (New York University Press, 2000).

Eleanor Nesbitt is Senior Lecturer in Religions and Education in the Warwick Religions and Education Research Unit, Institute of Education, University of Warwick. Her recent publications include, with Gopinder Kaur, *Guru Nanak* (Nesbitt & Kaur, 1999).

Jo Pearson is Research Lecturer in New Age Religions and Alternative Spirituality in the Department of Religious Studies at The Open University. She is co-editor (with Professors Richard Roberts and Geoffrey Samuel) of *Nature Religion Today: Paganism in the Modern World* (1998) and she completed her PhD thesis entitled "Religion and the Return of Magic: Wicca as Esoteric Spirituality" in early 2000.

Bilal Sambur completed his PhD at Birmingham University in Spring 2000.

Martin Stringer is Lecturer in the Department of Theology at the University of Birmingham and Director of the Worship in Birmingham Project. He published *On the Perception of Worship* (Birmingham University Press, 1999) and contributed to the *Journal of the Royal Anthropological Institute* (1999) and the *Scottish Journal of Theology* (2001). His current research is concerned with the ethnographic study of worship, the history of Christian worship, and the church and urban deprivation.

Helen Waterhouse is Lecturer in Religious Studies at the Open University. Her research interests to date are focused mainly on the practice of Buddhism in Britain and belief in reincarnation among British people. In addition to the publications cited in her contribution to this volume, she has published "Reincarnation and the New Age" (*Journal of Contemporary Religion* 14 (1), 1999) and, jointly with Tony Walter, "A Very Private Belief: Reincarnation in Contemporary England" (*Sociology of Religion* 60 (2), 1999). She is currently untertaking research on religion in Milton Keynes.

Combined Bibliography

Adler, M. *Drawing Down the Moon: Witches, Druids, Goddess-Worshippers, and other Pagans in America Today*. Boston: Beacon Press, 1979.

Agar, M. *The Professional Stranger*. New York: Academic Press, 1980.

Agassi, J. "Privileged Access." *Inquiry* 12, 1969: 420–426.

Al-Ghazali, Imam. *Ihya 'Ulum al-Din*. New Delhi: Islamic Book Service, 1996. Translated by E. E. Calverley as I. Al-Ghazali. *Worship in Islam: Al-Ghazali's Book of the Ihya on Worship*. Madras: The Christian Literature Society for India, 1925.

Allum, J. "That God in Everyone?" *The Friend* 156, 28 August, 1998: 9–10.

Ammerman, N. T. *Report to the Justice and Treasury Departments Regarding Law Enforcement Interaction with the Branch Davidians in Waco, Texas*. 1993.

Ammerman, N. T. "Waco, Federal Law Enforcement, and Scholars of Religion." In Wright, S. A. *Armageddon in Waco: Critical Perspectives on the Branch Davidian Conflict*. Chicago: University of Chicago Press, 1995: 282–296.

Anderson, B. *Imagined Communities: Reflections on the Origin and Spread of Nationalism*. London: Verso, 1993.

Anderson, N. *The Hobo*. Chicago: University of Chicago Press, 1923.

Arweck, E. *Responses to New Religious Movements in Britain and Germany, with Special Reference to the Anti-Cult Movement and the Churches*. PhD thesis, King's College London, 1999.

Baker, J. "Rhythm of the Masses." In Ward, P., ed. *Mass Culture: Eucharist and Mission in a Post-Modern World*. Oxford: The Bible Reading Fellowship, 1999: 33–53.

Bakhtin, M. *Speech Genres and other Late Essays*. Austin: University of Texas Press, 1986.

Barker, E. "'Brahmins Don't Eat Mushrooms': Participant Observation and the New Religions." *LSE Quarterly*, June 1987: 127–152.

Barker, E. *New Religious Movements: A Practical Introduction*. London: HMSO, 1989.

Barker, E. "Changes in New Religious Movements." In Fuss, M. *New Religious Movements. Vol. II*. Rome: International Federation of Catholic Universities, Center for Coordination of Research, 1991: 759–781.

Barker, E. "Presidential Address: The Scientific Study of Religion? You Must be Joking!" *Journal for the Scientific Study of Religion* 34 (3), 1995: 287–310.

Barton, S. *The Bengali Muslims of Bradford: A Study of their Observance of Islam with Special Reference to the Functions of the Mosque and the Work of the Imams*. Leeds: University of Leeds, 1986.

Bauman, R. *Let Your Words Be Few: Symbolism of Speaking and Silence among Seventeenth Century Quakers*. Cambridge: Cambridge U. P., 1983.

Bauman, Z. "Postmodern Religion?" In Heelas, P. (with the assistance of D. Martin & P. Morris), ed. *Religion, Modernity and Postmodernity*. Oxford: Blackwell, 1998: 55–78.

Bebbington, D. W. *Evangelicalism in Modern Britain: A History from the 1730s to the 1980s*. London: Unwin Hyman, 1989.

Bebbington, D. W. "Evangelicalism in its Settings: The British and American Movements since 1940." In Noll, M. A., Bebbington, D. W. & Rawlyk, G. A., eds. *Evangelicalism: Comparative Studies of Popular Protestantism in North America, The British Isles, and Beyond, 1700–1990*. Oxford, New York: Oxford U. P., 1994: 365–388.

Becker, H. S. *Outsiders: Studies in the Sociology of Deviance*. New York: The Free Press, 1963.

Beckford, J. A. *Cult Controversies: The Societal Response to the New Religious Movements*. London: Tavistock, 1985.

Beckford, J. "Religion, Modernity and Post-Modernity." In Wilson, B. R., ed. *Religion: Contemporary Issues*. London: Bellew, 1992: 11–23.

Bell, C. *Ritual Theory, Ritual Practice*. Oxford: Oxford U. P., 1992.

Bell, C. *Ritual: Perspectives and Dimensions*. New York, Oxford: Oxford U. P., 1997.

Berger, P. *The Heretical Imperative: Contemporary Possibilities of Religious Affirmation*. New York: Anchor Press (Doubleday), 1979.

Berger, P. L. *A Far Glory: The Quest for Faith in an Age of Credulity*. New York, London: Anchor Books, Doubleday, 1992.

Bhachu, P. "The Resocialisation of an Anthropologist: Fieldwork within One's Own Community." In Epstein, S., ed. *Female Ethnographers: Researchers Working within their own Communities*. Delhi: Hindustan Publishing Corporation, 1987.

Bocking, B. "Of Priests, Protests and Protestant Buddhists: The Case of Soka Gakkai International." In Clarke, P. & Somers, J., eds. *Japanese New Religions in the West*. Folkestone: Japan Library, 1994: 118–149.

Bocking, B. *A Popular Dictionary of Shinto*. Richmond, Surrey: Curzon, 1995.

Bonewits, I. *Real Magic*. York Beach, Maine: Samuel Weiser, 1989 (1st ed. published in 1971).

Boon, J. *Other Tribes, Other Scribes*. Cambridge: Cambridge U. P., 1982.

Bowen, D. *The Sathya Sai Baba Community in Bradford: Its Origin and Development, Religious Beliefs and Practices*. Leeds: Community Religions Project, University of Leeds, 1988.

Bowman. M. "Phenomenology, Fieldwork and Folk Religion." Occasional Papers 6. British Association for the Study of Religions, 1992.

Bourdieu, P. "Authorised Language: The Social Conditions for the Effectiveness of Ritual Discourse." In Bourdieu, P. *Language and Symbolic Power* (edited and introduced by John B. Thompson). Oxford: Polity Press, 1997: 107–116.

Brannen, J., ed. *Mixing Methods: Qualitative and Quantitative Research*. Aldershot: Avebury, 1992.

Brown, K. M. *Mama Lola: A Vodou Priestess in Brooklyn*. Berkeley: University of California Press, 1991.

Bruner, J. *Actual Minds, Possible Worlds*. Cambridge, Massachusetts: Harvard U. P., 1986.

Bruner, J. *Acts of Meaning*. Cambridge, Massachusetts: Harvard U. P., 1990.

Buber, M. *I and Thou*. New York: Scribners, 1970.

Cantwell Smith, W. "History of Religions—Whither and Why?" In Eliade, M. & Kitagawa, J. M., eds. *The History of Religions: Essays in Methodology*. Chicago: University of Chicago Press, 1959.

Cantwell Smith, W. *Towards a World Theology: Faith and the Comparative History of Religion*. Maryknoll, NY: Orbis Books, 1981.

Cashmore, E. *Rastaman: The Rastafarian Movement in England*. London: George Allen & Unwin, 1979 (1st ed.), 1983 (2nd ed.).

Causton, R. *Nichiren Shoshu Buddhism: An Introduction.* London: Rider, 1988.

Chaudhry, L. N. "Researching 'My People', Researching Myself: Fragments of a Reflexive Tale." *Qualitative Studies in Education* 10 (4), 1997: 441–453.

Christ, C. & Plaskow, J., eds. *Womanspirit Rising: A Feminist Reader in Religion.* San Francisco: Harper & Row, 1979.

Clarke, P. B. *Black Paradise: The Rastafarian Movement.* Wellingborough, Northants.: Aquarian Press, 1986.

Clarke, P. B. "Introduction: Change and Variety in New Religious Movements in Western Europe, c. 1960 to the Present." In Arweck. E. & Clarke, P. B. *New Religious Movements in Western Europe: An Annotated Bibliography.* Westport, CT: Greenwood Press, 1997: xxvii–xliii.

Clifford, J. & Marcus, G. M., eds. *Writing Culture: The Poetics and Politics of Ethnography.* Berkeley: University of California. Press, 1986.

Cohen, A. P. *Whalsay: Symbol, Segment and Boundary in a Shetland Island Community.* Manchester: Manchester U. P., 1987.

Cohen, A. P. *The Symbolic Construction of Community.* London: Routledge, 1989 (originally published in 1985 by Ellis Horwood, Chichester).

Cohen, A. P. *Self Consciousness: An Alternative Anthropology of Identity.* London: Routledge, 1994.

Coleman, S. "Words as Things: Language, Aesthetics and the Objectification of Protestant Evangelicalism." *Journal of Material Culture* 1 (1), 1996: 107–128.

Collins, P. J. *The Sense of the Meeting: An Anthropology of Vernacular Quakerism.* Unpublished PhD Thesis, Manchester University, 1994.

Collins, P. J. "The Meeting House and Its Meanings." *Friends Quarterly* 30, 1995: 194–207.

Collins, P. "'Plaining': The Social and Cognitive Practice of Symbolisation in the Religious Society of Friends (Quakers)." *Journal of Contemporary Religion* 11 (3), 1996a: 277–288.

Collins, P. J. "Auto/Biography, Narrative and the Quaker Meeting." *Auto/Biography* 4 (2/3), 1996b: 27–39.

Collins, P. J. "Quaker Worship: An Anthropological Perspective." *Worship* 72 (6), 1998: 501–515.

Conze, E. *A Short History of Buddhism.* London: George Allen & Unwin, 1980.

Corless, R. "How is the Study of Buddhism Possible?" *Method and Theory in the Study of Religion* 2 (1), 1990: 24–41.

Crowley, V. *Wicca: The Old Religion in the New Millennium.* London: Thorsons, 1996.

Culpepper, E. "The Spiritual Movement of Radical Feminist Consciousness." Needleman, J. & Baker, G., eds. *Understanding the New Religions.* New York: Seabury Press, 1978: 220–234.

Daly, M. *Gyn/Ecology: The Metaethics of Radical Feminism.* London: The Women's Press, 1978.

Dandelion, P. *A Sociological Analysis of the Theology of Quakers.* Lampeter: Edwin Mellen, 1996.

Davies, A. "Talking in Silence: Ministry in Quaker Meetings." In Coupland, N., ed. *Styles of Discourse.* Beckenham: Croom Helm, 1988: 105–137.

Dentith, S. *Bakhtinian Thought.* London: Routledge, 1995.

Denzin, N. K. *Interpretive Ethnography: Ethnographic Practices for the 21st Century.* London: Sage, 1997.

De Penter, J. "The Dialogics of Narrative Identity." In Bell, M. M. & Gardiner, M., eds. *Bakhtin and the Human Sciences.* London: Sage, 1998: 30–48.

Dillon, J. & Richardson, J. T. "The 'Cult' Concept: A Politics of Representation Analysis." *Syzygy* 3 (3–4), 1994: 185–197.

Dollarhide, K. *Nichiren's Senji-sho.* New York: Edwin Mellen, 1982.

Downton, J. V. *Sacred Journies: The Conversion of Young Americans to Divine Light Mission.* New York: Columbia U. P., 1979.

Eck, D. L. *Encountering God: A Spiritual Journey from Bozeman to Banaras*. Boston: Beacon, 1993.

Educational Department of Soka Gakkai. "Soka Gakkai and the Nichiren Sho Sect." *Contemporary Religions in Japan* 1 (1), n. d.: 55–70.

Eliade, M. "A New Humanism." In McCutcheon, R. T., ed. *The Insider/Outsider Problem in the Study of Religion*. London, New York: Cassell, 1999: 95–103.

Ellis, C. & Bochner, A. P., eds. *Composing Ethnography: Alternative Forms of Qualitative Writing*. London: Sage, 1996.

Ellis, C. & Flaherty, M. G., eds. *Investigating Subjectivity*. London: Sage, 1992.

Emerson, R. M., ed. *Contemporary Field Research: A Collection of Readings*. Berkeley, CA: University of California Press, 1983.

Evans-Pritchard, E. E. *The Nuer*. Oxford: Clarendon Press, 1940.

Evans-Pritchard, E. E. *Social Anthropology and Other Essays*. New York: Free Press of Glencoe, 1962.

Evans-Pritchard, E. E. *Witchcraft, Oracles and Magic Among the Azande*. Oxford: Clarendon Press, 1976.

Ewing, K. P. "Dreams from a Saint: Anthropological Atheism and the Temptation to Believe." *American Anthropologist* 96 (3), 1994: 571–583.

Faber, M. *Witchcraft and Psychoanalysis*. Rutherford: Fairleigh Dickinson U. P., 1993.

Fabian, J. *Time and the Other: How Anthropology Makes its Object*. New York: Columbia U. P., 1983.

Feuerbach, L. *The Essence of Christianity*. New York: Harper & Row, 1957.

Firth, R. *We, the Tikopia*. Beacon Press, 1963 (first published in 1936).

Firth, S. "Changing Patterns in Hindu Death Rituals in Britain." In Killingley, D.; Menski, W., & Firth, S. *Hindu Ritual and Society*. Newcastle: S. Y. Killingley, 1991: 52–84.

Firth, S. "Hindu and Sikh Approaches to Death" and "Cross Cultural Perspectives on Bereavement." In Dickinson, D. & Johnson, M., eds. *Death, Dying and Bereavement: A Reader*. London: Sage, 1993a: 26–32; 254–261.

Firth, S. "Cultural Issues in Terminal Care." In Clarke, D., ed. *The Future for Palliative Care: Issues of Policy and Practice*. Milton Keynes: Open U. P., 1993b: 99–110.

Firth, S. "The Good Death: Attitudes of British Hindus." In Jupp, P. & Howarth, G., eds. *Contemporary Issues in the Sociology of Death, Dying and Disposal*. London: Macmillan, 1996: 96–110.

Firth, S. *Dying, Death and Bereavement in a British Hindu Community*. Leuven: Peeters, 1997.

Firth, S. "Hindu Widows in Britain: Continuity and Change." In Barot, R., Fenton, S. *et al.*, eds. *Ethnicity, Gender and Social Change*. London: Macmillan, 1999a: 99–113.

Firth, S. "Spirituality and Ageing in British Hindus, Sikhs and Muslims." In Jewell, A., ed. *Ageing and Spirituality*. London: Jessica Kingsley, 1999b: 158–174.

Fox, M. *Creation Spirituality: Liberating Gifts for the Peoples of the Earth*. New York: HarperCollins, 1991.

Freilich. M., ed. *Marginal Natives at Work: Anthropologists in the Field*. New York: Wiley, 1977.

Gaiman, D. "Appendix: A Scientologist's Comment." In Bell, C. & Newby, H., eds. *Doing Sociological Research*. London: Allen & Unwin, 1977: 168–169.

Gardner, G. B. *Witchcraft Today*. London: Rider, 1954.

Gardner, G. B. *The Meaning of Witchcraft*. London: Aquarian Press, 1959.

Geertz, C. *The Interpretation of Cultures*. New York: Basic Books, 1973.

Geertz, C. *Local Knowledge: Further Essays in Interpretive Anthropology*. New York: Basic Books, 1983.

Geertz, C. *Works and Lives: The Anthropologist as Author*. Cambridge: Polity, 1988.

Gergen, K. *The Saturated Self: Dilemmas of Identity in Everyday Life*. New York: Basic Books, 1991.

Giddens, A. *Modernity and Self-identity*. Cambridge: Polity Press, 1991.

Ginzburg, C. *Ecstasies: Deciphering the Witches' Sabbat*. New York: Penguin, 1992.

Goldenberg, N. *Changing of the Gods: Feminism and the End of Traditional Religions*. Boston: Beacon Press, 1979.

Goldziher, I. *Introduction to Islamic Theology and Law*. Princeton, NJ: Princeton U. P., 1981.

Gordon, D. "Getting Close by Staying Distant: Fieldwork with Proselytizing Groups." *Qualitative Sociology* 10 (3), 1987: 267–287.

Goss, R. E. "'Buddhist Studies at Naropa': Sectarian or Academic?" In Williams, D. R. & Queen, C., eds. *American Buddhism*. Richmond, Surrey: Curzon, 1999: 215–237.

Griffiths, A. I. "Insider/Outsider: Epistemological Privilege and Mothering Work." *Human Studies* 21, 1998: 361–376.

Griffiths, P. J. *An Apology for Apologetics*. New York: Orbis, 1991.

Grimes, R. L. "Ritual Criticism and Reflexive Fieldwork." *Journal of Ritual Studies* 2 (2), 1988: 217–239.

Grimes, R. L. *Ritual Criticism: Case Studies in its Practice, Essays on its Theory*. Columbia: University of South Carolina, 1990.

Hammond, P. & Machacek, D. "Supply and Demand: The Appeal of Buddhism in America." In Williams, D. R. & Queen, C., eds. *American Buddhism*. Richmond, Surrey: Curzon, 1999: 100–114.

Hanegraaff, W. J. *New Age Religion and Western Culture: Esotericism in the Mirror of Secular Thought*. Leiden: Brill, 1996.; New York: SUNY, 1998.

Hanegraaff, W. J. "Empirical Method and the Study of Esotericism." *Method and Theory in the Study of Religion* 7 (2), 1995: 99–129.

Harré, R. *Social Being*. Oxford: Blackwell, 1979.

Harvey, G. "The Authority of Intimacy in Paganism and Goddess Spirituality." *Diskus* 4 (1) 1996: 34–48.

Harvey, G. & Hardman, C. *Paganism Today: Wiccans, Druids, the Goddess and Ancient Earth Traditions for the Twenty-First Century*. London: Thorsons, 1996.

Harvey, P. "Review of B. R. Wilson & K. Dobbelaere: *A Time to Chant*." *Sociology* 29 (2), 1995: 256–257.

Hayes, R. "The Internet as Window onto American Buddhism." In Williams, D. R. & Queen, C., eds. *American Buddhism*. Richmond, Surrey: Curzon, 1999: 168–179.

Headland, T. N., Pike, K. & Harris, M., eds. *Emics and Etics: The Insider/Outsider Debate*. London: Sage, 1990.

Heelas, P. *The New Age Movement: The Celebration of the Self and the Sacralization of Modernity*. Oxford: Blackwell, 1996.

Heelas, P., Lash, S. & Morris, P., eds. *Detraditionalization: Critical Reflections on Authority and Identity*. Oxford: Blackwell, 1996.

Heiler, F. *Prayer: A Study in the History and Psychology of Religion*. London: Oxford U. P., 1938.

Heilman, S. C. *Synagogue Life: A Study in Symbolic Interaction*. London: University of Chicago Press, 1973.

Heim, S. M. *Salvations, Truth and Difference in Religion*. New York: Orbis Books, 1995.

Hemminger, H. *Verein zur Förderung der Psychologischen Menschenkenntnis (VPM, IPM, GFPM)*. Vienna: Referat fÿr Weltanschauungsfragen, 1991.

Hobbs, D. & May, T., eds. *Interpreting the Field: Accounts of Ethnography*. Oxford: Clarendon Press, 1993.

Holquist, M. *Dialogism: Bakhtin and his World*. London: Routledge, 1990.

Homan, Roger. *The Ethics of Social Research*. London, New York: Longman, 1991.

Homan, R. E. & Dandelion, P. "The Religious Basis of Resistance and Non-Response: A Methodological Note." *Journal of Contemporary Religion* 12 (2), 1997: 205–214.

Howard, R. *The Rise and Fall of the Nine O'Clock Service*. London: Mowbray, 1996.

Humphrey C. & Laidlaw, J. *The Archetypal Actions of Ritual*. Oxford: Clarendon, 1994.

Hurtig, J. "Hispanic Immigrant Churches and the Construction of Ethnicity." In *Public Religion and Urban Transformation: Faith in the City*. Livezey, L. W., ed. New York: New York U. P., 2000: 29–56.

Hurvitz, L., transl. *Scripture of the Lotus Blossom of the Fine Dharma*. New York: Columbia U. P., 1976.

Hutton, R. "The Roots of Modern Paganism." In Harvey, G. & Hardman, C., eds. *Paganism Today: Wiccans, Druids, the Goddess and Ancient Earth Traditions for the Twenty-First Century*. London: Thorsons, 1996: 3–15.

Imtiaz, S. *A Comparative Study of Multilingual Pakistanis in Amsterdam and Birmingham*. Unpublished PhD Thesis, Centre for Research in Ethnic Relations, University of Warwick, 1998.

Imtiaz, S. & Johnson, M. D. R. *Healthcare Provision in the Kashmiri Population of Peterborough: An Initial Investigation of Issues of Concern*. Peterborough: North West Anglia Health Authority, 1993.

Introvigne, M. "The Secular Anti-Cult and the Religious Counter-Cult Movement: Strange Bedfellows or Future Enemies?" In Towler, R., ed. *New Religions and the New Europe*. Aarhus: Aarhus U. P., 1995: 32–54.

Iqbal, M. *The Reconstruction of Religious Thought in Islam*. Lahore: Sh. Muhammad Ashraf, 1998.

Jackson, R. *Religious Education: An Interpretive Approach*. London: Hodder, 1997.

Jackson, R. & Nesbitt, E. "The Diversity of Experience in the Religious Upbringing of Children from Christian Families in Britain." *British Journal of Religious Education* 15 (1), 1992: 19–38.

Jackson, R. & Nesbitt, E. *Hindu Children in Britain*. Stoke on Trent: Trentham, 1993.

Kalsi, S. *The Evolution of a Sikh Community in Britain: Religious and Social Change among the Sikhs of Leeds and Bradford*. Leeds: Community Religions Project, University of Leeds, 1992.

Kenna, M. E. "Changing Places and Altered Perspectives: Research on a Greek Island in the 1960s and the 1980s." In Okely, J. & Callaway, H., eds. *Anthropology and Autobiography*. London: Routledge, 1992.

Knott, K. *Hinduism in Leeds: A Study of Religious Practices in the Indian Community and in Hindu Related Groups*. Monograph Series. Leeds: Community Religions Project, University of Leeds, 1986a.

Knott, K. *My Sweet Lord: The Hare Krishna Movement*. Wellingborough: Aquarian Press, 1986b.

Knott, K. "Bound to Change? The Religions of South Asians in Britain." In Vertovec, S., ed. *Oxford University Papers on India: The Modern Western Diaspora*. Delhi: Oxford U. P., 1991: 86–111.

Knott, K. "Women Researching, Women Researched: Gender as an Issue in the Empirical Study of Religion." In King, U., ed. *Religion and Gender*. Oxford: Blackwell, 1995: 199–218.

Knott, K. *Hinduism: A Very Short Introduction*. Oxford: Oxford U. P., 1998.

Lakoff, G. & Johnson, M. *Metaphors We Live By*. Chicago: Chicago U. P., 1980.

Lazarus-Yufeh, H. *Some Religious Aspects of Islam*. Leiden: Brill, 1981.

Lévi-Strauss, C. *Tristes Tropiques*. Harmondsworth: Penguin, 1976.

Lewis, J. R. *Magical Religion and Modern Witchcraft*. New York: SUNY, 1996.

Lincoln, C. E. & Mamiya, L. H. *The Black Church in the African American Experience*. Durham, NC: Duke U. P., 1990.

Livezey, L., ed. *Religious Organizations and Structural Change in Metropolitan Chicago: The Research Report of the Religion in Urban America Program*. Chicago: The University of Illinois at Chicago, 1996.

Livezey, L. W., ed. *Public Religion and Urban Transformation: Faith in the City.* New York: New York U. P., 2000.

Lofland, J. *Analysing Social Settings.* Belmont, California: Wadsworth, 1971.

Loring, P. *Listening Spirituality. Vol 1: Personal Spiritual Practices among Friends.* Washington: Openings Press, 1997.

Luft, J. & Ingham, H. *The Johari Window: A Graphic Model for Interpersonal Relations.* California: University of California Western Training Laboratory, 1955.

Luhrmann, T. M. *Persuasions of the Witches' Craft: Ritual Magic in Contemporary England.* Basingstoke: Picador, 1994 (1st ed. published in 1989).

Lunn, P. "Inner Selves Outer Lives: Class, Religion and Interiority, and their Interaction with Gender Ideology and Attitude to Feminism in Two Groups of Women Adult Education Students." MA Dissertation in Interdisciplinary Women's Studies, Centre for Study of Women and Gender, University of Warwick, 1994.

Machacek, D. & Wilson, B., eds. *Global Citizens: The Soka Gakkai Movement in the World.* Oxford: Oxford U. P., 2000.

MacIntyre, A. *After Virtue.* London: Duckworth, 1985 (2nd ed.).

Malinowski, B. *Argonauts of the Western Pacific.* New York: Dutton, 1922.

Malinowski, B. *A Diary in the Strict Sense of the Term.* London: Routledge & Kegan Paul, 1967.

Martin, B. "Whose Knowledge? Methodological Problems and Procedures Arising from Sociology's Rediscovery of Religion." In Vassallo, M., ed. *Youth in Perspective: Methodological Problems and Alternatives in the Study of Youth.* Malta: The Euro-Arab Social Research Group, 1981: 85–114.

Martin, D. *The Breaking of the Image: A Sociology of Christian Theory and Practice.* Oxford: Blackwell, 1980.

Martin, D. *Tongues of Fire: The Explosion of Protestantism in Latin America.* Oxford: Blackwell, 1990.

Matsuda, T., ed. *A Dictionary of Buddhist Terms and Concepts.* Tokyo: Nichiren Shoshu International Centre, 1983.

McCormick Maaga, M. *Hearing the Voices of Jonestown.* New York: Syracuse U. P., 1998.

McCutcheon, R. T., ed. *The Insider/Outsider Problem in the Study of Religion: A Reader.* London: Cassell, 1999.

Merton, R. K. "Insiders and Outsiders: A Chapter in the Sociology of Knowledge." *American Journal of Sociology* 78, 1972: 9–47.

Metraux, D. *The History and Theology of Soka Gakkai: A Japanese New Religion.* New York: Edwin Mellen, 1988.

Needleman, J. & Baker, G., eds. *Understanding the New Religions.* New York: Seabury Press, 1978.

Needleman, J. & Faivre, A., eds. *Modern Esoteric Spirituality.* London: SCM Press, 1992.

Nesbitt, E. "Out of a Single Fire: Sikhs and Quakers." *Quaker Monthly* 59 (April), 1980: 75–78.

Nesbitt, E. "That of God." *Friends Quarterly* 24 (5), January 1987: 221–227.

Nesbitt, E. *"My Dad's Hindu, My Mum's Side are Sikhs": Issues in Religious Identity.* Charlbury: National Foundation for Arts Education, 1991.

Nesbitt, E. "On Being a Quaker and a Researcher in Religious Studies." *Quaker Monthly* 72 (August), 1993a: 160–162.

Nesbitt, E. "Transmission of Christian Tradition in an Ethnically Diverse Society." In Barot, R., ed. *Religion and Ethnicity: Minorities and Social Change in the Metropolis.* Kampen: Kok Pharos, 1993b: 156–169.

Nesbitt, E. "Living with Other Faiths: Reflecting [on] our own Sanskars." *Quaker Monthly* 73 (October), 1994: 205–209.

Nesbitt, E. "Of Faiths and Cultures." *The Friend* 155 (22), 1997: 11–14.

Nesbitt, E. "British, Asian and Hindu: Identity, Self-Narration and the Ethnographic Interview." *Journal of Beliefs and Values* 19 (2), 1998: 189–200.

Nesbitt, E. *The Religious Lives of Sikh Children.* Leeds: Community Religions Project, University of Leeds, 2000a.

Nesbitt, E. "Researching Children's Perspectives on their Experience of Religion." In Lewis, A. & Lindsay, G., eds. *Researching Children's Perspectives.* Buckingham: Open U. P., 2000b: 135–149.

Nesbitt, E. & Kaur, G. *Guru Nanak.* Norwich: Religious and Moral Education Press, 1999.

Niebuhr, H. R. *The Social Sources of Denominationalism.* New York: World, 1929.

O'Brian, J. & Palmer, M. *The State of Religion Atlas.* New York: Touchstone, 1993.

O'Flaherty, W. D. "The Uses and Misuses of Other People's Myths." In McCutcheon, R. T., ed. *The Insider/Outsider Problem in the Study of Religion: A Reader.* London: Cassell, 1999: 331–349.

Okely, J. *The Traveller-Gypsies.* Cambridge: Cambridge U. P., 1983.

Orion, L. L. *Never Again the Burning Times: Paganism Revived.* Prospect Heights, Illinois: Waveland Press, 1995.

Osborn, L. & Walker, A., eds. *Harmful Religion: An Exploration of Religious Abuse.* London: SPCK. 1997.

Otto, R. *The Idea of the Holy: An Inquiry into the Non-Rational Factor in the Idea of the Divine and its Relation to the Rational.* Oxford: Humphrey Milford, 1928.

Papanek, H. "The Woman Fieldworker in a Purdah Society." *Human Organisation* 23, 1964: 160–163.

Park, R. E. "The City as Social Laboratory." In Smith, T. V. & White, L. D., eds. *Chicago: An Experiment in Social Science Research.* Chicago: University of Chicago Press, 1968.

Pearson, J., Roberts, R. H. & Samuel, G. eds. *Nature Religion Today: Paganism in the Modern World.* Edinburgh: Edinburgh U. P., 1998.

Percy, M. *Words, Wonders and Power: Understanding Contemporary Christian Fundamentalism and Revivalism.* London: SPCK, 1996.

Percy, M. *Power and the Church: Ecclesiology in an Age of Transition.* London: Cassell, 1998.

Peshkin, A. "Odd Man Out: The Participant Observer in an Absolutist Setting." *Sociology of Education* 57 (October), 1984: 254–264.

Pike, S. M. "Rationalizing the Margins: A Review of Legitimation and Ethnographic Practice in Scholarly Research on Neo-Paganism." In Lewis, J. R., ed. *Magical Religion and Modern Witchcraft.* New York: SUNY, 1996: 353–372.

Platvoet, J. G. *Comparing Religions: A Limitative Approach.* The Hague, Paris, New York: Mouton, 1983.

Pollner, M. & Emerson, R. "The Dynamics of Inclusion and Distance in Fieldwork Relations." In Emerson, R. M. ed. *Contemporary Field Research.* Boston: Little Brown & Co., 1983: 235–252.

Pouillon, J. "Remarks on the Verb 'To Believe.'" In Izard, M. & Smith, P., eds. *Between Belief and Transgression: Structuralist Essays in Religion, History and Myth.* Chicago: The University of Chicago Press, 1982: 1–8.

Prebish, Charles S. "The Academic Study of Buddhism in America: A Silent *Sangha.*" In Williams, D. R. & Queen, C. S., eds. *American Buddhism: Methods and Findings in Recent Scholarship.* Richmond, Surrey: Curzon Press, 1999: 183–214.

Puttick, E. *Women in New Religions: In Search of Community, Sexuality and Spiritual Power.* London: Macmillan, 1997.

Quaker Faith and Practice: The Book of Discipline of the Yearly Meeting of the Religious Society of Friends (Quakers) in Britain. London: The Religious Society of Friends (Quakers) in Britain/Britain Yearly Meeting, 1995.

Rahman, E. *Islam*. Chicago: Chicago U. P., 1979.

Raj, D. S. *Shifting Culture in the Global Terrain: Cultural Identity Construction among Hindu Punjabis in London*. Unpublished PhD Thesis, University of Cambridge, 1997.

Rappaport, R. "Veracity, Verity, and Verum in Liturgy." *Studia Liturgica* 23, 1993: 35–50.

Rapport, N. J. *Diverse World-views in an English Village*. Edinburgh: Edinburgh U. P., 1993.

Rapport, N. J. *Transcendent Individuality: Towards a Literary and Liberal Anthropology*. London: Routledge, 1997.

Rasplica Rodd, L. *Nichiren: Selected Writings*. Hawaii: University of Hawaii, 1980.

Reader, I. "Aum Affair Intensifies Japan's Religious Crisis: An Analysis." *Religion Watch* 10 (9), 1995: 1–2.

REMID. "Stellungnahme zur gegenwärtigen Auseinandersetzung um die Scientology-Kirche [Statement Regarding the Current Controversy about the Church of Scientology]." Marburg: REMID, 1990.

Robbins, T., Anthony, D. & Curtis, T. "The Limits of Symbolic Realism: Problems of Empathetic Field Observation in a Sectarian Context." *Journal for the Scientific Study of Religion* 12 (3), 1973: 259–271.

Roberts, P. *Alternative Worship in the Church of England*. Cambridge: Grove Books, 1999.

Rochford, E. B. *Hare Krishna in America*. New Brunswick: Rutgers U. P., 1985.

Rubin, J. H. "The Other Side of Joy: Harmful Religion in an Anabaptist Community." In Osborn, L. & Walker, A., eds. *Harmful Religion: An Exploration of Religious Abuse*. London: SPCK. 1997: 81–98.

Said, E. W. *Orientalism: Western Conceptions of the Orient*. London: Penguin Books, 1995.

Saifullah-Khan, V. *Pakistani Villagers in a British City (The World of the Mirpuri Villager in Bradford and in his Village of Origin)*. Unpublished PhD Thesis, University of Bradford, 1974.

Salomonsen, J. *"I am a Witch—a Healer and a Bender": An Expression of Women's Religiosity in Contemporary USA*. Unpublished PhD dissertation, University of Oslo, 1996.

Sambur, B. *Prayer in the Psychology of Religion, with Special Reference to Al-Ghazali, Ibn 'Ata Allah, and Iqbal*. Unpublished PhD thesis, Department of Theology, University of Birmingham, 2000.

Schimmel, A. *Mystical Dimensions of Islam*. Chapel Hill: University of North Carolina Press, 1978.

Scott, J. *What Canst Thou Say: Towards a Quaker Theology*. Swarthmore Lecture. London: Quaker Home Service, 1980.

Seager, R. "Buddhist Worlds in the U.S.A.: A Survey of the Territory." In Williams, D. R. & Queen, C., eds. *American Buddhism*. Richmond, Surrey: Curzon, 1999: 238–261.

Shaw, R. "Feminist Anthropology and the Gendering of Religious Studies." In McCutcheon, R., ed. *The Insider/Outsider Problem in the Study of Religion: A Reader*. London: Cassell, 1999: 104–113.

Shimazono, S. "The Expansion of Japan's New Religions into Foreign Cultures." *Japanese Journal of Religious Studies* 18 (2–3), 1991: 105–132.

Shotter, J. *Cultural Politics of Everyday Life*. Buckingham: Open U. P., 1993a.

Shotter, J. *Conversational Realities*. London: Sage, 1993b.

Smart, N. *Dimensions of the Sacred: An Anatomy of the World's Beliefs*. London: Fontana Press, 1997.

Smith, J. Z. *Imagining Religion: From Babylon to Jonestown*. Chicago, London: University of Chicago Press, 1982.

Smith, L. T. *Decolonizing Methodologies: Research and Indigenous Peoples*. London: Zed, 1999.

Smith, M. *Al-Ghazali: The Mystic*. London: Luzac, 1994.

Soskice, J. M. *Metaphor and Religious Language*. Oxford: Oxford U. P., 1985.

Starhawk. *The Spiral Dance: A Rebirth of the Ancient Religion of the Great Goddess*. San Francisco: HarperCollins, 1979.

Steier, F., ed. *Research and Reflexivity*. London: Sage, 1991.

Stone, M. *When God was a Woman*. New York: Harcourt Brace Jovanovich, 1976.

Strathern, M. *Kinship at the Core*. Cambridge: Cambridge U. P., 1981.

Stringer, M. D. "Situating Meaning in the Liturgical Text." *Bulletin of the John Rylands University Library of Manchester* 73 (3), 1991: 181–195.

Stringer, M. D. "Towards a Situational Theory of Belief." *Journal of the Anthropological Society of Oxford* 27 (3), 1996: 217–234.

Stringer, M. D. *On the Perception of Worship: The Ethnography of Worship in Four Christian Congregations in Manchester*. Birmingham: University of Birmingham Press, 1999.

Taussig, M. *Shamanism, Colonialism, and the Wild Man: A Study in Terror and Healing*. Chicago: The University of Chicago Press, 1987.

Thomas, K. *Religion and the Decline of Magic*. Harmondsworth: Penguin, 1991 (1st ed. published in 1971).

Tomlinson, D. *The Post-Evangelical*. London: SPCK, 1995.

Turner, V. W. *The Ritual Process: Structure and Anti-Structure*. Chicago: Aldine de Gruyter, 1969; London: Routledge & Kegan Paul, 1969.

Turner, V. *Dramas, Fields and Metaphors: Symbolic Action in Human Society*. Ithaca, New York: Cornell U. P., 1974.

Turner, V. "Foreword." In Myerhoff, B. *Number Our Days*. New York: Simon & Schuster, 1978: xiii–xvii.

Turner, V. *From Ritual to Theatre: The Human Seriousness of Play*. New York: Performing Arts Journal Publications, 1982.

Turner, V. W. "Dewey, Dilthey, and Drama: An Essay in the Anthropology of Experience." In Turner, V. W. & Bruner, E. M., eds. *The Anthropology of Experience*. Chicago: University of Illinois Press, 1986: 33–44.

Valiente, D. *The Rebirth of Witchcraft*. Washington: Phoenix Publishing, 1989.

Van Gennep, A. *The Rites of Passage*. London: Routledge & Kegan Paul, 1960 (first published in 1908).

Van Maanen, J. *Tales of the Field: On Writing Ethnography*. Chicago: University of Chicago Press, 1988.

Van Maanen, J., ed. *Representation in Ethnography*. London: Sage, 1995.

Wagner, R. *The Invention of Culture*. Chicago: The University of Chicago Press, 1981.

Wach, J. "Spiritual Teaching in Islam: A Study." *Journal of Religion* 27–28, 1947–48.

Walker, A. *Restoring the Kingdom: The Radical Christianity of the House Church Movement*. London: Hodder & Stoughton, 1988 (2nd ed., 1st ed. published in 1985).

Wallis, R. *The Road to Total Freedom: A Sociological Analysis of Scientology*. London: Heinemann, 1976.

Wallis, R. "The Moral Career of the Research Project." In Bell, C. & Newby, H., eds. *Doing Sociological Research*. London: Allen & Unwin, 1977: 149–167.

Wallis, R. *The Elementary Forms of the New Religious Life*. London: Routledge & Kegan Paul, 1984.

Ward, P., ed. *Mass Culture: Eucharist and Mission in a Post-Modern World*. Oxford: The Bible Reading Fellowship, 1999.

Waterhouse, H. *Buddhism in Bath: Adaptation and Authority*. Leeds: Department of Theology and Religious Studies, University of Leeds, 1997.

Waterhouse, H. "Who Says So? Legitimacy and Authenticity in British Buddhism." *Scottish Journal of Religious Studies* 20 (1), 1999: 19–36.

Watling, T. *Negotiating Religious Pluralism: Ecumenism and the Development of Religious Identities in the Netherlands.* Unpublished PhD thesis, University of London, 1999.

Watt, M. *Muslim Intellectual: A Study of al-Ghazali.* Edinburgh: Edinburgh U. P., 1971.

Wedam, E. "'God Doesn't Ask What Language I Pray In': Community and Culture on Chicago's Southwest Side." In Livezey, L. W, ed. *Public Religion and Urban Transformation: Faith in the City.* New York: New York U. P., 2000: 107–132.

Whitehead, A. N. *Religion in the Making.* London: Cambridge U. P., 1930.

Whitworth, J. M. *God's Blueprints: A Sociological Study of Three Utopian Sects.* London: Routledge & Kegan Paul, 1975.

Williams, D. R. & Queen, C. S., eds. *American Buddhism: Methods and Findings in Recent Scholarship.* Richmond, Surrey: Curzon Press, 1999.

Williams, P. *Mahayana Buddhism.* London: Routledge, 1989.

Wilson, B. R. *Religious Sects: A Sociological Study.* London: Weidenfels & Nicolson, 1970.

Wilson, B. R. *Religion in Sociological Perspective.* Oxford: Oxford U. P., 1982.

Wilson, B. R. *The Social Dimensions of Sectarianism: Sects and New Religious Movements in Contemporary Society.* Oxford: Clarendon Press, 1990.

Wilson, B. R. & Cresswell, J. *New Religious Movements: Challenge and Response.* London: Routledge, 1999.

Wilson, B. R. & Dobbelaere, K. *A Time to Chant: The Soka Gakkai Buddhists in Britain.* Oxford: Clarendon Press, 1994.

Wilson, M. *Rituals of Kinship among the Nyakyusa.* Oxford: Oxford U. P., 1957.

Wittgenstein, L. *Philosophical Investigations.* Oxford: Blackwell, 1958.

Wright, S. A. *Armageddon in Waco: Critical Perspectives on the Branch Davidian Conflict.* Chicago: University of Chicago Press, 1995.

York, M. *The Emerging Network: A Sociology of the New Age and Neo Pagan Movement.* Lanham, ML: Rowman & Littlefield, 1995.

Index